# Managing People

# Managing People

A Guide for Department Chairs
and Deans

## Deryl R. Leaming

*Editor*
*Middle Tennessee State University*

Anker Publishing Company, Inc.

BOLTON, MASSACHUSETTS

**Managing People**

*A Guide for Department Chairs and Deans*

ISBN: 1-882982-53-3

Composition by Harvard Post Design Service
Cover design by Red Brick Design

Anker Publishing Company, Inc.
176 Ballville Road
P. O. Box 249
Bolton, MA 01740-0249

www.ankerpub.com

# Contents

# About the Editor

D eryl R. Leaming is former Professor of Journalism and Dean of the College of Mass Communication at Middle Tennessee State University. He earned his Ph.D. in Mass Communication from Syracuse University, his M.A. from the University of Nebraska, and his B.A. from Fort Hays State University. He is also a graduate of a special program at the Menninger School of Psychiatry. Dr. Leaming served for more than 20 years as a department chair and dean at several different universities. He is an active member of the Society of Professional Journalists, having also served on the society's national board and as a regional director. He and his colleagues at Marshall University won the coveted First Amendment Award from the society in 1993 for their courageous support of the university's student newspaper and the principles embodied in the First Amendment. He is the author of *Academic Leadership: A Practical Guide to Chairing the Department* (Anker, 1998), the editor of the online journal, *Academic Leadership*, and the author of many journal articles.

# Preface

The idea for this book began to take shape after I conducted workshops for chairs at many different universities. An overwhelming number complained to me about the unusual amount of time they give to helping faculty and staff members with problems. Most indicated this is what took up most of their time. They also complained about how poorly trained they were for handling many of the problems they were asked to solve. If you've been in a university administrative position any length of time at all, you can relate to these concerns. This book attempts to deal with the problems chairs and deans have in dealing with the everyday personnel management problems of faculty and staff.

The authors of the chapters of this book are chairs, deans, and vice presidents. During their combined experience of over 200 years, they have faced most of the problems with faculty and staff that you're likely to encounter during your tenure. In this volume, they share their experiences and offer advice based on personal experience and scholarly research.

## CHAPTER HIGHLIGHTS

The book commences with a discussion on understanding yourself. I chose this as a starting point because to understand others, you must first understand yourself. Chapter 1 examines what constitutes self-understanding and provides some strategies for improving it, including a behavior audit. Understanding others is critical to any leader, and Daniel W. Wheeler focuses on this in Chapter 2. As he examines strategies for working with others, Wheeler reminds us to be sincere and authentic, and that talking with people is a fundamental part of our work, not an add-on. Further, he says that we need to keep investing in and encouraging others to invest in relationships to create the environment we want. He says that those relationships don't happen naturally; courage, persistence, and good will combine to make a difference.

In Chapter 3, Lynn M. Little calls our attention to establishing a positive leadership approach. He outlines the fundamentals of the leadership process and tells us we need to challenge the process.

He discusses what chairs and faculty members want and tells us how important it is to figure that out. An important part of this chapter focuses on motivating faculty members, particularly in the context of satisfying basic human needs.

In Chapter 4, I discuss creating consensus among faculty, since in today's work environment, we cannot succeed unless we work together. My first suggestion is that when chairs or deans take a new position, they should take time to learn as much as they can about the college or department. What have been past practices? What is valued? Chairs and deans need to get to know the faculty and staff in their college or department. By learning all they can about the college or department and the faculty in it, chairs or deans can then formulate a vision and promote it whenever the opportunity presents itself. The chapter closes with useful tips to achieve consensus.

If you've ever worried about having to conduct departmental or college meetings, you need to read Chapter 5 in which Joan DeGuire North discusses how to use meetings to create cohesion. Her chapter is practical advice at its best, providing clear guidance for what we all could do to have more productive meetings. She points to ways we can develop shared leadership in conducting meetings, and she provides useful methods of shaping the structure of meetings to produce better results, combat boredom, and influence collegiality. She brings the chapter to an end with this statement: "Our meetings should be wonders to behold." Using her advice might make it possible to have such meetings in our departments or colleges.

Thomas McDaniel's extensive experience—as department chair, division head, dean, vice president for academic affairs, provost, and interim president—enables him in Chapter 6 to discuss with comfort and authority the different types of detractors and how best to deal with them. He provides a welcome touch of levity when he discusses Dilbert and dysfunction. He says that Dilbert "keeps us humble, honest, and in touch with what is really going on in our workplaces." He brings his chapter to a close with a solid discussion of faculty morale.

Stripping away negative defenses is the topic of Chapter 7, which is handled adroitly by Elliott Pood. He points out that defensiveness has certain measurable costs, both professionally and personally. He explains the importance of understanding something about the defensiveness cycle. Out of this discussion comes a useful explanation of defense by denial, defense by justification, and defense by attack, which is followed by the development of strategies for ending the defensiveness. He gives us steps to use to help increase assertive communication and thus reduce the tendency to defensiveness.

Ben Bissell is a psychologist who acts as an independent consultant, and he's had years of helping clients deal with conflict. He works with a model that enables people to solve problems without anyone getting hurt. In Chapter 8, Bissell discusses the various types of difficult individuals, how they behave, and how we might respond productively to their behavior in order to avoid, manage, and possibly resolve conflict.

In Chapter 9, Howard B. Altman looks at dealing with troubled faculty members. He draws on his vast experience and scholarship in this field to help us better understand what we as administrators can do to help those faculty members who are troubled. Altman defines troubled faculty as "those whose job performance and/or relationships with students and colleagues have deteriorated from their normal pattern as a result of emotional stress." Unfortunately, many of us have worked side-by-side with faculty members who fit this description. He points to the ways colleges and universities are responding to the problems presented by troubled faculty, who are, he says, just a small percentage of our faculty. Altman gives us the telltale signs that signal trouble and then addresses what can be done to help them. His section "Providing Help for Troubled Faculty" offers ideas and hope for those of us who want to reach out to offer a helping hand.

Baron Perlman and Lee I. McCann team up to write Chapter 10, which helps us improve the odds of hiring the right person. In doing so, they remind us of the importance of treating all applicants in a professional manner. Perlman and McCann say that the recruitment process should start with a process of "getting your house in order," and they explain the meaning and purpose of doing that. Then they tell us how to plan so that our recruitment satisfies our intent. Knowing what constitutes a good fit is explained in detail so that when we hire a person we will get an individual whose qualifications best fit the department's defined needs. The major issues involved in recruiting are covered in this informative chapter by two experts in the field of faculty recruitment.

In Chapter 11, Nancy Van Note Chism discusses how evaluations can be used to enhance faculty performance and satisfaction. She sees evaluation as a constructive process that is essential for teaching improvement and quality instruction, and she tells us what steps we can take to promote climate changes with respect to evaluation of faculty performance. Chism talks about the usefulness of feedback for ourselves as well as for others. She writes that "You must be authentic in your convictions that evaluation is worthwhile and necessary and that the feedback component, in particular, is essential for learning and growth." She writes about mentoring in this chapter, with the recommendation that rather than attempting to suggest one mentor for the new faculty member, it might be helpful to think in terms of a network of expertise, with different coaches for different aspects of the faculty role.

Faculty morale should always be of concern to chairs and deans, and I address the matter of morale and morale problems in Chapter 12. I look at the causes of low morale, and what chairs and deans can do to improve it. In the chapter is a list of characteristics of high morale colleges, which I found to be instructive. Finally I look at the role of deans and chairs in maintaining faculty morale.

In Chapter 13, this volume concludes with a summary of what we might do to better manage faculty and staff in order to achieve our visions and dreams and to feel that we have positively affected our institutions and the individuals that comprise them. This is, in my judgment, a worthy goal that will pay dividends.

## ACKNOWLEDGMENTS

I am deeply indebted to the contributing authors of this volume. Reading their chapters provided me with a sense of profound humility as I marveled at the depth of their knowledge. I learned much from them, as I believe you will. My humility was less encompassing when I was able to acknowledge and was reminded of the pride I took credit for because I was smart enough to ask such a great group to contribute to this effort! Each brings an abundance of experience and study from which to draw on for the chapter he or she contributed.

Several years ago when I served as Dean of the College of Liberal Arts at Marshall University, Alan B. Gould, then the provost, suggested I put together a manual for chairs to help them better understand their many different duties and responsibilities. It was then that I took up the project that resulted in *Academic Leadership: A Practical Guide to Chairing the Department*. I am indebted to Alan Gould for his confidence in me. My newly acquired interest in helping deans and chairs exercise more positive leadership has been particularly gratifying.

My special thanks go to a longtime friend, Dr. George T. Arnold of Marshall University, who read my early chapters. As always, George, your help and friendship are constant reminders that I am a person of good fortune. I also wish to thank Susan and Jim Anker for their unwavering support of my work. They have been wonderful to work with, and I have much respect for the work they do to help academic administrators.

# About the Contributors

**Howard B. Altman** is Professor and Director of the Linguistics Program at the University of Louisville, where he has taught since 1973. He received his Ph.D. from Stanford University in 1972. A specialist in faculty and department chair development, he has published extensively and consulted at numerous higher education institutions in these areas, as well as in his original discipline of foreign language education. He serves as a member of the advisory boards for *Academic Leader*, for *the Journal of Staff, Program, and Organizational Development*, and for the Kansas State University National Conference for Academic Chairpersons, and is a past member of the board of directors of the Professional and Organizational Development Network in Higher Education.

**Ben Bissell** is a speaker, writer, teacher, therapist, and businessman. He is president of his own consulting firm, LuBen Associates, located in Henderson, Nevada. His Ph.D. was earned at the University of Tennessee, Knoxville. He continued his postgraduate work at the Medical College of Virginia where he taught courses on the emotional care of patients and worked with department staffs on how to manage conflict. He has continued to further his interest in group dynamics and currently teaches over 150 programs a year to companies, organizations, schools, and hospitals. For the past six years he has taught a course for school principals from around the world at Harvard University's Graduate School of Education. He has received Congressional recognition and been called "The Michael Jordan" of his profession. He says his real training comes from growing up in the mountains of Eastern Kentucky—an area noted for the storytelling that Ben has mastered well.

**Nancy Van Note Chism** is Associate Vice Chancellor for Professional Development and Associate Dean of the Faculties at Indiana University Purdue University, Indianapolis, where she is also Associate Professor of Higher Education. Previously, Dr. Chism was Director of Faculty and TA Development and Associate Professor of Educational Policy and Leadership at The Ohio State University. She has been involved in directing or participating in several major funded projects, including the National Consortium on Preparing Graduate Students as College Teachers (Pew Charitable Trusts), The Ohio State Cluster Preparing Future Faculty Program (Pew Charitable Trusts), and the Gateway Engineering Education Program (National Science Foundation). She is a past president of the Professional and Organizational Development Network in Higher Education, an organization devoted to improving college teaching, and in 1998 she received the highest award of that association. Dr. Chism is the author of 30 edited books, book chapters, and journal articles on teaching and learning in higher education and developing faculty and teaching assistants as teachers, with particular emphasis on multicultural teaching and program evaluation. She has made more than 50 presentations nationally and internationally on teaching and learning issues in higher education, including invited addresses at universities and conferences, and has consulted at more than 20 campuses on improving college teaching and evaluating improvement efforts. At Ohio State, she was named Ameritech Faculty Fellow in 1997, and received the Outstanding Teaching Award of The Ohio State College of Education, the Outstanding Service Award of the Graduate Student Association, and the Distinguished Service Award of the Graduate School. She earned her Ph.D. from The Ohio State Univerity in Educational Policy and Leadership.

**Lynn M. Little** is Chair of the Department of Medical Laboratory Sciences at the University of Texas Southwestern Medical Center at Dallas, where he also serves as Assistant Dean for Academic Affairs. He teaches in the areas of health care education, interdisciplinary heath care, medical laboratory management, and leadership. Throughout his career, Dr. Little has served in many leadership capacities, including chair of the University of Texas System Faculty Advisory Council, president of several state and regional medical technology and allied health professional associations, on the national board of directors of the Association of Schools of Allied Health Professions, in leadership positions in the biotechnology industry, and as a commissioned officer in the U.S. Public Health Service.

**Lee I. McCann** is Professor of Psychology at the University of Wisconsin, Oshkosh, where he has served as department chair and Associate Vice Chancellor. He received his Ph.D. in experimental psychology from Iowa State University. His research interests include social communication of dietary preference in rats, implicit learning in humans, psychology curricula, and faculty career development. He is a consulting editor for the journal *Teaching of Psychology*, co-editor (with Baron Perlman and Susan McFadden) of the book *Lessons Learned: Practical Advice for the Teaching of Psychology* (1999, American Psychological Society), and the Teaching Tips column in the *APS Observer*. He is also co-author (with Baron Perlman) of *Recruiting Good College Faculty: Practical Advice for a Successful Search* (Anker, 1996).

**Thomas R. McDaniel** is Professor of Education and Vice President for Academic Affairs and Provost at Converse College. He came to Converse in 1971 as Chair of the Department of Education and Director of Graduate Studies. In 1984, he was named Charles A. Dana Professor of Education. In 1993–1994, he served Converse as Interim President. Dr. McDaniel received his Ph.D. from Johns Hopkins University, where he was elected to Phi Beta Kappa. In all, he is a member of 12 national honorary fraternities. Among Dr. McDaniel's 150-plus publications are six books and 20 textbook chapters, as well as articles in over 50 different journals in education, humanities, and the social sciences. He has served on the editorial boards of such professional journals as *The Capstone Journal of Education, The Clemson Kappan*, and *Academic Leader*. Currently, he serves as executive editor for *The Clearing House*. His latest book, co-authored with Nan McDaniel and Sandra Thomas, is *At Home in South Carolina*, a third-grade social studies text adopted by the state in 1991 and 1999. His commentary on the Gospel of Luke was published in 2000. He serves on a number of local and regional committees and boards, and he has made presentations to scores of educational and civic organizations, both locally and nationally.

**Joan DeGuire North** has served as Dean of the College of Professional Studies at the University of Wisconsin, Stevens Point since 1985. Previously, she held administrative posts at two private colleges, directed the faculty development segment of a national grant, and was an early pioneer in the faculty development movement. She was the founding president of the Professional and Organizational Development Network in Higher Education in the early 1970s. She has written on faculty evaluation, post-tenure review, campus support for teaching, and faculty vitality.

**Baron Perlman** is both a Rosebush and University Professor in the Department of Psychology at the University of Wisconsin, Oshkosh and a fellow in the APA's Society for the Teaching of Psychology (Division 2). He received his Ph.D. in clinical psychology from Michigan State University in 1974. He has a longstanding interest and involvement in faculty development, and chaired the university's Faculty Development Board and was a Mentoring Committee member. He is co-author of three books: *The Academic Intrapreneur* (with Jim Gueths and Don Weber, Praeger, 1988); *Organizational Entrepreneurship* (with Jeffrey R. Cornwall, Irwin, 1990); and *Recruiting Good College Faculty: Practical Advice for a Successful Search* (with Lee McCann, Anker, 1996). He is editor of the Teaching Tips column in the *APS Observer*. The columns recently appeared in book form, *Lessons Learned: Practical Advice for the Teaching of Psychology* (Perlman, McCann, & McFadden, eds.) published by the American Psychological Society (1999). His current research focuses on undergraduate teaching from two perspectives. The first illuminates the teaching preparation and ongoing mentoring and development of faculty who teach, and the place of teaching in the recruitment process. Recent University of Wisconsin Undergraduate Teaching Improvement Council and APA Division 2 grants supported work with UW, Oshkosh faculty and the writing of a training manual, *Peer Review of Teaching* (with Lee McCann). The second provides curricular data useful for individual faculty and departments in their policies, curricular decisions and undergraduate teaching. Two journal articles presenting a national study of the undergraduate psychology curriculum recently appeared in *Teaching of Psychology* (with Lee McCann) supported by a grant from the APA.

**Elliott A. Pood** is Dean of the College of Arts and Sciences and Professor of Communication at the University of North Alabama. Prior to accepting his recent post, Dr. Pood was Chairman of the Department of Radio-Television/Photography and then served as Assistant Dean of the College of Mass Communication at Middle

Tennessee State University. Dr. Pood received his Ph.D. in Organizational Communication from Florida State University. Before joining UNA and MTSU, Dr. Pood served as Associate Professor and Director of the Institute for Communication Research and Consulting at the University of North Carolina, Greensboro. Dr. Pood specializes in organizational communication with a research/consulting specialty in organizational conflict management. He has published over 60 articles and professional papers on the subjects of organizational communication or mass communication and has won awards for his research from the International Communication Association. He has also served as a consultant to over 75 different public agencies and private corporations.

**Daniel W. Wheeler** is Professor of Extension and Higher Education, and Coordinator, Office of Professional and Organizational Development at the University of Nebraska, Lincoln. He has coauthored four books and numerous articles on department chairs and faculty development, and has consulted extensively nationally and internationally with higher education institutions.

# Understanding Yourself 1

*Deryl R. Leaming*

> *Above all else, academic deans and department chairs—and all leaders—must come to terms with and accept who they are.*

L eaders who never come to understand themselves are destined for failure. This is especially true when leaders fail both to understand who they are and to accept themselves. Effective leaders cannot be overly sensitive to criticism, and individuals who do not accept who they are tend to be defensive. They recoil at criticism, perhaps to the extent of considering revenge. Such people, whatever their titles, will not attract many followers.

Self-understanding is a lifetime process, ongoing and recursive and flexible. Leaders must constantly search for better self-understanding and welcome opportunities that will assist them in such a quest.

So if we accept the notion that good leaders have good self-understanding, the question that remains is how do we gain self-knowledge? Short of spending a lot of time and money for psychoanalysis, what can we do? Of course there is no simple or single answer to this question. However, there are some relatively simple things we can do to help us achieve a better understanding of ourselves. In this chapter, I offer a few examples of rather simple things we can do to help us achieve better understanding of ourselves.

## KNOW AND ACCEPT YOURSELF

Above all else, academic deans and department chairs—and all leaders—must come to terms with and accept who they are. For a moment, think about leaders you've known, both those you admired and those you thought to be inadequate. Did any of the leaders you admired seem uncomfortable with who they were? Did any manifest insecurity? What about those who you thought were inadequate or not up to the task? Chances are good that the

1

leaders you have admired and respected are secure and comfortable with themselves, whereas those who seem to be weak and less-than-adequate leaders are likely to be insecure, without a sufficient self-knowledge and acceptance.

The simple and plain truth is that we cannot be leaders unless others look up to and want to follow us, and the likelihood of that happening when we are not secure in who we are is remote. Everything about us—our words, actions, body language, and very demeanor—is exposed to others whenever we are out in front as leaders. Thus, if we are insecure and unhappy with who we are, others sense this. Not only do we not have as much confidence in ourselves when we are insecure; it soon becomes obvious that others lack confidence in us as well. Insecure people tend to be defensive and overly sensitive and do not respond well to criticism, and—as we know—all those who make decisions will sooner or later be criticized.

Deans and chairs who dare to do something are prepared for opposition—especially when risk is present. They often take a courageous stand, suggesting that even if something isn't broke, it should be fixed nonetheless. Deans and chairs—who have the courage of their convictions and are ready to be ridiculed and opposed—should be open and forthcoming with faculty and staff members and not back down in the face of inevitable resistance. Deans and chairs must have confidence supported by being at ease with who they are. Competence never substitutes for insecurity.

Bennis (1989, p. 53) reminds us that by "the time we reach puberty, the world has reached us and shaped us to a greater extent than we realize. Our family, friends, school, and society in general have told us—by word and example—how to be," and he points out something especially important when he adds that "people begin to become leaders at that moment when they decide for themselves how to be."

Let's accept for a moment Bennis's premise that leadership really begins at that moment when people decide for themselves how to be. Have you decided "how to be"? Do you know how to go about deciding how to be? Even though we accept Bennis's premise, we must realize that believing it and acting on it are vastly different concepts, with the latter being complex and, for many, seemingly unachievable.

## STRATEGIES FOR SELF-UNDERSTANDING

Let's pause for a moment to reflect on the question of what we might do to gain insights into who we are and how to work toward feeling comfortable with that person so that we will be in a position to provide enlightened leadership.

If you're anything like me, you've struggled over the years with the elusive and perplexing problem of trying to understand yourself. More than likely you've been to conference after conference where you've been subjected to discussions and tests of one kind or another that purport to help us better understand who we are. Again, if you're anything like me, you're still searching for better self-understanding.

Does this mean that these sessions and exercises have been useless? Of course not. Indeed, what we soon discover is that coming to terms with ourselves, and understanding who we are never ends; it's a lifetime pursuit. We still need more than self-improvement sessions. We need a useful way of helping to better understand who we are and developing the wherewithal to accept ourselves—knowing, of course, that even if we come to terms with who we are, we still can find room for improvement.

### The Behavior Audit

My solution is that all of us who are leaders or aspire to leadership positions should begin by administering to ourselves regular behavior audits. Let me illustrate:

We must begin by asking ourselves tough, direct questions and answering them as honestly as we know how. While in Table 1.1 there are 20 questions, there is nothing sacred about that number; you may choose to have more or even fewer than 20. You should do these on a weekly basis, though other periods are acceptable and can be equally useful. You should arm yourself with a short journal during the week so that you can provide more helpful answers.

At times it also is a good idea to have a friend who you can trust to be honest with you look at your behavior and answer some of these same questions. You want the complete, unvarnished truth, even if it is painful to accept. By examining your behavior this way, you have an opportunity to redefine yourself, which is something leaders must do.

## TABLE 1.1 BEHAVIOR AUDIT QUESTIONS

1) What action(s) did you take during the week that you are proud of?

2) What did you do during the week that you are not especially proud of?

3) For those things you did that made you proud, what did you do right, and how can you duplicate this behavior in the future?

4) Did you accomplish during the week what you set out to?

5) How did your accomplishments come about? Did you make them happen? If so, how?

6) How did your failures occur? How did you let these responsibilities fall through the cracks? Was it your fault or the fault of others?

7) Were you honest and forthright with all those with whom you interacted? (You must not pull any punches here, as this is an especially important question for all leaders to ask themselves.)

8) What did you do this week to fulfill your vision, and how well did you communicate this vision to others?

9) How would you rate your decision-making ability if you scored it on a 1–10 scale, with 10 being high?

10) Are there things you could do or change next week so that you could honestly give yourself a higher decision-making score?

11) How effectively did you communicate with all those who report to you and those to whom you report? If you used the same scoring system as in question #10, what score would you give yourself?

12) Did you do any strategic planning this week?

13) What can you list as evidence of building consensus and fostering teamwork?

14) Are you willing to look at how your college should change, and are you honestly prepared to advocate change? Or is it your tendency to favor the status quo?

15) How well did you interact with others? Did you consult others when decisions had to be made? How well did you involve others in the college's business?

16) Are you empowering others and giving them a sense of ownership of the college?

17) Have you been fair to others, giving them the benefit of the doubt?

18) Have you successfully put yourself in the shoes of those who disagree with you? Could these persons have been right?

19) Have you been upbeat and cheerful? Do others enjoy your company?

20) What part of who you are needs to be changed immediately, and what goals should you have for the coming week to make these changes happen?

## The Circle of Concern and the Circle of Influence

Stephen Covey (1989) has developed a way for helping us better understand ourselves. His approach centers on where we focus our time and energy. He explains that each of us has a wide range of concerns—our health, our children, problems at work, etc. He demonstrates this with his creation of the "circle of concern." As we examine those things within our circle of concern, it becomes obvious that there are some things over which we have no real control and others that we can do something about. Those that we can do something about can be identified within a smaller circle of influence.

Covey notes that proactive people take responsibility for their own lives. Their behavior is a function of their decisions, not their conditions. They can subordinate feelings to values. They have the initiative and the responsibility to make things happen. On the other hand, reactive people are driven by feelings, by circumstances, by conditions, by their environment.

Most leaders are proactive people who focus their efforts in the circle of influence, working on the things they can do something about. The nature of their energy is positive, enlarging, and magnifying, causing their circle of influence to increase.

Reactive people behave differently. They operate mostly in the circle of concern, focusing on the weakness of other people, the circumstances over which they have no control, and the problems of the environment. Covey (1989, p. 83) says, "Their focus results in blaming and accusing attitudes, reactive language, and increased feelings of victimization. The negative energy generated by that focus, combined with neglect in areas they could do something about, causes their circle of influence to shrink."

As long as our attention is focused on the circle of concern, we accomplish little beyond increasing our own feelings of inadequacy and helplessness. When we work in our circle of influence, on the other hand, we begin to create positive energy. As leaders, we must strive to work within our circle of influence, taking responsibility for our actions and behavior. We can be happy and accept those things that at present we can't control, while we focus our efforts on the things we can. Covey implores us to keep our commitments, to be a light and not a judge, to be a model and not a critic. More importantly, he says we should be part of the solution and not part of the problem. If we are proactive leaders, we will work almost exclusively out of our circle of influence. That should be our goal.

### The Descriptive Me

Let's look for a moment to a more structured way to have friends tell us how they view us. A good exercise is to have three or four friends rate you on the following statements and then compare his or her answers with how you respond. This is an exercise I call "The Descriptive Me." Reprint the scale in Table 1.2 and give it to three or four individuals whom you know well and who you believe will respond honestly.

This exercise can be done in an hour or so, and to me it is well worth the time. But we can't stop at that point if we are seriously

## TABLE 1.2 THE DESCRIPTIVE ME

Respond to each statement below by marking it on a scale of 1–5, with 1 being strong disagreement with the statement and 5 indicating strong agreement.

1) The subject is someone you can trust.

2) The subject is a decisive person.

3) The subject has strong leadership qualities.

4) The subject is a charismatic person.

5) The subject is capable of getting things done.

6) The subject has a solid vision of the future.

7) The subject has an even temperament.

8) The subject is courageous.

9) The subject is able to influence others.

10) The subject has a wide range of knowledge.

11) The subject has the ability to build confidence.

12) The subject is able to see what the needs of others are.

13) The subject is an effective communicator with many different audiences.

14) The subject is described by others as someone others turn to for advice.

15) The subject challenges the status quo and is willing to make changes and take risks.

interested in understanding ourselves and coming to terms with who we are. If we want to be confident leaders, much more is necessary. You should post your weekly self-improvement goals in a spot where you must look at them several times each day, and you should assess your progress daily. For the purpose of illustration, let's assume that you have a confrontation with a colleague. Afterwards, you should ask yourself how well you handled your differences. Were you honest? Did you become defensive? Did you keep your dispute on a professional level? Were you able to achieve a resolution to the problem? If you had to do it all over, what changes would you make in how you handled yourself and the situation? What can you learn about yourself from this experience?

### Questions to Ask Yourself

Pema Chodron (2001, pp. 12–13) asks important questions which can help us better understand ourselves when she writes, "[H]ow do I react when my beliefs about the government are challenged? How about when others don't agree with how I feel about homosexuality or women's rights or the environment? What happens when my ideas about smoking or drinking are challenged? What do I do when my religious convictions are not shared?"

Chodron goes on to make many valid points and suggestions that can help us with our quest to learn who we are and why we are the way we are. She points out that we all have a variety of habitual tactics that we use to avoid life as it is. Perhaps we have just as many tactics to hide from better understanding ourselves. Do we really want to know who we are?

I mentioned that there are other techniques we can use to help gain self-understanding. There is nothing so helpful, in my judgment, as developing the ability and know-how of self-introspection. It takes intensive concentration and time, but once achieved enables us to look deep within ourselves to find demons that haunt us and perhaps have been bedeviling us since we were toddlers. Once we discover these demons, we then can reach deep within to pull them out, so that we can look at each one squarely between the nasty scoundrel's eyes. Having done this, it is possible to slay them and get rid of them for good. This level of self-introspection allows us to come to a much better understanding of who we are.

## CONCLUSION

As most of us have heard since we were young, "Those things in life that are worth anything are worth working for." Understanding yourself is not excluded from this bromide, of which our parents would often remind us. Indeed, it is a formidable—but worthwhile—task which is, in my opinion, a prerequisite to the development of any of the other leadership skills. Self-understanding is the starting point for becoming a skillful leader.

## REFERENCES

Bennis, W. (1989). *On becoming a leader.* Cambridge, MA: Perseus Books.

Chodron, P. (2001). *The places that scare you.* Boston, MA: Shambala.

Covey, S. R. (1989). *The seven habits of highly effective people.* New York, NY: Simon & Schuster.

# Understanding and Communicating with Others  2

*Daniel W. Wheeler*

> *With those with whom we experience an affinity, genuineness, and interest seem natural and relatively straightforward. Interactions are usually read correctly or, if not, one is given the benefit of the doubt.*

In the first chapter you were presented with the importance of having a greater self-understanding in order to fulfill your roles and to be more effective with others. Although this chapter focuses on understanding others, you are encouraged to continually reflect for yourself that you are a part of the responses of others.

Given the commitment to understanding others, this chapter addresses the following areas:

- Some assumptions that can create problems
- Communication process within a context
- Types of conversations
- Understanding why others make changes
- Additional strategies to develop effective communication processes

Because chairs may have little actual training in the process skills of understanding others, various frameworks and strategies are interwoven into this overall scheme for understanding others. However, let's begin with some common assumptions that may result in difficulty understanding others.

***Others are motivated by the same things and in the same ways as I am.*** Some may be, but we also know that people are complex and motivated by a range of factors, some of which remain constant and others which change over time.

***Some people won't change.*** Most will, but their requirements may be quite different than ours, or our assumptions about what is necessary may be ill-founded.

*I have little leverage to make people do anything.* Even with concerns about academic freedom, unionization, and litigation, chairs can have tremendous influence through setting the agenda, persuading, and being persistent. However, you have to have the courage to suggest changes and to help people see why those changes are necessary.

*Upper administration will not support my efforts.* If they understand what you are doing and why it is important in terms of the department and the future, they should be supportive.

*This person's behavior is unrelated to me.* Often untrue! You may be part of the stimulus/response which often involves a negative or positive force in these interactions.

Given that we often make assumptions or misinterpret behavior, what can we do to be more effective in working with others? Let's examine some strategies.

## COMMUNICATION WITHIN A CONTEXT

With those with whom we experience an affinity, genuineness and interest seem natural and relatively straightforward. Interactions are usually read correctly or, if not, one is given the benefit of the doubt.

However, in situations in which there is distrust or little affinity, chairs and deans face greater challenges. Even though we may believe that relationship building should be a 50–50 proposition, the greater pressure is on the administrators because the institution needs the relationship to work—the consequences are too great when it does not.

So, if an administrator wants to reach beyond the 50–50 norm, what premises are necessary?

• Find out the person's interests, whether it's in your area of interest or not. Everyone has a passion, whether about their work or outside of work, and relating around the passion builds relationship of openness and trust.

• Think of your development of understanding in a similar vein to how you would address a research, teaching, or service problem or question. Your curiosity can help break down barriers, particularly if you are sincere about your interest.

• Understand that talking with people is a big part of your work; it's not an add-on or nicety. Conversations are investments in the human interaction bank—if you don't invest, there is nothing to withdraw when things are more difficult. As a faculty member suggested in a study of department chairs about his highly admired chair, "he talks to people about everything for a living" (Creswell et al. 1990).

• If you believe there is distrust, or you sense a distance between you and your colleagues, have a frank conversation and indicate what you intend to do and what you would like them to do. Ask your colleague to think about the situation and then get together with him or her at another time, not more than a week later, to follow up on the conversation. Often the person is more receptive.

• No matter what strategy you use, you must be sincere and authentic. If you can't do that, no strategy will be successful, as the person will see through it. It doesn't matter whether you hired the person, like him, or want him as part of your departmental family—he is part of your unit, and you have to deal with him. And, just to stir the pot, punishment is usually ineffective, particularly if the person is willing to accept the punishment (loss of merit or privileges). You also have the potential to make the person into a martyr, with the other faculty turning on you because even though they want something done, they are offended by your methods. Part of the reaction is if you would do this to them, you might do it to me!

## ESTABLISHING THE CONTEXT

In exchanges with others, you need to establish a context for the discussion. Some of the levels to be addressed include:

*Interests and needs.* What is important to the faculty member, professionally and personally? Where is his or her passion? Will it fit professionally? If not, what are the options?

*Departmental or unit needs.* What are the priorities? How can the interests fit into departmental needs? If the interests do not address needed innovations and new directions, would any of these interests help resolve the maintenance needs (just keeping things going) of the department?

*Institutional priorities.* If the individual interests aren't aligned with departmental needs, do they align with institutional needs? If so, is there some way to make the opportunity meet these institutional needs? Who could help make this happen?

*Open conversations.* If the person just wants to talk about whatever is on his or her mind, can you just listen, be empathetic, and suggest possible options?

Unless the context is established, conversations will tend to go off on tangents or into areas that will not move the situation forward.

## SUGGESTED RULES OF ENGAGEMENT

*Listen.* So often people believe they are good listeners, yet they are either talking or waiting to say their piece rather than concentrating on what the person is saying. Listening takes concentrated effort and commitment. Especially in situations in which you are pressed, listening is difficult. But a rule to remember is, listening now may prevent problems later. A few minutes of listening is an investment in prevention. Anything less will send the wrong message.

*Clarify, don't assume.* So much of what happens is based upon assumptions and categorizations, or at worst, stereotypes. Assumptions are often based on previous experience such that even if someone is open to or interested in change, or reinventing himself or herself, previous perceptions often control what is possible. On the positive side, specialists such as faculty are educated to make categorizations, but human beings are more complicated than most of what scientists often address. The impression is if I can put you in this box and keep you there, then I don't have to consider anything different—it allows me to protect myself or keep you within the boundaries I have created. Then sometimes we turn around and blame the person for not changing!

## WHOSE PROBLEM IS IT?

A well-known and recently revised management article by William Oncken, Jr. and Donald W. Wass (1999) suggests that people often take on others' problems (described as taking monkeys on your back). Chairs and deans, as authorities, can be pulled into situations in which someone wants them to solve their problem. In some ways, the administrator may become the mother or father figure who is expected to take on the child's (the faculty member's) problem. As Oncken and Wass describe, "Getting control over time and content of what you do is appropriate advice for managing management time. The first order of business is for the manager to enlarge his discretionary time by eliminating subordinate-imposed time" (p. 178).

If adult, responsible interactions are the goal, then chairs and deans should not resolve others' issues. As a chair said to me recently, "I will not clean up faculty messes. If they create them, then they can clean them up." Administrators can become so burdened by these problems that they don't get to the issues they should address.

### How to Avoid the "Monkey on Your Back"

*Recognize your own propensity to take on others' problems.* Some of us, in our efforts to help others avoid pain or to avoid pain ourselves, may jump in. Or, we may believe it is our way to be liked, which most of us have in some quotient.

*Recognize those staff who are prone to drop "monkeys on your back."* Certainly there are some who seem to relish having someone else take care of them. Once you know the pattern, prepare yourself for how you will handle the situation. Reframe what you will do.

*Clarify the issue.*

*Explain why you don't see this as your problem, and that it is their problem.*

*Suggest what you are or aren't willing to do.*

*Listen and help them reflect on the problem.* Your response may not be well received, particularly if others have played the "save me" role before. Be prepared to repeat your message and to hold firm.

After a few interactions, you will usually find your department members will quit using the strategy. They may or may not take you up on your suggestions for what you are willing to do, or they may come back at a later time after they have gotten over their anger or resentment. In recalcitrant situations, you may have to persevere for a considerable time period, and they may suggest to others that you are not very helpful or are not doing your job. Others will understand it is not your responsibility, and you are helping by not taking someone else's problem on your back.

Remember, this pattern doesn't know hierarchical boundaries, as departmental members may use the strategy but so can higher administrators. Although the political ramifications may be greater with higher administrators, you can't allow this pattern to be established.

Some would no doubt refer to this strategy as "tough love," which became popular in relationships between parents and children around issues such as drug use and other high-risk situations. Whatever it's called, it's common with those who focus on rights but not the responsibilities. It's required to prevent some counter-effective behaviors and to build individual responsibility.

## OPTIONS

A major role in the support and encouragement of others is helping others to see options—whether of large or small magnitude. For example, a chair or dean may suggest a whole new direction or capitalize on a suggestion made by the faculty member, or, on a smaller scale, suggest behaviors such as listening more carefully to a particular faculty member, that will result in a different relationship. There may be no greater gift than helping someone move beyond his or her communication cul-de-sac. Then again, you have to be sincere in wanting to help and in offering options since, in the short term, such a possibility may demand administrative creativity (changing someone else's assignment for this person to be able to realize his or her option, which often means gaining a commitment from someone else to take on the tasks).

## CONSEQUENCES

Today, many people talk about their rights and privileges but not their responsibilities. Consequences build responsibility. Sometimes faculty can be quite irresponsible because they feel protected by rights such as tenure and academic freedom. If they abuse their responsibilities, then they need to understand the consequences. Some examples follow. If a staff member is abusive to others (students, colleagues, or you), then what happens if there are no consequences? It will build a pattern of continued irresponsibility. The range of possible consequences/actions you might take may include:

*Confront the person about the inappropriateness of his or her actions.* Suggest what the appropriate departmental values and behaviors are.

*Suggest what will happen if he or she continues the present behavior.* One possibility includes a written warning in the personnel file for not meeting professional obligations.

*Take action if the faculty member continues and let him or her know that you have taken the action.*

*If the behavior still persists, move to the next level of consequences, which may involve a higher level of authority or more formalized procedures.* Don't let threats of legal action or a sense of blackmail prevent you from doing what has to be done because the strategy will be used repeatedly if it was successful.

## COMMITMENTS

Any conversation suggests that there may be commitments made—actions or behaviors agreed to or strategies to consider. To be sure that both or all of the parties are on the same page, it is important to summarize in writing what you believe has been agreed upon, including a specific time frame for that agreement. Not only does such a document often prevent misunderstandings, it also builds trust. Even if something is agreed to that is distasteful, a faculty member will probably respect you for clarifying the situation. In any event, such clarification is necessary in effective communication.

## FOLLOW-UP

Once commitments are made, follow-up is important to insure that they are honored. Today it may be even more important as there is some indication that many employees avoid commitments (they may say they are committed, but they keep their options open).

*Revisit time commitments.* Certainly there may be reasons that the time frame may have to be adjusted, but those who have made a commitment should be expected to explain why the adjustments are necessary and how they will fulfill the obligation.

This basic process of communication encourages clarity, trust, and clear responsibility. However, it requires consistent effort and some courage to implement.

## UNDERSTANDING WHY OTHERS MAKE CHANGES

In today's environment, conversations often revolve around discussion about change. Why do people make changes, and how can you use this understanding to help them make changes? The following are some reasons that prompt people to consider making changes in their lives:

- Self-interest
- The greater good
- Making a difference

### Self-Interest

Economists often suggest that self-interest motivates all behavior. Certainly observing many academics, one would believe this premise, and it should be taken into account in understanding behavior. This pattern is also suggested by transactional relationships—behaviors based upon the quid pro quo agreements (Bass, 1985). A well-known saying in academe is that "the politics are so vicious because the stakes are so small." The major problem with this kind of motivation is that one only does what one is rewarded for. It also suggests that faculty expect others to have control over the reward system or their common refrain will be "I only do what I get rewarded for."

### The Greater Good

Over time, statesmen and great moral leaders have appealed to the greater good as a motivator. They have been able to create a vision in which others are willing to invest. Deans and department chairs play an important role in articulating and helping others interface with the vision.

The sense of investing in something beyond self-interest has been captured and well documented in transformational behaviors in leadership. These clusters of behaviors, measured by the Multi-factor Leadership Questionnaire (MLQ), suggest the importance of visions of the future, new ideas, and meaning making in changing situations. Considerable research indicates that those who are more transformational will make greater commitments to organizational goals, work harder, and be more satisfied (Avolio, 1999). Chairs should make every effort to appeal to faculty on this wider basis.

*Making a Difference*

In my various conversations in consultations with faculty, making a difference comes to the forefront as a motivator. In changing times, people express concerns about whether their present activities do make a difference. Here is the opportunity to move to the bigger picture—the vision of the future—to define behaviors that will make a difference and to let go of other activities that are no longer meaningful or that no longer make a difference.

## OTHER STRATEGIES THAT PROMOTE CHANGE

In a situation with a combination of authority and relationships, chairs can do several things to enable development.

*Give permission.* Even though we are dealing with bright people, the socialization process is intense. This means that chairs and deans can play an important role in giving permission to faculty to make changes that may address institutional needs but conflict with disciplinary needs. This tension will always be part of what chairs and deans have to address.

*Understand the role of preferences in making changes.* Different personality types have different needs or requirements to make changes. As a chair or dean, you should know that intuitive personality types respond to challenges. If the challenge is sufficient, they will accept it and won't care about such details as job descriptions or clear expectations. On the other hand, those with a primarily sensing personality type will want more structure and clear expectations. Job descriptions will be helpful.

Another important difference is whether one has a preference for thinking or feeling. For individuals whose personality type relies on a preference for thinking, steps need to be clear and have a clear rationale. Relationships may have some effect, but they are not primary. Those with a feeling preference focus primarily on how ideas and actions affect personal dimensions, and they want a harmonious work environment. Chairs and deans should become knowledgeable about personality indicators such as the Myers-Briggs Type Indicator (MBTI), and should strive to understand the preferences of others as well as their own.

*Consider motivational knowledge.* The classic work in motivation is Maslow's Hierarchy of Needs. Certainly this framework provides some useful ways to think about needs, but some further work in this area is more focused.

Barbuto (1999) has developed a five-component motivational scale, the Motivational Style Instrument (MSI), which addresses various ways people are motivated.

1) *Intrinsic process motivation:* focused on task pleasure and enjoying their work

2) *Instrumental motivation:* concerned with tangible rewards and a "what's in it for me?" orientation

3) *External self concept–based motivation:* concerned with others' opinions and meeting their expectations

4) *Internal self concept–based motivation:* focused on their own internal standards of behavior and motivation

5) *Goal internalization motivation:* committed to moral causes in which principles guide choices

The MSI suggests that we cannot assume that others are motivated the same way we are. For example, many faculty members are oriented to the internal self-concept, but some are not. The MSI provides specific ways to engage others' motivations. However, once again, whatever tools and strategies are chosen, one must be sincere in the interactions and in using privileged information to help people move forward in their professional and personal lives.

*Be a gadfly.* Creswell, et al. (1990) suggest that academics can become stuck or entrenched in what a colleague refers to as academic cul-de-sacs (Schuster, 1990). Even though we are working with intelligent professionals, we have all observed a number of people who just don't monitor their own careers and make decisions while they have options. They often need encouragement and permission to take new perspectives and move in new directions.

An important role you can play as a department chair or dean is to be a gadfly—to challenge, encourage, and cajole departmental members to gain new perspectives and have different experiences. This may include different conferences and workshops, forging new relationships and collegial associations, and just encouraging new ways to look at things both professionally and personally. If you do it enough, your department or college members will come to expect it and won't get so locked into entrenched behaviors.

## TYPES OF CONVERSATIONS

Some conversations are easy to have and others are not. One might divide them into three types: 1) difficult conversations, 2) "soft" conversations, and 3) hard conversations.

### Difficult Conversations

*Explaining the rules of the game have changed.* Many who have been at an institution for a while find that they struggle with their performance at the institution and are often angry with the changes. A common refrain is "It's unfair to change the rules." One helpful strategy is to redefine what is sometimes referred to as the "psychological contract" (Creswell et al., 1990; Schein, 1978), in which an understanding is developed from where things were, and then enables people to visualize where they can go from here. It is important that the chair not engage in blaming or defending previous chairs, but help the faculty member come to some closure about the past so that he or she can move forward.

*Working with people we don't like.* Nearly everyone has someone they would just as soon avoid or not work with because of characteristics that translate to "we just don't like them or like to be around them." Particularly if they were not in our academic area as a faculty member, we often had the luxury of avoiding them. However, as a chair or dean, we may have no choice but to work with them. So how do we forge a constructive professional relationship?

*Focusing on goals.* Sometimes conflict is the result of different ways of doing things—using different processes. If we can agree on the goals and their outcomes, then often we can be on the same page. We may need to let go of the means question (especially if the person has demonstrated a track record of success).

*Helping them see the impact of their behavior.* If you see this as a teaching situation, you might want to mix in some feedback about how their behavior affects you and suggest an alternative. Sometimes this can lead to a coaching situation, or even a contract to work on the issue.

*Acknowledging that you can work together and not necessarily like one another.* One aspect of being a professional is the ability to work with others even if we don't particularly like them. I can still focus on the professional business at hand and learn to ignore the rest. Sometimes it just helps to put issues on the table and agree to proceed professionally.

*Defining what's unacceptable.* We need to help people see what are acceptable and unacceptable patterns of behavior. Quite often we are either surprised or repulsed by some of the behaviors of people we observe. Yet we have to help some of our colleagues understand that they have to change behaviors to meet professional expectations that seem to be either unknown or ignored.

*Recognizing fundamental value differences.* We constantly face value differences that may be triggered by any of the following differences: 1) ends, 2) means, 3) values, and 4) personality. Certainly ends and means are the easiest to address, especially if they can be made explicit. The most difficult are the personality differences because they often are a result of differences in style. If people can agree on ends and, even better, ends and means, then style can become a minor issue—just agree to differences in style and focus on how to achieve goals.

*Talking about taboos.* Some faculty may have different standards of personal issues (dress, language, cleanliness) and/or professional issues (plagiarism, professional differences, civility). In informal conversation one often hears "he/she should know better" or "don't parents teach their kids social etiquette anymore?" The result may be a faculty member with brilliant professional credentials who may be unsuccessful or have questions raised because of these more personal/social habits or behaviors.

Somehow, fair or not, the department chair or dean ends up with the problem, or the opportunity, to make these into learning situations—the teachable moment, if you will. Here the situation of being both an authority and a colleague can create even more complexity in having a conversation. On the one hand, if you use the authority to guide and direct, the reaction may be a complaint of violating academic freedom or freedom of choice. However, speaking as a colleague will mean you are counting on your sense of concern and persuasion to help leverage the behavior change desired.

In some situations in which the behavior clearly is a non-fulfillment of duties (coming to class drunk or not even showing up for class), the chair or dean uses his or her authority to see that obligations are met. Anything short of that action would be negligent.

However, many behaviors are more subtle and do not suggest a lack of fulfillment of duties—just an interference with or difference as to what is involved in the obligations. In these cases, one might consider the following criteria in deciding whether to have these difficult conversations: 1) the effect on department (students, colleagues, and staff), 2) the consequences to the faculty member if the behavior continues, and 3) the likelihood that if not addressed, this will become a more difficult problem.

Say, for example, that a faculty member in your department is reportedly verbally abusive to a secretary not directly under your supervision. A number of other faculty and staff who have observed the abusive behavior have come to you suggesting the behavior is inappropriate and creates a morale problem in the department. Neither of the two parties comes to you for help or counsel.

In your analysis of the situation, you assess that you have a good relationship with both the faculty member and the staff member; with people coming to you, you know that this is already a problem and will probably get worse (you've heard rumors that the staff member may leave). You are aware more people are questioning why something isn't being done (which usually means why someone in authority—namely you—isn't doing something).

Because your relationship with the faculty member is good, you can probably risk more in your approach. You may be able to ask him if he is aware of the perceived situation, how it is affecting the department, and what might be done to address it. If the faculty member acknowledges the problem, the situation may have a straightforward resolution.

However, if there is no acknowledgment of the situation, or if you have a poor relationship with the faculty member, then you might be forced to suggest the parameters of the situation you will accept—abusiveness to anyone in the department is not tolerated and, if it is not stopped immediately, corrective action (reprimands, change of supervisory assignment) will be taken. Essentially the person is put on notice for a zero-tolerance policy that will lead to abrupt action.

If you take this course, there may be a strong reaction, with accusations of infringing on academic freedom, breaking procedures, and possible grievances or legal action. In response, you have the opportunity to take the high road, suggesting if the problem is addressed, nothing more will be necessary. However, if the offending faculty member refuses to admit that there is a problem, confirm for all that you want to continue the professional relationship and that you believe the situation can be resolved by a change in the person's behavior.

These difficult situations provide the opportunity for you to take giant steps in authenticity and credibility. Those in the department are going to respect you because you resolved a situation that created a departmental morale problem, you demonstrated effective human interaction skills, and you added to the quality of life for the combatants as well as the entire department. The whole episode demonstrated your commitment, courage, and leadership—aspects you can continue to draw upon because of the trust of others.

### Conversations about "Soft" Things

The soft stuff often makes chairs and deans nervous because there are multiple outcomes, and the conversations are wide ranging. Yet these are conversations about motivation—the transformational dreams, hopes, feelings—the basis of passion. We have to learn to tune into these conversations. They lead to the concrete proposals and the plans that make a difference. They keep people motivated.

Especially for those socialized in the hard sciences, these conversations will be difficult. This is not the raw material of formulas and precise work, which, at times, frustrates those who want everything tied up neatly. But they are a necessary part of management and professional development.

### Conversations about Hard Things

The conversations about the hard stuff are often easier for chairs and deans. This includes outcomes, plans, and actions. Here administrators often believe that they are on familiar ground— with subject matter they can operationally define and actions for which they can hold people accountable.

In your conversations, it is crucial that you create the atmosphere in which the conversations about hopes and dreams can be translated into the management accountability language that includes the more familiar plans and products.

## WHERE DO I SPEND MY TIME?

We all know that we only have so much time to spend, so how do we decide how to spend it? I suggest that you spend time focusing on the following: things that people are excited about, progress, people expressing and/or demonstrating support, the teachable moments, deeper conversations, and willingness to take responsibility.

Things that waste precious time are when someone tries to foist their problems onto you and when you find yourself going over the same ground (complaints and historical situations) more than once. Instead, refocus such conversations by using the following process: 1) invite individuals to reflect on what they have said (some paraphrasing by you would probably be helpful); 2) ask what they want you to do (sometimes they just want someone to listen); 3) spell out what you are willing to do and not do; and 4) discuss their options.

## MEANS OF COMMUNICATION

With the level of activity and expectations in today's work environment, making time to relate face-to-face will continue to be a challenge. What are some guidelines about various means to enhance successful communication?

*Face-to-face conversations.* Even with all the marvelous—in some ways seductive technology—make sure you deal with important communication face-to-face. This includes personal interactions, personnel actions, and conversations about the important things in life.

*Email.* Many conversations and dialogues can be enhanced through email exchanges. Much of the normal business (committee meetings and idea exchange) is now conducted by email because it is easy to do and people can respond any time. Be careful not to rely on it just because it is easy, or to use it for things that should be done face-to-face.

*Telephone.* If one cannot communicate face-to-face, the telephone is an important communication device. At least it has a personal aspect and allows exchange in a way that allows some sense of the person's response.

Of course, the stronger the relationship, the less important the means of communication. If the trust is there, then even if there are miscommunications, you are often given the benefit of the doubt.

## WINDING UP

As the leader of your academic unit, you are expected to be a model of reasonableness, fairness, and trust. Others can get by with a lesser standard for relating, but you are always under inspection for appropriate behavior. If you can stay focused on what the cultural expectations and goals are, as well as the departmental or college results, then relationships become more important and integrated into the life of the unit. You need to keep investing in— and encouraging others to invest in—relationships to create the environment you want. It doesn't happen by accident or just naturally. It takes courage, persistence, and good will to make a difference.

Good luck to all of us.

## REFERENCES

Avolio, B. J. (1999). *Full leadership development: Building the vital forces in organizations.* Thousand Oaks, CA: Sage.

Barbuto, J. E., & Scholl, R. W. (1999). Development of new scales to measure an integrative taxonomy of motivation sources. *Psychological Reports, 82,* 1011–1022.

Bass, B. M. (1985). *Leadership and performance beyond expectations.* New York, NY: Free Press.

Creswell, J. W., Wheeler, D. W., Seagren, A. T., Egly, N. J., & Beyer, K. D. (1990). *The academic chairperson's handbook.* Lincoln, NE: University of Nebraska Press.

Oncken, Jr., W., Wass, D. L., & Covey, S. R. (1999, November-December). Time Management: Who's got the monkey? *Harvard Business Review, 77* (6), 178–187.

Schein, E. H. (1978). *Career dynamics: Matching individual and orgnizational needs.* Reading, MA: Addison-Wesley.

Schuster, J. H., & Wheeler, D. W. (Ed.). (1990). *Enhancing faculty careers: Strategies for development and renewal.* San Francisco, CA: Jossey-Bass.

# Establishing a Positive Leadership Approach

**3**

*Lynn M. Little*

> *The leader stands on a precipice, looking forward, looking backward, looking in all directions. Looking forward, to search for a pathway to the future. Looking backward, to assess the terrain already covered. Looking in all directions, to see the possibilities and the dangers on the periphery. The leader stands on a precipice, not a summit—the visibility is limited, the footing treacherous.*

Chairs and deans must have good leadership skills in order to be successful. The reality, however, is that too many of them arrive in leadership positions with only a vague understanding of leadership and poorly developed leadership skills. No wonder people don't lead well when they have never been taught how to do so.

For over 11 years, I have led the Department of Medical Laboratory Sciences at the University of Texas Southwestern Medical Center at Dallas. Before I took this position, my background had been in clinical microbiology and public health laboratory management; I had never served as a full-time faculty member before becoming chair. I have been successful in leading this department, not because I had worked my way up through the conventional ranks of academia, but because I knew the academic discipline, and I knew how to lead people (though, as I discovered, I had much to learn). What also has helped me to develop as a leader has been that, for the past decade, I have taught leadership to doctoral students in education at Nova Southeastern University. What I have learned from this experience, I apply daily in my position as chair of my department.

In this chapter, I will deal with some fundamental principles of leadership, as well as examples from my own experience to show how these principles may be put into practice in leading an academic department or school. A good place to start in understanding leadership is what I call the fundamental leadership process.

## THE FUNDAMENTAL LEADERSHIP PROCESS

I adapt this process from the seminal work of Kouzes and Posner, who, in their book, *The Leadership Challenge: How to Keep Getting Extraordinary Things Done in Organizations*, speak of the following five practices of exemplary leadership (Kouzes & Posner, 1995).

### 1. Challenge the Process

Assessing the condition and initiatives of the department or college is the first task of deans or chairs when they assume a new position, and assessing any new undertaking is what established chairs or deans must do in order to challenge the process. Challenging the process begins by asking the question, "Why are we doing what we are doing?" and trying to answer these three questions: 1) What are we doing now? 2) Why are we doing it? 3) How can we do it better? The answers to these questions will tell the chair what the initiatives of the department are, who the champions of those initiatives are, and what the barriers to those initiatives are.

*My example.* When I arrived at UT Southwestern Medical Center in 1990 as chair of the Department of Medical Laboratory Sciences, I asked the faculty members, "What are we doing now?" with respect to curricula and students. I learned that our medical technology program included not only an accredited, 12-month, senior-year, professional curriculum, but also an optional junior-year curriculum. (The junior-year curriculum was optional in that students could either enter our school after their sophomore year and take all their junior-year prerequisite courses with us, or they could choose to attend another senior college or university to complete these courses.)

Because all our senior students took the same professional curriculum and completed the program 12 months later, regardless of whether they had taken their junior-year prerequisite courses with us, I asked the question, "Why do we need to offer junior-year courses at all, when our students can get these prerequisite courses elsewhere?" (Why are we doing that?) "Why not concentrate our faculty members' time and our departmental resources into teaching only the 12-month, senior-year, professional curriculum?" (How can we do it better?) I shall return to this example later.

## 2. Inspire a Shared Vision

The leader—whether chair, dean, provost, or president—is charged with the responsibility of being the keeper of the vision. To some extent, the followers expect the leader to "go to the mountain top," survey the horizon, and come down from the mountain top with a vision of how to progress toward achieving the group's aims and goals. But the leader may not be the most visionary person in the department or school, and no single member of the group will be able to see as clearly the pathway to the future as will the group as a whole, working together. The definition of synergy, that "the whole is greater than the sum of the parts," applies to the visioning process. The leader's job is to guide the visioning process, so that the vision developed will be the clearest possible and acceptable to all team members. To the extent that the followers are involved in the visioning process, the vision will become clearer, and the followers will support the vision because, having created it, they own it.  What people own, they will support.

*My example.* Getting back to my own experience as a new chair, the faculty members—not wanting to appear unwilling to follow the new chairperson's vision—consented to my idea of eliminating the junior year, so that we could concentrate on strengthening our accredited, professional, senior-year curriculum. After all, the leader is supposed to know what he is doing, right?

As I would learn in the ensuing year, this was a poor decision. Actually, I had made two flawed decisions as a leader. The first was not to encourage full participation by all members of our team in deciding whether to continue or discontinue the junior year. And the second was to discontinue the junior year! Acting essentially in isolation, I had chosen a faulty course. I was to learn later that two very good reasons existed for continuing our junior year: 1) to create a needed pool of qualified applicants for our senior-year program, and 2) to acclimate our future senior students to a clinical orientation to their studies, which is necessary for student success in our senior-year program. Had I been conscientious in inspiring, and then following, a shared vision, I could have avoided these mistakes.

## 3. Enable Others to Act

Once a vision has been set, the leader must ensure that the necessary resources are made available for followers (faculty members or chairs) to act. A vision without resources is merely a dream of what could be. All human endeavor requires the use and consumption of resources. If the leader is truly serious about his or her team's ability to accomplish goals, the resources must be found and made available to team members.

*Authority.* One such resource is authority. The leader may help grant new authority through the promotion process, or the leader may share his or her own authority, so that the faculty member is empowered to act on the authority of the department chair or dean.

*My example.* In the year following the one in which we had discontinued our junior year program, working now as an integrated team, our faculty made the wise decision to resurrect the junior year curriculum. And because previously we had not had sufficient credit hours available in the junior year to provide all the students' needed prerequisite courses, we set about creating relevant new courses. Because they could see the importance of offering these additional courses as a way of achieving our mission of creating fully prepared, entry-level medical technologists, our faculty members accepted the added responsibility of teaching these additional courses, without our department adding any new faculty members!

### 4. Model the Way

It can be said that, in the final analysis, a leader can lead only by example—everything else is just pushing. The leader can lead by setting the standards of behavior, conduct, and achievement that he or she expects of all group members. One rule for the leader to remember: Group members, on the whole, will not rise above the standards that have been set for them by the leader (though they often may fall below them). So aim high in setting standards for yourself and your group. All of us learned to model the behavior of our leaders (parents, older siblings, etc.) as children. This behavior is thoroughly ingrained in the human psyche. Followers will continually assess and model the behavior of their leaders. For leaders, there is no place to hide from this scrutiny. The follower's expectation that the leader will model the true behavior that he or she requires holds the leader to a very high standard of conduct at all times.

*My example.* Once I had modeled the way by demonstrating to the faculty members that I valued their input and was willing to fully consider their ideas and to implement group decisions arrived at through consensus, the faculty members were willing to accept me as their partner, so that we could work together toward a fuller understanding of how to meet the department's needs and challenges and how to solve its problems.

### 5. Encourage the Heart

If the leader sets high standards, faculty members will be challenged to rise above their previous levels of accomplishment in teaching, scholarship, and/or service. However, the higher the goal, the greater the chance for failure. It is imperative for the leader to provide moral support for the followers (faculty members or chairs) and to emphasize that the best definition of failure is simply "the last attempt before succeeding." Failure (with a lower case "f") is never permanent and represents only a temporary setback which provides further insight into what won't work in a given situation. Failure (with a capital "F") becomes permanent only when the person who stumbles refuses to get back up and try again. (This point, by the way, illustrates why persistence is the secret to success in life. The person who refuses to fail, and continues to try until he or she succeeds, cannot fail, by definition.)

*My example.* As a final note on the saga of the junior class, this class has grown stronger and more vital to our mission with each passing year. We have continued to add more courses to the junior-year curriculum in order to strengthen it. Because we have expanded the junior class curriculum at the same time that we have continued to offer the senior class curriculum with no additions of new members to our faculty, our faculty members sometimes grow weary of trying to meet all commitments and keep all the balls in the air at the same time.

To help to keep faculty spirits high in the face of an ever-increasing workload, we have instituted an annual retreat for our department. On the Friday following the end of the spring semester in May each year, we all gather in a plush conference room across campus from our offices for a full day to reflect on the past year and look ahead to the coming one. We take time out in the middle of the day for a leisurely lunch in the faculty club on campus. Because we function now essentially as a family, we are all comfortable with one another, and we use the time to kick back, relax, and recharge our batteries. On other occasions, we make trips to the faculty club for lunch at departmental expense, or we have cake in the departmental break room, to celebrate birthdays, children's graduations, and other important events in faculty members' lives, as a way of celebrating our camaraderie and encouraging the heart.

As mentioned previously, these five practices of exemplary leadership constitute what I call the fundamental leadership process. These practices are required for leading people, projects, departments, and schools. The dean or chair who would be successful must master these five practices.

## WHAT DO CHAIRS WANT AND NEED?

What do chairs want? Whether you are reading this chapter as a chair, a faculty member, or a dean, it is important to understand what a chair wants from those for whom he or she is responsible (the faculty members of the department) and to whom he or she is responsible (the dean). Kouzes and Posner (1995), while they were associated with the Leavy School of Business and Administration at Santa Clara University, asked more than 10,000 managers what they admired and looked for in their leaders. In order of preference, they wanted leaders who were 1) honest, 2) competent, 3) forward-looking, and 4) inspiring. In a separate study, Kouzes and Posner asked a large number of managers what they looked for in employees. In order of preference, they wanted employees (followers) who were 1) honest, 2) competent, 3) loyal, and 4) dependable.

### Honesty and Competence
It is interesting that the two most sought after traits, both in leaders and in followers, were honesty and competence. I believe that I speak for other chairs in saying that these are the two most important traits that chairs look for, both in faculty members and in deans. Not that chairs don't expect many other important characteristics in those who report to them, and to whom they report, but these two are the most fundamental. You can't get very far in establishing a dependable working relationship with someone if you can't trust that person to be honest with you and with others. And you can't get very far in helping to develop faculty members or yourself if the other person in the relationship does not rise to a baseline level of competence.

## A Productive, Satisfying Environment

Chairs want an equitable and happy working environment in which they can lead others (faculty members) to new heights of accomplishment in their endeavors as teachers, scholars, and good citizens of the academic and extended community. They want the opportunity to continue to be active in the areas of teaching, scholarship, and service in which they excelled before becoming chair. They want the resources that they need to accomplish the mission and goals of individual faculty members within their departments, as well as the mission and goals of the school and the university. They want the opportunity and ability to ensure that the students, who are taught by them and their faculty members, are properly taught and are adequately prepared for a career in their field, or success in graduate or professional school.

## Recognition and Respect

Chairs want, at a minimum, understanding and appreciation from their dean for the job they do, day in and day out, in attempting to manage and lead a group of faculty members with diverse personalities at various stages of development and/or burnout in their respective careers. Ideally, they want sufficient resources, respect, and validation from their dean to feel that they are doing at least an adequate job in carrying out the myriad responsibilities in leadership, management, administration, and scholarship inherent in their positions. At the end of the day, they want to feel at least minimally competent (and on a good day, highly competent) in discharging their duties as chair, scholar, colleague, mentor, and fellow human being.

## Skills

What skills does the chair need, if he or she hopes to fulfill these wishes? Vision. Good listening skills. Good communication skills. Persuasiveness. The ability to create goodwill and trust among faculty members. The ability to support the dean (administration), when feasible, and the ability to protect the department from the dean (administration), when necessary. The ability to prioritize, and to see and pursue the big picture without losing sight of the importance of meeting today's challenges. The ability to inspire, on a good day, and to commiserate, on a bad day. The ability to set realistic, achievable goals. The ability to set the bar high enough, without setting it too high. The ability to sense who needs special care and handling at a point in time and to provide that level of attention without shortchanging others. The ability to achieve balance in meeting all the challenges that a chair faces.

## WHAT DO FACULTY MEMBERS WANT AND NEED?

What do faculty members want? They want the chair's attention when they need it, and to be left alone when they don't need it. They want the chair to go to bat for them with the dean, with other faculty members in their own department, with other faculty members in other departments, and with the system at large to help them get what they need to accomplish their professional goals. They want pay raises and promotions on a regular basis, despite institutional shortfalls in funding and periods of their own under-productivity.

Faculty members want upgrades in computer hardware and software, teaching assignments and schedules that will accommodate their busy lives, and an office with a window. They want the chair to point the way, and to show them how to do the things they don't know how to do, but not to "show them up" in showing them how to do those things. They want to be kept informed of what is going on around the school but not to be overburdened with administrative duties or other service work. They want to be recognized for their teaching ability, envied for their scholarship, appreciated for their service work, loved by their students, and admired by their chair and dean. They want to be able to balance their professional needs with their personal needs, to be given time off when they ask for it, and to be brought up-to-date when they return.

## HOW CAN A CHAIR PROVIDE FOR THESE NEEDS?

How can the chair possibly hope to provide for all these needs of faculty members? By remembering when he or she was in their positions and being sympathetic to, and understanding of, their needs. By providing resources where they exist, explanations where they do not exist, and good humor, always. By remembering what keeps faculty members happy fundamentally (the freedom to pursue ideas and to teach others what they know), and working hard to provide an environment in which those things can take place. By being patient with oneself, being patient with one's faculty members who are respectful and well intentioned (and offering remedial training for those who are not), and by being patient with the inevitable anachronistic idiosyncrasies that make a university a university. By building trust with faculty members, by being straight with them, caring for them, building a sense of teamwork, inspiring a vision with them, sharing leadership with them, working in the trenches, establishing balance, and being patient, patient, patient.

## MOTIVATING FACULTY MEMBERS

How does one motivate faculty members, in particular those who have tenure, those who are burned out, and those who have tenure and are burned out? Motivation of followers is essential to the success of any leader and can be very difficult within the constraints and realities of an academic department. In her book, *Strengthening Departmental Leadership* (1994), Ann F. Lucas says "Setting goals with individuals and providing feedback on performance in a supportive climate are the strongest forces a chair can use for motivating faculty." I agree that these activities should help to motivate most faculty members. Others have said that no one can motivate anyone else, rather that motivation must come from within oneself. Perhaps this is true, but I have learned valuable lessons on motivating others from John Kotter, professor of organizational behavior at the Harvard Business School, and author of *A Force for Change: How Leadership Differs from Management* (1990).

Kotter tells us that all people have the following five human needs and that leadership must satisfy the basic human needs of followers for a sense of 1) self-esteem, 2) achievement, 3) recognition, 4) belonging, and 5) having a sense of control over one's life. If these five human needs are satisfied, followers (even faculty members) will be motivated to follow the lead of the leader.

How can the leader provide for the satisfaction of these five human needs? By fulfilling the following responsibilities of the leader.

• Communicate the vision in a manner that stresses the values of followers. This provides a sense of self-esteem and belonging.

- Involve followers in deciding how to achieve the vision. This provides a sense of achievement and control over one's life.
- Enthusiastically support the efforts of followers in achieving the vision through feedback and coaching. This provides a sense of self-esteem, achievement, and belonging.
- Publicly recognize the efforts of followers and reward their successes. This provides a sense of recognition, achievement, belonging, self-esteem, and control over one's life.

Following these steps with your faculty members will provide a strong impetus for them to get on board with you in taking actions that will lead toward achievement of the department's and/or school's vision.

In his book, *Academic Leadership: A Practical Guide to Chairing the Department* (1998), Deryl Leaming discusses a department chair's responsibility to faculty. The most relevant for this discussion are:

- Counseling and guiding faculty; encouraging outstanding teaching, research, and other professional activities; organizing faculty meetings and departmental committees to further the business of the department.
- Promoting faculty development, including encouraging faculty members to attend professional conferences, join professional organizations, travel, etc.
- Protecting faculty rights, including recommendations of personnel matters such as leaves of absence, sabbatical leaves, research grants, etc.
- Giving periodic appraisal for recommending reappointment, tenure, promotion, and salary adjustments.
- Fostering productive, interpersonal, professional relationships among faculty of the department (p. 26).

My own analysis leads me to believe that motivation depends on giving people what they want, or at least an environment in which they can get what they want. What do people want? Happiness. And what is happiness? I believe that happiness is a feeling of joy and self-satisfaction that derives from a sense of personal growth and making progress toward achieving goals. I believe that personal and professional growth and progress toward goals have five similar components.

Professional growth requires the following five components:

1) Meaningful work to do
2) A sense of being in control
3) Reasonable goals and challenges
4) A sense of accomplishment
5) A feeling of being valuable

Personal growth requires the following five components:

1) Meaningful relationships
2) A sense of being in control
3) The opportunity to give love
4) The opportunity to receive love
5) A feeling of being valued

Most people's motivation derives from the sense of happiness that they feel by giving and receiving to meet the inherent needs of themselves and other people.

## CREATING A POSITIVE BIAS FOR FACULTY MEMBERS

The key to success in most things is to do the necessary preparation before a project begins to help ensure its steady progress so that it can be accomplished, on time and on budget, with a minimum of delays, mistakes, and rework.

This principle applies to leadership. For example, when I need to hire a new faculty member, I advertise widely and winnow the list of applicants down to as many as three or four applicants who appear to be the most competitive in meeting the basic requirements for the position. Then I interview each person at length, not only to learn what I can about the person, his or her background, strengths, weaknesses, interests, and expectations for the position, but also to bias the applicant.

By this, I mean that I explain as fully as I can what is good and what is not so good about the department. I never want to hire someone on false pretenses. Not only would that be unethical, it almost surely would doom the new hire to failure, or at least demoralization, since I would be unable to deliver on promises that could not be kept. If the department may face budget cycles in which raises may not be given, I want to inform the candidate of that possibility. If the department may face space constraints or supply and equipment shortages, I want to inform the candidate of that possibility. I try to bias the candidate into believing that things may be a little worse in the department than I believe them really to be, so that I can trust the candidate's decision, should he or she conclude that the opportunities here outweigh the liabilities.

Then, when a new faculty member has been hired, in the beginning I spend many hours biasing the new hire to my way of thinking. As the leader of the department, and therefore the keeper of symbols and values, I want to bias the new faculty member with respect to the prevailing culture. Call it acculturating, although true acculturation probably requires interaction with others in the department over time. I want the new faculty member to be biased to my values, my expectations, and to my (positive) view of the department and our work, before some less optimistic member of my faculty may gain access to our new colleague and bias him or her in some negative way.

I also want to bias the new faculty member to believe that he or she can come to me at any time, to discuss any matter of importance to him or her. I want to bias the new colleague from the beginning into believing that I am friend, not foe and that my job fundamentally is to help him or her succeed. This approach to departmental leadership has reaped rich rewards for me in building trust with new faculty members and in keeping the department moving in the direction in which I think it should be moving.

## THE BOTTOM LINE ON LEADING AN ACADEMIC UNIT

In this chapter, I have talked about how I came to lead an academic department, the fundamental leadership process, what chairs really want, what faculty members really want, how to provide what faculty members want, how to motivate faculty members, and the importance of biasing faculty members.

Leadership is paradoxical, in many ways. While the fundamental principles of leadership, I believe, are easy to understand, in practice it almost always is mind-bogglingly complex and difficult. The reason for this difficulty, principally, is that leadership always takes place in a dynamic setting, and it always involves human beings. The dynamic nature of leadership means that the leader must face new, sometimes previously unknown, challenges every day. The fact that leadership involves human beings, each with his or her own needs, expectations, biases, understandings, and misunderstandings, means that leadership almost always is challenging at best and disastrous at worst.

For me, the bottom line on leadership of an academic unit (or of any other group, for that matter) is for the leader to know himself or herself, to be schooled in the idiosyncrasies of human nature, sensitive to the needs of others, fair minded, honest, caring, well intentioned, willing to place the needs of others ahead of his or her own, and willing to treat others as you would have others treat you. If this latter point reminds the reader of the Golden Rule, then we are thinking of leadership along the same lines. I hope that the reader finds these observations and musings useful in the noble pursuit of leadership in an academic setting.

Happy leading!

## REFERENCES

Kotter, J. P. (1990). *A force for change: How leadership differs from management.* New York, NY: Free Press.

Kouzes, J. M., & Posner, B. Z. (1995). *The leadership challenge: How to keep getting extraordinary things done in organizations.* San Francisco, CA: Jossey-Bass.

Leaming, D. R. (1998). *Academic leadership: A practical guide to chairing the department.* Bolton, MA: Anker.

Lucas, A. F. (1994). *Strengthening departmental leadership. A team-building guide for chairs in colleges and universities.* San Francisco, CA: Jossey-Bass.

# Creating Consensus Among Faculty

**4**

*Deryl R. Leaming*

> *At every opportunity you need to talk about your plans. You must show how your plans can be accomplished, how they are real. Nothing will delay you more than voicing a vision that others see as unattainable.*

Today's leaders must strive to create consensus if they are to realize their goals, see their visions become reality, and become effective leaders. This is true no matter what kind of environment leaders work in. I believe this to be especially true for all of us who are academic leaders.

In *Leadership Reconsidered* (Astin & Astin, 2000), the authors rightly point out that "Practically all of the modern authorities on leadership, regardless of whether they focus on the corporate world or the nonprofit sector, now advocate a collaborative approach to leadership" (p. 4). This, it seems to me, is critical in higher education, and I believe department chairs and deans must be ever mindful of the need to engage faculty and to lay out plans to them in an effort to achieve consensus.

The authors of *Leadership Reconsidered* also make note of the fact that:

> Most institutions of higher learning in the United States are organized and governed according to two seemingly contradictory sets of practices. We have both the hierarchical model and the individualistic model.
>
> When we get to the bottom of the rung in the professional hierarchy, we find something very different: Individual faculty members, who on paper appear to fall *under* chairs, actually enjoy a great deal of autonomy in their work and seldom take orders from anyone (especially chairs!). (p. 5)

We know this is true, and any dean or chair who fails to reconize this is in for a rough time. We have all known chairs or deans who have tried to operate or lead from position authority alone, and we have watched their failures—every one of them! It is often a painful thing to witness.

So, how do you best work with faculty to get their support for accomplishing goals that you believe are in the best interests of students in your departments or colleges? In this chapter, I will address these questions by first presuming that either the dean or chair is new. Further, for purposes of illustration and laying out ideas for effective consensus building, I will challenge these leaders to take over the leadership role of a college or a department that is floundering. In a nutshell, both change and leadership are needed—unfortunately not a rare situation.

## RESEARCH THE SITUATION

Even when it's obvious that change is in order, any leader would be foolish to approach making any change without first learning a lot about the college or the department. This means studying the history and examining why the unit has become what it is today. Who are the people within your unit, and what can you do to recognize their value and worth? Warren Bennis (1997) reminds us of what Alfred North Whitehead once said: "Every leader, to be effective, must simultaneously adhere to the symbols of change and revision and the symbols of tradition and stability" (p. 10). Taking the time to learn a lot about any organization and the people who work within it is advice that we should heed. Indeed, we ignore it at our peril. Leaders who make the mistake of coming in and announcing change without first acknowledging the value and worth of the organization and its people are doomed to failure. They will succeed in accomplishing their goals only by running roughshod over those who believe—and rightfully so—that they have a big stake in the organization. Many will do all they can to sabotage the leader's efforts.

The essential principle here is to take your time. Dust off old files that give the story of the unit and study them carefully. Talk to everyone in the college or department, especially giving time to those who have been a part of the academic unit for a considerable period. What can they tell you about the culture and history? Listening is a critical skill for any leader, and in this situation it is a must. Kouzes and Posner (1995) write that "The first task in enlisting others is to identify our constituents and find out what their common aspirations are. No matter how grand the dream of an individual visionary, if others don't see in it the possibility of realizing their own hopes and desires, they won't follow. Leaders must show others how they, too, will be served by the long-term vision of the future, how their specific needs can be satisfied. . . . If leaders need one special talent, it's the ability to sense the purpose in others. By knowing their constituents, by listening to them, and by taking their advice, leaders are able to give voice to constituents' feelings" (p. 129). This last point seems to me to be particularly important: that we as leaders are able to give voice to the feelings of those in our academic units.

According to Bennis and Nanus (1997), "Over and over again, the leaders we spoke to told us that they did the same things when they took charge of their organizations—they paid attention to what was going on, they determined what part of the events at hand would be important for the future of the organization, they set a new direction, and they concentrated the attention of everyone in the organization on it" (p. 81).

The purpose of learning all you can about the academic unit and its people is so that you can begin formulating a vision of what the unit can be. Notice that I used the word "people" instead of "faculty." It is important to know how staff members feel if you are to succeed in changing the college or department. Try to determine how those in the organization define the common purpose. My guess is that you are likely to get many different views of what this is. To some faculty members, it will be research; to others, it will be teaching. Others—particularly staff—are likely to voice their idea of the organization running smoothly, of deadlines being met, and of the need for order.

When I became dean at Middle Tennessee State University, I issued an invitation for all faculty and staff members to make an appointment to visit with me in my office for about 15 to 30 minutes so they could tell me about themselves. I told them the time was theirs—that they could talk about anything they wanted, but I indicated that I also wanted to know something about their teaching and research interests and that I would be interested in hearing what they considered the college's strengths and weaknesses. Most importantly, I told them that I was going to listen only.

When I wasn't seeing faculty and staff in my office, I was attempting to learn as much as I could by reading and listening as I walked around campus. Over the course of several weeks, I saw every faculty and staff member except one, a longtime loner who after eight years has never set foot in my office. From the many conversations I had, I began to get a sense of the frustration that many felt regarding the lack of standards and the way leadership decisions had been made. Most described a kind of seat-of-the-pants and whoever-got-to-the-dean-last style of management. I selectively use the word "management" rather than "leadership." One important distinction made in today's literature regarding these two words is that managers protect the status quo whereas leaders seek to cultivate change. Astin and Astin (2000) write, "We believe that leadership is a process that is ultimately concerned with fostering change. In contrast to the notion of management, which suggests preservation or maintenance, 'leadership' implies a process where there is movement—from wherever we are, not some future place or condition that is different" (p. 8).

## FORMULATE A VISION

Deans and chairs must develop a vision of where their college or department should be going. In other words, what is the principal agenda? Where should the focus of energy be directed? As a dean or chair, you must develop an idea in your mind of a possible and desirable future for the college or department.

If you are taking charge of a department or college in need of management and leadership, you might develop for your academic unit a vision that begins with the idea that you must put in place policies that elevate your standards and written procedures that everyone clearly understands. You could go on to have as your target or goal the idea of raising standards across the board for teaching, scholarship, and service, while providing the best possible learning environment for all your students. When your department or college hires faculty and staff members, are they looking for the best and the brightest, or are they content to hire only those who will not make them look bad? One element of your vision could be changing the culture through the hiring process, whereby new faculty members would immediately challenge existing faculty members with the level of their teaching, research, and service.

As the dean or chair in this situation, you must challenge the status quo. Kouzes and Posner (1995) suggest making "a list of all the practices in your organization that fit this description: 'That's the way we've always done it around here.' For each one, ask yourself, 'How useful is this in helping us become the best we can be? How useful is this for stimulating creativity and innovation?' If your answer is 'absolutely essential,' then keep it. If not, find a way to change it. Review all the policies and procedures" (p. 55). This is where I found myself when I took over my last deanship. I had many of those who came to my office for our first visit say, "We want someone who will just leave us alone. We don't want to make any changes."

## ESTABLISH AN IMPROVEMENT ORIENTATION

One of the ways academic leaders can begin to create consensus is to encourage faculty and staff members to embrace the idea of improvement as part of the vision you are formulating. Improvement should always be foremost in our thoughts and actions. Improvement must be entrenched in the rhetoric of the leadership—in speeches, in vision statements, in organizational goals. Most importantly, the quest for improvement must be given meaning through actions. Faculty and staff members are more likely to be able to deal with change if they see that it is necessary to bring about improvement of the department or college.

## HELP FACULTY MEMBERS DEVELOP A SENSE OF OWNERSHIP

Another key to creating consensus from the start is helping others to develop a sense of ownership. Faculty and staff members need to feel that the department belongs to them. This means that whenever changes are to be made, faculty and staff must be involved because they have a stake in whatever happens.

You can help faculty and staff members to gain a sense of ownership by dealing them in on all major decisions of the department.

By asking them "What is the best thing for us to do for the good of the department?," you give them a sense of ownership. Conversely, you can undermine their sense of ownership by making decisions without listening to and incorporating their voices. They want a say in how things are done in the department or college, and they become better workers when they are consulted regularly about matters of importance.

One way of developing faculty ownership in your department or college is to get them involved in formulating problems and challenges. Just because you are the department chair or dean does not mean that you alone are responsible for any problems within your unit. Getting everyone in the department involved in identifying problems and developing solutions is a good way to get everyone on the same team.

### Set Standards and Publish Them

Too many chairs and deans would rather not talk about standards. Instead, they assess individuals and their accomplishments on some sort of ad hoc basis. The trouble with this is that either the leader has no standards, or the standards are unknown. Faculty members, of course, need to have some say about what standards apply, especially in tenure and promotion cases. By serving on a committee to develop promotion and tenure guidelines—and other policies, for that matter—faculty will feel ownership in them. They will feel more comfortable when they are expected to follow guidelines or apply them to others in the department or college. Standards must also be well publicized. Everyone has a right to know what the standards are, and they should have copies of all policies of the department and college.

## GET OTHERS TO BUY INTO YOUR VISION

Once you have formulated a vision, the very first thing you must do if you are going to move a department or college forward is to get others to buy into that vision. You must sell your ideas. As a leader, you must show others how they will be served by the long-term vision of the future—how their specific needs will be satisfied. You must show faculty and staff members how they will become an integral part of the department or college of the future.

At every opportunity, you need to talk about plans. You must show how they can be accomplished, how they are real. Nothing will delay your progress more than voicing a vision that others see as unattainable. Thus, you must lay out in specific terms exactly how you would like to accomplish your goals and realize the vision.

Talk to every faculty and staff member. You need to spend time with them, not just to explain your vision, but rather to listen to them to see what concerns they have. If you listen carefully and are sensitive to them, you will find out much about their fears, and this will provide ways of dealing with them.

### Use Whatever Tools You Can to Promote Your Vision

Successful leaders have a well-thought-out vision of where they want their organization to go. If they know how to share this vision, they can pull people toward them. One thing that ought not to be overlooked is the need to be clear about purpose. Your faculty members want to be challenged, and they are attracted to a leader's vision and goals because they recognize that through them, they and the department or college can become permanently better. Every leader knows the importance of having a vision, but that's only half of it. The other half is ensuring that others know what your vision is. By communicating the vision, you have a chance to get a consensus among those you lead. Achieving this consensus cannot be over emphasized: Successful departments and colleges have consensus on a set of overall goals. No one will follow you simply because you decide you want to lead: You have to have a clear idea of where you want to the take the department or college, and then you must promote it to your department or college to convince faculty and staff that your goal is worthwhile.

### Recognize that People Come First

Effective leaders take an interest in the people who work for them. They get to know their family situations and outside interests, and they drop by each person's office from time to time. Leaders must be visible. Make contact regularly with all people in your unit, and be supporting, reinforcing, and motivating. Know what each faculty member is doing in the way of research and have a good understanding of that research. You'll find that faculty members love to talk about their research, and you need to give them that chance.

*Build trusting relationships.* Look for every opportunity to establish trust between your colleagues and yourself. More often than not, it's the little things we do throughout the day—day in and day out—that help us build trusting relationships. It is the stop in the hall to talk to a faculty member about an upcoming conference he or she will be attending, the small talk that occurs as you get yourself a cup of coffee, or the extra time you give to helping a faculty member find additional funds for a piece of equipment that goes a long way toward developing trust between faculty and staff members and yourself.

*Don't be afraid to admit your mistakes.* As a leader, you must take responsibility for your actions. If you are going to take credit for success, then you also must accept responsibility for failure. You cannot hope to gain the respect of faculty and staff in your college or department if you shift blame for your mistakes. Your faculty and staff will be willing to follow you provided you are honest, and admitting your mistakes shows that you are. Failure to do this will cause others to lose respect for you and distrust your leadership.

## UNDERSTAND THE NATURE OF POWER

Leaders cannot lead effectively without power, and we know that those who have made a difference or who have made the greatest contributions are the ones who use power wisely. They understand power and how it can help them achieve goals. They use it judiciously, which is something that takes wisdom and restraint. To lead well, deans and chairs need to be strong but gentle and be sensitive enough to know when they need to be tough, or when being gentle is more appropriate.

### Do Not Try to Force People
Understand that you can't force people to do very much. This idea is essential to the understanding of what effective leadership is about. People have to want to participate. One way of getting people to follow your lead is to gain their respect. If your faculty and staff respect you, they usually will do what you want. They

will have confidence in your vision and goals. What will make you successful is an ability to inspire; it makes consensus possible. Lead through voice rather than position. As a chair or dean, you do have position power; however, personal power or authority derived through voice is much more potent. The underlying issue in leading from voice is trust. Bennis (1994, p. 160) lists four ingredients leaders have that generate and sustain trust:

1) *Constancy.* Whatever surprises leaders themselves may face, they don't create any for the group. Leaders are all of a piece; they stay the course.

2) *Congruity.* Leaders walk their talk. In true leaders, there is no gap between the theories they espouse and the life they practice.

3) *Reliability.* Leaders are there when it counts; they are ready to support their coworkers in the moments that matter.

4) *Integrity.* Leaders honor their commitments and promises.

### Be Trustworthy

Everything you do as a leader must show that others can trust you. If you do not follow through on your promises, faculty and staff will soon learn you are not to be trusted. Everything you do must show that you are a person who can be trusted. You must show that you can be counted on if you are going to create a consensus and provide support for accomplishing goals that you articulate. Leaders cannot play games with people if they are to be trusted. You must put everything on the table and speak honestly to people. They must know that they can count on your word.

### Share Power

To achieve their goals, it is also important that leaders share their power. When deans and chairs empower faculty and staff members, they have more confidence, they become more efficient, and they will work harder for their chair or dean. Moreover, they are better team members. We see chairs and deans who just don't get it: They don't understand that by sharing power, they gain power. They are the ones who fear that giving away power diminishes it. Nothing could be further from the truth; the more you empower others, the bigger you become in the eyes of your faculty and staff.

Leaders must understand and share power. With power of voice and vision, they can accomplish a lot; without it very little. Furthermore, deans and chairs can possess all kinds of leadership qualities and still not succeed unless they understand power. Power, if used properly, will hold all of the other qualities together. It can energize and enable us to use our resources. When leaders use power well, they show faculty and staff members that they can be trusted. When leaders abuse power, they find their work far more difficult.

## Use Power Properly

The abuse of power causes others to build defenses that are almost always destructive in nature. Whether it's position power or person power, a chair or dean cannot be seen as someone who abuses power. Likewise, the power of a chair or dean must be reinforced by those above him or her. One of the worst things that can happen is for the power of either the dean or the chair to be undermined by those to whom these individuals report. This can happen in a number of ways. Most often it happens when a decision is not supported by the dean or vice president for academic affairs. A single such occurrence may do no harm, but if it happens regularly, the dean or chair loses position power, and his or her chances of creating consensus for a vision fade.

Just as a dean or provost can do much to undermine the power of a chair or dean, chairs and deans can abuse their power and thus hurt their chances of becoming effective leaders. This can happen when leaders hoard information, a common manifestation of the reluctance to share power. It also can happen for any of the following reasons:

• Consistently failing to recognize the work or accomplishments of others in your department or college
• Regularly making inaccurate comments
• Being untruthful or being reluctant to admit mistakes
• Being inflexible. There will be times when you must change your plans or course of action. If you feel so strongly wed to an idea that you cannot abandon it to take advantage of something more promising, then you will likely have difficulties as a leader who advances an academic unit. Even seeing other promising possibilities is difficult for some. Leaders must be alert to promises and challenges that others often overlook.

## STRATEGIES FOR ACHIEVING CONSENSUS

Here are some useful strategies for achieving consensus within your department or college, many of which I have already touched upon. These strategies are presented as an array of techniques that optimize the likelihood of achieving consensus.

### Make Communication a Priority

Faculty and staff members need to know what is going on, and they need to hear it directly from you. I can't emphasize this point enough: Department chairs or deans who do not communicate effectively and fully with all faculty and staff members within their departments or college will run into problems regularly. Just as you need to provide information to faculty and staff members, you need to listen to what they have to say. In other words, sharing information is only half of the equation. Listening is the other half.

One of the most important things a leader can do is to develop a communication plan and implement it. How will you get important information to those in your department or college? What information will you need to share? What regular means of communication will you employ? These are just some of the questions you'll need to answer before completing a communication plan.

**Distribute information.** In my role as dean, I try to share information with all employees of the college. I do this in a number of ways. First, I provide information to chairs at our weekly executive committee meetings, and I ask them to share information with members of their faculty. Also, the minutes of this weekly meeting are distributed to all faculty and staff members within the college.

**Post news.** I also publish an online weekly newsletter that I call the *Monday Morning Memo* (see Figure 4.1). It includes any information I have that I believe others in the college need to know. This includes announcements of upcoming events and information about what faculty members are doing, including articles they've published, workshops they have been invited to give, family news, awards they've won, and so on. I also include university information that I get from meetings I attend.

**Write memos.** In addition to the online newsletter, I send out what I call *An Occasional Memo* (see Figure 4.2) to address issues of

## Figure 4.1
## Monday Morning Memo – February 5, 2001

HERE'S WISHING A happy birthday to the following faculty and staff who have birthdays this month:

| | |
|---|---|
| February 1 | Mike Alleyene |
| February 7 | Bob Wyatt |
| February 26 | Don Parente |

TOM HUTCHISON'S WIFE, Lynne, has released her first novel in a trio of books scheduled for release this year from Kensington Publishers. Lynne is a 1999 graduate from the School of Journalism. The book is a historical romance entitled *Summer's End*. Lynne and Tom will be hosting a book signing at Books-A-Million in Murfreesboro on Friday, February 9 from 5–7 p.m. and invite all Mass Comm faculty to attend. (We plan on all going out for adult beverages after the signing.) Lynne is writing under the pseudonym Lynne Hayworth. You can find out more about her books at http://www.lynnehayworth.com.

I WILL BE off campus most of the week attending a national conference for chairs in Orlando where I will present a workshop. If you need anything from my office during my absence, see Matthew O'Brien, Ami Gullett, or one of the secretaries.

FORMER VICE PRESIDENT Al Gore will begin teaching at MTSU as a Seigenthaler Chair holder next week. Please pass this on to your students: Students interested in the community building class to be taught by the former Vice President may begin registering on Monday, February 5, according to officials in the registrar's office. Students may register in the James

Union Building, Room 123 on February 5 and 6 from 8 a.m. to 7 p.m., and on February 7 from 8 a.m. to noon. The class will be limited to 125 currently enrolled students, who are juniors, seniors, or graduate students. If more than 125 students register, a lottery will be used to determine which students will be admitted into the class. The two-hour class is titled "Creating Family-Centered Communities" and will begin at 4 p.m. Monday, February 12. The interdisciplinary course will meet once a week for ten sessions, with one week off for spring break. A longtime advocate and supporter of building strong families and communities, Gore will lead the way in teaching and establishing the curriculum for an interdisciplinary course based on community building. "There is no curriculum that I know of that offers a holistic approach to what kinds of skills are needed to build a healthy and strong community," Gore told the 14-member planning group during a January 29 meeting at Middle Tennessee State University. "This is intended to be something brand new. I am really interested in seeing this come about. If we get it right, it would be a great experience for these students. I think it's an idea whose time has come." For more information students may go to the MTSU News and Public Affairs web site at http://www.mtsu.edu/~proffice.

RALPH WILEY, AN award-winning author, journalist, and screenwriter, will be speaking in Beverly Keel's class on February 7 at 3:40 as a part of the African American History Month.

QUOTE OF THE WEEK: "It seems to me that one should read only books which bite and sting one. If the book we are reading does not wake us up with a blow to the head, what is the point of reading? A book must be the axe which smashes the frozen sea within us."

— *Franz Kafka*

## FIGURE 4.2
## AN OCCASIONAL MEMO – SEPTEMBER 29, 2000

THERE ARE THOSE defining moments in our lives that help us more fully illuminate other parts of our lives, or so it seems to me. And my recent experience has been one such defining moment. Taking many matters into consideration, I am announcing at this time my resignation as dean, effective the end of this academic year.

This has been a relatively easy decision for me to make, and I have passed on to Barbara Haskew a letter of resignation.

I want to take this opportunity to thank each faculty and staff member in the college for allowing me to be your dean for the past seven years. Despite any differences we may have had over the years, I have great respect for the faculty and staff of this college. Furthermore, I am convinced we have made great strides in developing as one of the nation's premier mass communication colleges. I could provide a long list of our accomplishments, all of which are the payoffs of labor and dedication of many individuals and groups working together for the good of our students. Again, I thank you.

Dr. Haskew has indicated she will soon begin an effort to search to fill the dean's position, and I know she will involve faculty in the search and selection process. I will continue this year to serve you with the effort and dedication I have in the past. Furthermore, I will continue to press for the college to maintain standards, which I have fought to put into place. In my judgment, these standards serve the students, faculty, and staff well.

I hope we can continue to develop policies that help new faculty members understand clearly our expectations of them. Also, I plan to continue my efforts to bring them comfortably into the college family and to help them move smoothly toward tenure and promotion. We owe them no less.

My hope for the College of Mass Communication is that a dean will be selected who will take the college to the next level of excellence. In my judgment, this college is on a solid course to achieving great things. I hope those in the college who are advocates for the future and who serve as agents of change will continue to exert influence. As I said when I addressed the faculty in August, I cherish the past and enjoy studying it, but the future holds great excitement for all mass communication. If we embrace change and put aside our fears, then there are no limits to what this college can become. I am convinced of that. I believe the college has positioned itself nicely by getting out in front of many other programs across this country. The excitement in the college leads me to believe that faculty and staff will keep up the outstanding work required for the College of Mass Communication to reach ever higher levels of excellence. I have good feelings toward each person in this college. Thus, it's easy for me to wish each of you the very best. May you have fulfilling, exciting careers as you mold tomorrow's mass communicators. Your responsibility is great and your cause noble.

Deryl Leaming

the moment. If a matter comes up that I need to share before my next issue of the *Monday Morning Memo,* I use *An Occasional Memo* to get out this information.

*Hold faculty meetings.* In addition to these techniques, I use college-wide faculty meetings when I want to both share a lot of information with faculty members and get their immediate reactions.

I cannot say enough about the importance of developing, maintaining, and regularly evaluating a solid communication plan. Seek out faculty members and ask them if they believe they are getting enough information. Leaders must value openness and resist any temptation to use information as a weapon of control. If you question whether certain information should be shared with faculty, share it: It is better to err on the side of providing too much information than not enough.

Just as you must communicate often and effectively, you must share information regarding budgets, planning, and matters that affect the lives of those in your departments or colleges. I have known chairs who are not comfortable sharing budget information, and, generally speaking, faculty members become suspicious of them. They don't earn the trust of their faculty unless they are willing to be open.

### Listen

Leaders must remember the importance of listening. If you are a careful listener, you will quickly find out what concerns the faculty and staff, and you can address these concerns in your communication. Faculty and staff members want you to know what's on their mind. Your job is to listen. By doing so, you show respect for others, a key ingredient in others' respect for you. Remember also that people listen more attentively to those who listen to them. So much of the literature that deals with the art of communication fails to include anything about listening, yet listening is one of the most critical skills for any leader. Mallard (2000) reminds us that it is a time-consuming task. She says that "listening serves two purposes: 1) gathering facts and information, and 2) demonstrating care and concern (p. 11)." She also points out that "listening is the skill most overlooked in management books as well as college curricula." Certainly, if you are to be an effective communicator, you must learn how to listen. Keep in mind that unless you listen carefully, you may miss important information that others are trying to tell you.

### Develop Sensitivity to Others

If you are to become an effective leader, you must get a sense of what people want, what they value, and what they dream about. Kouzes and Posner (1995) report that researchers from the Center for Creative Leadership have substantiated the importance of sensitivity. "Insensitivity to others is cited in their studies as the primary reason why successful executives tumble off the track to the executive suite" (p. 190). "Managers who focus on themselves and are insensitive to others fail, because there's a limit to what they can do by themselves" (p. 191).

How does one go about developing sensitivity to others? It is not something you're taught in formal courses, yet it is requisite to leading effectively and to achieving consensus. Most who rise to leadership positions have this skill, although many of us can do more to make it a more prominent part of who we are and how we behave. It seems to me that whenever you are thinking about taking any action that will affect others, you need to ask yourself how you would react to someone whose similar decision affects you. Are you truly able to put yourself in the shoes of others? This is a must if you are to be sensitive to others.

*Treat others as you would be treated.* Most of us learned this as children, and it has a lot to do with leadership. Its meaning reaches beyond religion or ethics, going to the very heart of leadership. People do not willingly follow leaders who are unconcerned with how they are treated. Treating others the way you would want to be treated shows that you value others.

*Be patient with others.* As a leader you must allow yourself to be patient with others, even if you are impatient with yourself. Being patient with others also means that from time to time you must overlook others' minor mistakes, or at least not overreact to them. Costly mistakes must be dealt with, and those who make the same mistakes repeatedly require counsel. However, a show of impatience toward faculty and staff will not help you when you must count on them to help you realize your goals.

*Maintain a positive attitude.* No one likes to work around people with negative attitudes. You must look at the positive side and see ways of accomplishing your goals and getting others to help you. If you are negative, you will alienate people and diminish your chances of creating consensus among faculty and staff.

*Treat everyone fairly.* Do not show favoritism. Treat everyone fairly, though at times doing so is difficult. Some faculty and staff members are difficult to like; consequently you may have a tendency to treat them differently, but avoid this at all costs. Others will lose respect for you if they see that you are not treating everyone fairly. I have found it interesting that even when you do not actually show favoritism toward any faculty or staff members, you may still be accused of doing so. There will likely be faculty and staff members who are much warmer toward you than are others in the department or college, and this is too often incorrectly interpreted as favoritism. You must be careful in all your actions not to give even the slightest sign of favoritism.

*Support and defend faculty and staff.* Talking up for faculty and staff is something that all effective leaders practice. Take every opportunity to promote your faculty and staff. Let your vice president for academic affairs and dean know of the accomplishments of your faculty and staff members, and support them if they come under fire. Give them the benefit of the doubt if they come under attack.

Another way to support faculty and staff is to provide information about sources of support for them. Post fellowship, leave, and grant opportunities, and remind faculty of deadlines for sabbaticals, grant applications, and the like. Further, nominate or identify individuals who might receive awards, honors, or other support.

### Make Others Feel Important

There is no greater motivator of human behavior than making others feel important. It's more powerful than money, promotion, working conditions, or almost anything else. There are many little things you can do to make each faculty and staff member feel important, and most of those things cost little or no money.

Business leaders who have been particularly successful understand this. One example is Mary Kay, founder and CEO of Mary Kay Cosmetics, who built a $300 million company starting with a $5,000 investment. She insists that one of her secrets is that she imagines that every person she sees has a sign on his or her head. The sign reads: "Make me feel important." And she says she does everything she can to obey the sign's request. Faculty and staff members will follow you when you make them feel important, not when you make yourself feel important.

*Ask others' opinions.* One thing you can do is to ask others what they think of something. Showing that you value the opinion of faculty and staff members makes them feel important.

*Give credit for work well done.* Take note of good work, and let those who are responsible for it know that you appreciate their efforts. Leaders must keep their eyes open for those who go above and beyond the call of duty or get special recognition. In my weekly *Monday Morning Memo,* I announce accomplishments of faculty. Recognition as a way of life should be deeply etched in the way we conduct ourselves as leaders.

### Develop Self Understanding

The ability to create consensus requires understanding—of self and others.

*Be comfortable with yourself.* Leaders often face ridicule and criticism, and such negative comments are easier to handle if you are comfortable with who you are. If you are secure, you can accept criticism without feeling the need to lash out.

As an example, some years ago, I latched onto the idea of mini-courses long before they were popular; in fact I had never heard of them. But shorter courses that don't have a place in the curriculum made a lot of sense to me. When I first inquired about offering mini courses, I was told that I couldn't. When I asked why, I got the standard answer: "We just don't do things like that."

It made no sense to me that every course had to last for 15 weeks; I wanted to offer a series of courses that would each run for five weeks. Finally, I was given permission to experiment with them. To get enrollment, I advertised them as important for their subject matter and boldly announced that learning was more important than grades. One chairman in our college made fun of the idea and said something to the effect that our department was just offering a bunch of easy courses and we didn't have high grading standards. The criticism hurt, but I was undaunted by it, mostly because I was secure in what I was doing. I was comfortable with who I was at the time. Otherwise, I might have given up on the mini course idea, which turned out to be immensely popular positive learning experiences, and student after student told me how much they got out of these courses.

Leaders will face similar situations, plenty of them. And they must be prepared to withstand criticism or even ridicule. Leaders must rise above criticism and have faith in what their goals are. They need to be comfortable with who they are.

*Don't allow yourself to be petty.* Effective leaders need to rise above pettiness. It is sometimes tempting to fall into that trap, but you must not allow yourself to do so. Leadership is not about getting even.

*Lead by example.* Everything you do or say sends a message, sets a tone, or gives others the idea of what direction to take. As a department chair or a college dean, you are highly visible. Say something stupid, and you'll be quoted often. Do something unintelligent, and you may be mocked. Conversely, you have a chance to influence the behavior of others if you set a good example of leadership. You can cause others to become better communicators by being an effective communicator yourself, or you could cause others to be sensitive if you display that quality. Indeed, all the qualities of leadership that you show others will influence how others behave. And if you are to be an effective leader, you must set an example that others choose to follow.

### Think Big

Thinking big is an attitude we can cultivate, an attitude that sees people, places, and things bigger and better than they see themselves. As a visionary leader, you will seek opportunities where others do not. Indeed, others may see problems where you see opportunities, and you'll see answers where others have not yet formed the questions. Allow your imagination to work: It will promote big thinking. It allows you to create a vision and give you something to shoot for. Big thinkers can transform departments and colleges, and they can inspire others to want what's best for the overall program. Leaders believe in people and want people to be their best. As a big thinker, challenge tradition and the prevailing wisdom, and you will nurture curiosity in yourself and in others.

### Be a Risk Taker

If you are to become an effective leader and create consensus, you must be a risk taker. Some of your faculty and staff members will never understand how you can take risks. But they'll admire you for sticking your neck out. And they'll be pulling for you to win. Risk taking is an indispensable part of leadership because being overly cautious and indecisive kills opportunity. Taking risks complements thinking big.

Leaders also must help others take risks. You need faculty and staff members who will try something new instead of sticking with what is comfortable. Indeed, those who are not willing to take risks are the foot draggers when it comes to creating change. You should encourage and reward risk taking, and above all not punish those who fail. One way to encourage risk-taking behavior is to cultivate a sense of ownership. By allowing faculty and staff members to help formulate plans and establish tasks, you give them ownership. When faculty and staff members feel ownership, they are more likely to take risks than they might be if they believed that college or department plans and tasks belonged only to the dean or the chair. You also need to give others permission to take risks and to make mistakes.

### Be Courageous

Finally, creating consensus among faculty and staff members requires courage. But what is courage in academics? After all, you are not putting your life on the line as police officers do. Still, there is much that you can do to show courage.

*Be ethical.* Defend what is right even when it is easier to cut corners. Faculty and staff members will quickly notice those who do not show the courage required to be ethical.

*Stand up for your beliefs.* As a leader, you will have many opportunities to stand up for what you believe, or to put your job on the line in favor of doing the right thing.

*Seek the truth.* Sometimes accepting the truth is not easy; indeed it may get in the way of your plans or threaten your emotional security, but a leader needs to be a truth seeker.

*Seek humility.* Just as you must seek the truth even when it can undermine your plans, you must seek humility. You must be humble if you are to be a leader that others respect. As T. S. Eliot noted, "Humility is the most difficult of all virtues to achieve."

*Resist pressure from detractors.* Do not be sidetracked or abandon your goals or vision. One of the most courageous things you can do is to be steadfast in your belief, to know who you are, and where you want to go. You will likely have plenty of detractors. You must stand up to them if you are to be a leader who creates consensus.

*Speak out.* Just as you must resist pressure from those who try to damage your dreams or destroy your goals, you must not be afraid to speak out for what you believe and to stand up for faculty and staff members in your department or college. You must have courage to speak out in the face of ridicule or intimidation.

Courage is not an old-fashioned notion. In the face of change, courage is more necessary than ever before. Courage, along with other traits outlined in this chapter, will help you create the consensus needed to build an outstanding department or college. You can make a difference if you work to get others involved and to rally around your ideas. Creating a consensus, or fostering teamwork, is not an option for academic leaders. You won't get far trying to lead through intimidation. If you are to succeed, you must depend on strong leadership skills and work hard to bring about a consensus.

## REFERENCES

Astin, A., & Astin, H. (2000). *Leadership reconsidered: Engaging higher education in social change.* Battle Creek, MI: W. K. Kellogg Foundation.

Bennis, W. (1994). *On becoming a leader.* Cambridge, MA: Perseus Books.

Bennis, W. (1997). *Managing people is like herding cats.* Provo, UT: Executive Excellence Publishing.

Bennis, W., & Nanus, B. (1997). *Leaders' strategies for taking charge.* New York, NY: Harper Business.

Brown, W. (1985). *13 fatal errors managers make and how you can avoid them.* New York, NY: Berkley Books.

Kouzes, J. M., & Posner, B. Z. (1995). *The leadership challenge: How to keep getting extraordinary things done in organizations.* San Francisco, CA: Jossey-Bass.

Mallard, K. (2000, Winter). Lending an ear: The chair's role as listener. *The Department Chair: A Resource for Academic Administrators, 10,* 11–13.

# Using Meetings
# to Create Cohesion   **5**

*Joan DeGuire North*

*Structuring discussion with these or other tech-
niques such as brainstorming forces the visual
display of individual thoughts so that the group
gains a tangible picture of its collective opinions
at the moment.*

Early in my career, when I chaired a committee on committees, little did I imagine that meetings would become a lifelong professional obligation. I don't even like meetings. But fate wasn't going to permit me to avoid them.

Since the early 1970s, this Woman of La Mancha has been throwing spears at academe's meeting practices, pleading in workshops or in practice for better ways to accomplish results in groups (North, 1980).

Some campus personnel can duck the call for service in local or campus committees, but one's own department meetings always loom. In addition to all the problems associated with meetings in general, department meetings sometimes feature senior colleagues who huff and puff and threaten to blow away junior colleagues, as well as the chair. I know several chairs who are routinely nauseated the morning of department meetings, anticipating public humiliation at worst and wasting people's time at best. Intimidating meetings have kept more than one new faculty member from peeping one word in their first year. Misunderstandings from meetings have been known to incubate factions with long lives, and boredom from meetings has glazed over generations of academicians' eyes. Yet, a successful meeting or exciting retreat can produce both new directions and renewed collegiality. Department heads and deans interested in improving their people management skills can hardly overlook the conduct of effective meetings.

What makes meetings so difficult? First, discussion protocols seem to have only two variations: endless talk or Robert's Rules, which will be discussed later in this chapter; the different purposes for meetings are not always well served by either end of that continuum. We need to use a greater variety of discussion and decision-making tools, especially tools that promote participant satisfaction. Second, meetings suffer the same A–Z ailments of any human-to-human interaction: listening blocks, power differentials, clouded clarity, differing styles, hostility, hidden agendas. Meetings amplify the pitfalls. And yet, we expect the chair to monitor all of this, serve as referee, psychologist, mother, tiger-tamer while at the same time trying to follow and focus the discussion. Chairs need help steering through interpersonal mine fields during meetings, especially if they want to achieve results and promote departmental cohesion. Finally, meetings are doomed for failure when we squeeze complex issues into our 50-minute free classroom periods, like Cinderella's sisters with her glass shoe. Instead, meetings should be structured to fit their purpose; form should follow function.

Books on how to improve meetings provide many new tools and insights for department chairs and deans (see for example Mosvick & Nelson, 1987; Hammond, 1996). In this chapter, I will suggest looking differently at three aspects of meetings: discussions/making decisions, leadership roles, and the structure of meetings.

## SHAPING DISCUSSIONS

In 1876 when U.S. Army General Henry Robert wrote "The Rules of Order," he attempted to bring order to the chaos that must have characterized meetings of his day by making parliamentary procedures available in print form. Today we still have the same options: unregulated discussion or formal parliamentary procedure. While there may be times when free-flowing discussion is warranted, often department members long for their meetings to carve out decisions from the endless goo of discussion. Likewise, there may be reasons for using formal parliamentary procedures in department meetings, but those rules may not necessarily foster department inclusion, cohesion, and collegiality.

Since Robert's era, advances have been made in group dynamics that can provide new insights and additional structures for moderating the discussion and coming to conclusions (www.agric.gov.ab.ca/ruraldev/rurallea/r2tps2.html). Many of these structures pay particular attention to promoting good group dynamics, which can lead to better department cohesion. The structures suggested below are a sampling of many possible ways to lasso group opinions and provide wider group participation in meetings without reverting to the more formal Robert's Rules.

### Nominal Group Technique

Nominal group technique (NGT) (Delbecq, 1975) was developed in the early 1970s to bring a group together to reach conclusions in a different kind of way. NGT is organized so that think time is balanced with talk time; all individuals contribute, not just those comfortable with talking in groups; and a wide variety of ideas can be displayed. (See http://128.143.238.20/services/CSA/nomi nal.htm.) This approach is more structured than brainstorming and more participative than voting. The NGT steps I use, slightly adapted from the original, follow.

*Step one.* State a question or issue and ask the group members to work alone by writing their own responses in phrases. Topics that might be appropriate for this technique include: "What directions might our department take in the next five years?" or "How can we reduce credits to degree?"

*Step two.* After three to five minutes, record the ideas, one idea per person at a time, on a large flip chart or board. No discussion or evaluation of the ideas should occur during this step.

*Step three.* Lead the group in discussing the ideas one at a time, especially for clarification. Often, groups will eliminate duplication or cluster ideas.

*Step four.* Assign group members a certain number of points and ask them to come up to the board (in any order or no order) to divide those points among the ideas they like the most, with no limit on how many points can be assigned to any one item. The number of points each person is given to allocate depends on the size of the group; I suggest about two to three times the number of participants, so for a group of 10 participants, each individual might have 25 points to divide.

*Step five.* Tally the results and encourage group discussion of the findings. If the group desires, refine the answers and distribute points one more time.

There are many variations on this overall design, but the essential elements are: silent generation of ideas that are displayed for all to see; distribution of preference points; and discussion of results (Hammons & Murry, 1995). I have used this technique for small groups, mid-sized groups of 30, and large groups of 80 or so. With large groups, a team of group leaders makes the process more efficient.

### Inventing Criteria

Inventing criteria (Merry & Allerhand, 1977) helps a group choose among options by directing the group's attention to the most important criteria the options might meet. For instance, a physical education department might consider expanding by creating new programs in adventure education or athletic training or adaptive physical education. Using this process, the department would first identify criteria that would be important to the decision, such as student interest, adequate staffing, needed facilities. Then the options could be examined according to each criterion. Because the focus moves from the options themselves to the decision criteria, the technique can often diffuse arguments for and against specific options. Other typical issues, which might suit this technique, are "Which classroom should be renovated first?" or "Which proposal(s) for professional development should be funded?" Here is how the technique works.

1) List options on a board or flip chart in a matrix design (see Figure 5.1).

2) The group identifies criteria by which the ideas should be judged and lists them on the matrix. If some are more important than others, they should be so noted.

3) Each individual rates each idea by each criterion, using high-medium-low or a numerical system to show how well each idea is supported by each criterion. Summarize the individual votes into summary votes for each box.

4) Discuss the results.

In this example, the adaptive physical education option meets criteria better than the other options, especially since it meets what was identified as the most important option—staffing.

### Results

Structuring discussion with these or other techniques, such as brainstorming, forces the visual display of individual thoughts so

## FIGURE 5.1
## CRITERIA MATRIX SHEET

|  | Facilities | Funding | Staffing Most Impt. | Student Need | Timing | Etc. |
|---|---|---|---|---|---|---|
| Adventure Ed. | High | Medium | Low | High | High | |
| Athletic Training | High | Low | Low | ? | ? | |
| Adaptive Phys. Ed. | High | High | High | High | High | |
| Option D | Etc. | | | | | |
| Option E | | | | | | |
| Option F | | | | | | |
| Etc. | | | | | | |

SOURCE: MERRY & ALLERHAND (1977).

that the group gains a tangible picture of its collective opinions at the moment. While this may seem small, it provides group members with the assurance that each person, no matter how shy or low on the power totem, contributed; that domination is demininished or eliminated altogether; that the discussion will not be funneled into an adversarial yes or no vote; that the collective is addressing collective issues. In other words, structuring discussions contributes to the group feeling like a connected group.

Structuring discussion also promotes efficiency by reducing time wasted in meetings. Most structured discussion processes provide a limit on general discussion by directing the group to some form of visual display of opinions. This governor for discussion generally eliminates soliloquies and filibusters, and discourages verbal domination, which take up so much time in many meetings.

And, sometimes the variety provided by structured discussion processes actually makes meetings seem like fun.

## SHAPING LEADERSHIP ROLES

All too often, the responsibility for achieving results in meetings falls on the backs of the chairs, deans, or other conveners. Meeting members watch—with curiosity, amusement, or fear—to see if he or she can pull it off, how often members expect the convener to make the meeting work. So the convener juggles all the tasks associated with getting people to agree, with getting things done in time, with ensuring full participation, and with making arrangements. These multiple tasks stretch the abilities of even the best convener to attend to content, process, and arrangements at the same time, thus risking the meeting's success. The-chair-does-all model masks the members' individual responsibility for the success of the meeting, taking them off the hook. To get the best out of meetings, different roles should be identified and assigned to various members. Many departments already recognize the value of separating meeting roles when they appoint or enlist someone to assume the recording role.

### Role Differentiation
Perhaps the most obvious role differentiation required for productive meetings is between getting the tasks accomplished and assuring that the members have a positive experience. While not completely opposite objectives, the two goals can lead in very different directions. The task orientation focuses on speedy completion without much leeway for contemplating participation

patterns. The group orientation considers the needs of individuals in the group even if the task doesn't get accomplished in a speedy manner. Often chairs concern themselves with completing the tasks at hand at the expense of group participation and satisfaction. All too often departments that do not give some special attention to both process and participation receive negative reactions to meetings:

> Too frequently people's reactions to most meetings are disappointment and frustration. Disappointment that tasks weren't completed. Frustration that the potential benefits of any group . . . were effectively negated by one or more problems such as: domination by one or two members, failure to tap the talents of group members, a pervasive sense of having been manipulated, pressure for conformity to pre-determined answers/solutions. (Hammons & Murray, 1995, p. 10)

I suggest that four different people in meetings assume four different roles: organizer, completer, facilitator, and recorder.

*Organizer.* The organizer, usually the chair, handles the agenda, logistics, and details. Normally, the organizer leads the meeting. The organizer might also confer with the completer and facilitator in planning the meeting with both efficiency and satisfaction in mind.

Because the organizer is usually the power figure—department chair or dean or director—the organizer is the only one who can build a permissive climate for the group to fully participate, without which none of the remaining suggestions make sense (Mosvick & Nelson, 1987). A chair who dominates meetings or who tolerates only agreement might be better served conducting meetings in front of his or her bathroom mirror.

*Completer.* The completer's focus is helping or nudging the group to accomplish the tasks at hand. This person pushes for conclusions and uses a variety of techniques to urge the group to finish its task. This person might summarize where the group is in the discussion by listing the things already decided and what still lies ahead. This person might note when the group has strayed from the agenda or ask to separate issues. The completer could suggest a straw vote or a new decision-making technique or recommend that a subgroup make recommendations on an issue. The completer role is difficult because it requires great concentration both on the topic under discussion and on the flow of the conversation.

*Facilitator.* The facilitator's focus is to ensure the positive involvement of the group. The facilitator tries to assure that all members contribute to discussions and that people hear each other. In addition, he or she serves as a champion of each person and watches for opportunities to celebrate individual and group successes. The facilitator seeks to build and reinforce a sense of community. Humor can also be an effective tool for a facilitator. The facilitator can help the organizer by suggesting meeting designs that open participation and by helping to curtail the natural tendency of the organizer to do most of the talking. This difficult role requires concentration not only on the meeting topics but also on interpersonal nuances and patterns of participation.

*Recorder.* The recorder produces a record of the group's conclusions. The recorder is often an ally of the completer, attempting to make sense of the flow of the discussion. He or she can play a unifying role by keeping track of conclusions, options, or discussions on a visible board, so that all members can watch their progress; having all eyes on one set of notes reminds the group of their collective purpose. The use of visual recording devices such as white or black boards or flip charts makes ideas common property and removes the association with the person originating the idea. It also recognizes that the idea was received by the group. Without this public recording, often ideas just hang in the air, neither accepted nor rejected.

Details about how these roles might be implemented will vary, but factors a group will want to consider include: how people are chosen for the roles, how long a person serves in the role, what kinds of resources/training might be available for those new in the roles.

As group members serve in one or more of the roles, their sense of responsibility for the group grows, group perceptions of one another broadens, and individuals can experience themselves in new ways within the sociology of the department. With this shared leadership for the collective business of the group, the role of the chair becomes less lonely and formidable as the diffused light replaces the spotlight on the chair.

## SHAPING THE STRUCTURE OF MEETINGS

With schedules as tight as they are, department chairs can become giddy isolating even one time period when all members are free to attend department meetings. Therefore, it comes as no surprise that department meetings are usually held at the same time and are of the same duration, format, and in the same place. And yet, the tasks for meetings can vary from simple announcements to complex problem solving, leading inevitably to wasting time on the one hand (discussion expands to fill the time allotted) or inadequately addressing larger problems on the other. Careful thought about shaping the structure of meetings can produce better results, combat boredom, and influence collegiality.

### Some Basic Advice

*Meet only when necessary.* Organize meetings so that form follows function. Meet only when topics suggest that exchange is desirable, not merely to make announcements. Vary the time of the meetings if possible, scheduling half- or full-day retreats for elaborate or lengthy issues and 16- or 23-minute meetings for briefer items.

*Get the group's opinion.* Take the temperature of the group regarding their opinions on how well the meetings are working (Nikola, 1999). Use a continuum from 1 to 16 to ask members where they think recent meetings rate on producing results or encouraging collegiality or using time well. Do these evaluations on paper or on a board at least annually. The follow-up to the rating should be a question about how the group could improve the meetings.

*Be creative with your space.* Spice up meetings with creative use of space. Space is a powerful symbolic tool, which can be used to increase departmental cohesion and to make department meetings more pleasant. Rooms where seats are arranged in lecture style tend to inhibit colleague-to-colleague discussion and encourage a more formal talking arrangement in which everyone talks to the chair. Sometimes using different rooms helps mix up the normal seating patterns and therefore breaks up a predictable response pattern. Going off campus to a retreat setting often helps members shed traditional distances from each other and work on problems with new perspectives.

*Avoid monotony.* Vary the structure of the agenda, shifting traditional topics around. If subcommittees normally report first and then the group goes to new business, reverse them on occasion.

*Try using a fish bowl design.* In a fish bowl design, the committee meets in a circle in the center of a room with one extra chair. Observers sit in chairs around the inner circle to listen to the discussion. If an observer wishes to join the committee's discussion, he or she moves to the extra seat in the inner circle to join the discussion and leaves when finished.

*Entice with food.* Occasionally, arrange for food to be available before, during or after departmental meetings. Food heightens the congeniality of the group, sometimes breaks tensions, and increases attendance.

## CONCLUSION

Academic institutions, more than any other type of organization, should be on the forefront of being really proficient at encouraging, monitoring, and using group discussion on issues. Our meetings should be wonders to behold.

All too often we take meetings for granted, assuming that no special efforts or skills are necessary for a group to sit together, talk, and make decisions. However, like parenting or teaching, participating in a meeting, especially a department meeting, is a complex human interaction with multiple goals, histories, and personalities, with an intricate subtext and high stakes attached to success or failure.

Meetings are the one place in which all members of the group interact, establish their collective norms, and create their collective identity. Meetings provide flagship opportunities to create positive experiences. And yet, all too often meetings at their worst spawn a gang mentality or cover over honest disputes with a thick film of melted sugar.

Department meetings are like meals in a family, times that the group convenes as a unit. Like a dinner setting, department meetings can be nightmarish experiences, or they can establish and reinforce group norms that promote group cohesion. Like dinners, they take some planning, concentration, and effort to achieve the best results. Let's be as creative, organized, and determined about our meetings as we are about our teaching. Bon appétit!

## REFERENCES

Delbecq, A. L., Van de Ven, A. H., & Gustafson, D. H. (1975). *Group techniques for program planning*. Glenville, IL: Scott Foresman.

Hammond, S. A. (1996). *The thin book of appreciative inquiry*. Plano, TX: Thin Book.

Hammons, J. O., & Murry, J. W. (1995, Winter). Applying group decision-making to meetings. *The Department Chair*, (5) 3, 10–11.

Merry, U., & Allerhand, M. E. (1977). *Developing teams and organizations*. Reading, MA: Addison-Wesley.

Mosvick, R. K., & Nelson, R. B. (1987). *We've got to start meeting like this!* Glenview, IL: Scott, Foresman.

Nikola, M. P. (1999, Winter). Maximize departmental collaboration through effective facilitation and meeting management techniques. *The Department Chair*, (9) 3, 6–7.

North, J. (1980, Summer). Guidelines and Strategies for Conducting Meetings. *POD Quarterly, 2*, 79–91.

# Winning Over Your Detractors

**6**

*Thomas R. McDaniel*

> *On every faculty you will have some irreducible minimum of chronic complainers. These faculty may have a cynical view of life in general and probably complain about everything no matter where they are.*

A nyone in a college leadership position—department chair, dean, provost, or president—will encounter detractors. Such critics may be motivated by spite, malice, revenge, envy, ambition, or a wide variety of maladaptive behaviors. Or perhaps their views and values simply conflict with yours. Why is this the case for leaders? Who are these detractors in the academic world? What can a department chair or dean do to deal with detractors? In this chapter we will explore such questions with the dual goals of understanding (perhaps even appreciating) the "detractor dynamic" and arriving at some solutions and strategies for the beleaguered leader.

I have been a department chair, division head, dean (arts and sciences), vice president (academic affairs), provost, and interim president over the course of my 37 years of academic administration. All of these leadership positions have presented me with "detractor dilemmas" aplenty, and the dynamics are always the same, even when the players are changed. As a regular columnist for the journal *Academic Leader*, I have been writing a monthly advice column for deans called "The Dean's Dialogue," in which I find myself returning time and again to one aspect or another of the "detractor dynamic." If only our critics would become allies—or at least leave us alone to do our jobs—how pleasant and satisfying academic administration would be!

And so, in this chapter I am going to draw on my own experience, on the advice I have proffered to fellow administrators (especially from my column for *Academic Leader*), and on what other authorities (Bennett, Higgerson, Leaming, Lucas, and Tucker, among others) have concluded about the "detractor dynamic." I will outline what I think are the essential elements at work in the structure of academic institutions and departments when individuals seem hell-bent on undermining an administrator's effectiveness. While all deans and department chairs have detractors, and conflict is a normal aspect of administration, we who labor in the academic vineyard simply must know how to deal with our critics. To fall prey to detractors is to fail in the fine art of academic administration. While much of my advice will focus on deans, that advice applies equally to department chairs and other academic administrators.

## DETRACTORS

Who are these so-called detractors who bedevil deans and department chairs? They come in many guises (and disguises) and do not lend themselves to a one-size-fits-all description. In fact, detractors may come and go, wax and wane, depending on circumstances and events. A detractor today may be an ally tomorrow (and vice versa). The challenge for academic administrators is 1) to recognize detractor symptoms in any individual, 2) to convert detractors into supporters, and (if conversion fails) 3) to nullify the negative consequences of detractors who cannot be won over. No simple task—but an imperative for the successful academic leader.

Consider a handful of detractor types. This is not a comprehensive catalog by any means, but it will start you thinking about the kinds of detractors in your own academic world.

### The Second-Guessers
The second-guesser detractors are the Monday morning quarterbacks of the academic world. From where they sit, safely protected from the consequences of decision-making, the administrator should have foreseen the consequences of decisions now gone awry. The second-guessing syndrome makes for good faculty lounge gossip and somehow elevates the detractor as one who surely would have made better decisions.

### The Chronic Complainers
On every faculty there will be an irreducible minimum of chronic complainers. These faculty may have a cynical view of life in

general and probably complain about everything no matter where they are. For such individuals, the administrator is a natural target. Be assured that attending to criticisms will only reinforce the complainer's conviction that only because of the critic's complaints did the administrator come to his or her senses.

### Pretenders to the Throne
There are many individuals in the academic community who believe they are better suited for the administrator's job than you are. If only those who empowered the administrator had the wisdom to rethink that choice, what a better place this campus would be! Pretenders are usually wiley enough to hide their secret ambition but also shrewd enough to let it be known that they are available should an opening in the administrator's office suddenly occur.

### Troublemakers
Like the chronic complainers, troublemakers seem to thrive on negativity. In fact, they are not happy until there is some sticky-wicket problem on campus—even a crisis—to keep the academic life, well, interesting. Troublemakers often delight in announcing bad news and then stepping back to see who sweats. They are a curious lot, but no academic community is without them.

### Noble Shaman
The noble shaman can be the administrator's greatest allies or greatest adversaries. These individuals are, in fact, blessed with special powers of wisdom, insight, and good judgment. So long as they are on your side, you may have wonderful counselors to help you and the institution succeed. But a shaman gone awry can be a detractor of enormous influence on the campus. If such an individual basks too much in the reflected glory of your appreciation, the afterglow may put you in the shadows (McDaniel, November 2000).

You can probably identify a few of your colleagues who can be tagged with these labels. They no doubt have redeeming virtues. (If none occur to you, remember Emerson's observation: "A weed is a flower whose virtues have not yet been discovered.") You may also discover other types not identified in the short list above. While dwelling on the identification of detractors should not be an obsessive preoccupation (bordering on paranoia), remember that some of your detractors might really try to do you in.

## THE DETRACTOR DYNAMIC: BUREAUPATHOLOGY IN ACADEME

Let us turn now to the academic workplace climate in which detractors not only survive but thrive. What is it about academic institutions that seems, in a perverse way, to encourage and nurture detractors of academic leaders? Among the leading causes is what is sometimes called "bureaupathology."

Perhaps it is obvious that the contemporary college and university have taken on many of the bureaucratic features of other complex organizations—from business and industry to governmental agencies. Bureaucracy, its putative inventor Max Weber (1946) declared, has all of the advantages of the machine: rationality, order, efficiency, uniformity of its moving parts, standardization, speed of performance, and repetition of function. In bureaucratic organizations a system of general rules—universalistic and impersonal—circumscribes the conduct of officials. The entire structure of the organization is formalized so that individuals have little personal influence on the conduct of the duties of the office. Consequently, organizational relationships—such as those between presidents and deans, deans and department chairs, department chairs and faculty—are standardized and depersonalized.

The specific nature of the bureaucracy, Weber observed, "develops the more perfectly the bureaucracy is 'dehumanized,' and the more completely it succeeds in eliminating from official business love, hatred, and all purely personal, irrational, and emotional elements which escape calculation" (p. 239).

Bureaupathology is the institutional disease of an organization that has become so machine-like and dehumanized that personal relationships, individuality, creative expression, and social goals of community life are ignored, abused, and snuffed out. When efficiency, standardization, and rules—given new force by contemporary demands for accountability and productivity—override human values (like freedom and creativity), the organization can become dysfunctional. When that happens, the organization reflects the very opposite of its bureaucratic intention: It becomes inefficient, disorderly, aberrant, and unproductive. Bureaucrats (already a term of derision) like deans and department chairs become mere functionaries and mindless rule-keepers. They become depersonalized effigies of a nameless and faceless authority—"they," "the powers-that-be," "the administration."

It is this dysfunctional, irrational climate that sets up any bureaucratic leader for criticism. One of the best satirical treatments of bureaupathology at work is the popular comic strip "Dilbert." Let's examine how a prototypical modern detractor like Dilbert functions in the dysfunctional organization where bureaupathology is the norm. Here is how I described that comic experience in an *Academic Leader* essay (McDaniel, 2000).

*Dilbert and dysfunction.* Cartoonist Scott Adams casts a cynical eye on the work of managers, supervisors, CEOs, and other leaders who (giving proof that the Peter Principle works) find creative forms of incompetence to visit upon hapless workers, like Dilbert, Wally, and Alice. In the Dilbert collection *Casual Day Has Gone Too Far* (Adams, 1997), Dogbert (his "management consultant") explains leadership: "Leaders start their careers as morons; they are drawn to meetings like moths to a porch light; they prevail in all decisions because they are impervious to logic or coffee . . . " (p. 7).

What dean or department chair does not see just a touch of himself or herself in the administrative shenanigans of the pointy-haired boss who bedevils Dilbert and his coworkers or in the equally dysfunctional, if not downright malevolent, Catbert (the evil human resource director) and Dogbert? Let me remind you that Adams found in his first annual Dilbert Survey that the most annoying management practice cited by employees was "Idiots Promoted to Management." But surely, you know the difference between a computer and an Etch-A-Sketch.

What wisdom can academic administrators glean from Dilbert? In his book *The Dilbert Principle* (1996), Adams teaches those of us who live in the rarefied ethers of the Adminisphere that certain leader behaviors and attitudes promote organizational success and others inhibit it. When Dilbert encounters management at its worst (which is most of the time), we can see how and why so many leadership practices go awry. But we can also see how opposite practices might improve morale, efficiency, accountability, productivity, quality, and creativity.

## AVOIDING BUREAUPATHOLOGY

So, what can we who are in the academic adminisphere learn from detractor Dilbert's dyspeptic dilemmas? Here are a few lessons for deans and chairs.

### Stay out of the Way

Much of the caustic humor of Dilbert flows from the pointy-haired boss's ignorant, awkward, and unwarranted intrusions into the work process. He is a micro-manager from hell. In one strip, a new "bungee boss" is lowered into the office declaring, "Hi-I'm-your-new-boss-let's-change-everything-before-I-get-reassigned, oops-too-late-goodbye." And then the attached bungee cord snatches the bungee boss out of the office. Dilbert remarks, "I think he made a difference." One of the important rules for any administrator is the physician's axiom: First, do no harm. Whose way should you stay out of today?

You might consider, for example, whether or not your presence in a meeting of, say, the English Department is perceived as support or intrusion. Just because you have administrative oversight for academic programs does not mean that you have special wisdom to impart to faculty members who have been working on curriculum reform for several weeks. If your presence seems to distract the faculty, you might simply listen attentively for a few minutes and move on to someplace where your contributions may actually make a positive difference. Micro-managers usually mean well but often undermine real productivity. Faculty are more likely to want your support than your advice. Effective leaders know the difference and act accordingly.

### Stay off Bandwagons

One of Dilbert's themes is the prevalence of administrative panaceas: Total Quality Management (TQM), reengineering, visioning, recognition programs, rightsizing—the list is long. Administrators are portrayed as fad-happy cutting-edgers who think that leading is always a matter of introducing yet another magic bullet that usually ends up lodged in someone's foot. But hey! We are out in front! Characters in the strip often play the language game to turn bandwagon slogans back on the administration. In one Dilbert calendar cartoon, Dilbert asks do-nothing Wally for "a bullet point for your monthly accomplishment." Wally replies, "Put me down for 'leveraged synergy across all technology platforms.'" Dilbert says, "That was your accomplishment last month?" Wally's final comment is, "It's more of a journey than a destination." Is your administrative journey made via bandwagons?

Deans and department chairs usually have more opportunities than faculty to attend conferences devoted to management miracles and may come back to campus with new enthusiasm for the latest panaceas. Let's say that you have just returned to campus with new insights into the importance of collaborative teaching, partnering with a purpose, or distance education. The dynamic conference speakers made their concepts sound so compelling and the implementation so simple that you were confident your faculty would be as enthusiastic as you are. Be assured that is not likely the case. Your faculty did not share your "near life experience" at the conference, and they have very different priorities in their workplace. Furthermore, they have seen far too many bandwagons driving through the campus with snake oil salesmen touting unproven cures for student dyspepsia and institutional dysfunction. Effective leaders know that skepticism and temper their enthusiasms accordingly.

### Stay in Touch with Reality

The outrageous, over-the-top humor in virtually all Dilbert strips derives from a workplace environment as bizarre as any Kafka novel or Pirandello play. Adams' dark humor is primarily directed at the Alice-in-Wonderland quality of the modern corporation, a place where idiots lead and geniuses cope with the absurdity of administrative policy and practice. What should be an environment that promotes efficiency, creativity, and productivity in the looking glass world of Dilbert turns out to be a nightmare for employees:

> *Pointy-Haired Boss:* "Here's the company vision and business plan."
> *Dilbert* (reads): " 'Vision: Empowered employees working toward a common plan.' Sounds good. . . . But the business plan is blank."

*Pointy-Haired Boss:* "It's confidential."
*Dilbert:* "How am I supposed to know what to do?"
*Pointy-Haired Boss:* "I'll yell at you if you do the wrong thing."

From the "Seven Habits of Highly Defective People" to the predictably insane advice of consultants (who will always recommend that you do what you are not doing now), Dilbert keeps us humble, honest, and in touch with what is really going on in our workplaces (McDaniel, September 2000).

One of the ways that academic leaders can stay in touch with reality is to get to know faculty and administrative colleagues on a personal basis and in informal settings outside the college campus. There is an informal communication structure in the workplace itself that often bypasses administrators; it should not be underestimated as a source of reality checking. A dean or department chair needs to have confidants to have confidence that administrative policy and practice actually work. You have to rise above the rumor mill, the academic grapevine, and the petty politics in your institution—but you better be in touch with what those sources of information are telling you about the workplace reality. Detractors have little patience with administrative ignorance.

One of the things we should keep in mind is that faculty members on the whole are among the least bureaucratically compatible people on the planet. They tend toward independent action and idiosyncratic (sometimes esoteric) research interests; they have creative minds; they gravitate toward personal interactions with students and colleagues and resist meetings of all kinds; they are often free spirits who reject punching time clocks and conforming to rules; they are inclined toward informality and are uncomfortable with regulated formality. Is it any wonder that the bureaucratized academy has become a breeding ground for administrator detractors? Bureaupathology may explain much of the detractor dynamic in higher education, but it does not excuse administrators from taking on the challenge of improving the workplace climate.

## FACULTY MORALE

A related phenomenon that effective deans and department chairs must attend to as they work to win over their detractors is the illusive concept commonly called faculty morale. If bureaupathology explains the institutional climate in which detractors thrive, faculty morale gives the academic administrator a measure by which to assess the detractor dynamic in a given department or college.

During my years as an academic dean in an independent liberal arts college, I often pondered the quixotic quality of faculty morale. What is it? How do you measure it? Are there ways to improve it? Indeed, I was regularly asked by the president and board chair, "How is morale among the professors, Tom?" I would try to look wise as I replied: "Remember the rule—faculty morale is always at an all-time low." But I know that answer was inadequate. Here is what 30-plus years as an academic leader have taught me about faculty morale.

### What Is Faculty Morale?

Beats me. I think the term is a code word that conveniently conveys one professor's perception which that professor tends to project on the faculty in general. But as Mark Twain once commented, "No generalization is worth a damn—including this one." Often this code is used as a sort of faculty weather report and, like many weather reports, gets more play when there is a storm brewing. However, just as the weather may be bad somewhere, elsewhere the sun is shining. The same shift in student enrollments that hurts morale in the physics department helps morale in the business department: It's an ill wind that blows no good. Call faculty morale the highly subjective individual and collective perception faculty have about the weather in their part of the academic world. Some might call it a "happiness reading." Remember: Unhappy faculty members are the most likely to be your detractors.

### How Do We Measure Faculty Morale?

Another perplexing problem. Because morale varies from time to time and place to place within each institution, it is difficult to assess. Faculty don't usually like to claim high morale because that takes the pressure off the dean or department chair to satisfy whatever need is current, from a new computer to better office accommodations to a lower course load to the ever-present better salary. Deans and department chairs have to keep an ear close to the ground while not overreacting to faculty complaints. Sometimes administrators can measure morale on campus against benchmark surveys and studies.

For example, *The American College Teacher,* a survey (Sax, L. J.) of 33,785 faculty members at 378 colleges, reports that the faculty is getting older, and older faculty feel more stress from technology than younger faculty, that the faculty in general are satisfied with their jobs (75%, up from 69% in 1989), and nearly 50% are happy with salaries, but that almost 34% have thought about leaving campus life in the last two years. And only 58% were satisfied with their relationship with administrators. Such findings give deans and chairs benchmark temperature readings on various aspects of faculty life that affect morale.

### Are There Ways to Improve Faculty Morale?
Certainly. As elusive and indefinable as the concept is, good academic leaders find ways to optimize faculty morale or they perish. As the axiom says, "Old deans never die; they just lose their faculties." And lose them they will if they—and provosts, division heads, department chairs—do not establish an action plan explicitly designed to promote optimum faculty morale. Of course, that includes efforts to improve salary and working conditions, but the extensive research on faculty job satisfaction and morale makes it clear that the professoriate, more than most professions, is motivated by qualitative factors and workplace considerations: autonomy, achievement, respect, responsibility, freedom, collegiality, and support for creative research and teaching. Deans need to understand those motivations and to support institutional efforts to respond to them. That includes working in concert with department chairs to make faculty morale a priority. The result will be an organization less victimized by bureaupathology and Dilbert's dyspeptic dilemmas.

## AN ACTION AGENDA FOR DEANS AND CHAIRS

It is possible to design strategies to promote a culture that nurtures high faculty morale. This requires more than quick-fixes and band-aids, more than recognitions and rewards, more than friendly pats on the back. Deans and chairs should go beyond faculty development programs—faculty often resent being "developed"—to thinking in terms of faculty vitality. Developing an action agenda requires administrators to take some risks and expect some recrimination, especially from those who are dean detractors. As the saying goes, "No good dean goes unpunished." It is easier to take on the stance one of my colleagues does when he proudly calls himself "Dr. No": no to new ideas, no to creative research, no to funding unproven teaching experiments.

I rather like the persona of another colleague who calls herself "the dean of exceptions." She is willing to say yes, even when that decision may break precedent or rule—if a yes advances faculty morale. The risks, of course, include failed experiments, grumbling about favoritism, and questions about "what have you done for me lately?" Good deans and other middle managers are willing to take these lumps in the interest of a proactive agenda to promote faculty vitality. They need the help of department chairs to turn ideas into actions. In an excellent publication from the Council of Independent Colleges (CIC) entitled *A Good Place to Work,* Austin, Rice, and Splete (1991) evaluate the research on faculty morale and identify a host of factors that characterize faculty vitality at selected high morale colleges. A dean might well begin with suggestions from this study.

The CIC study found morale highest in independent liberal arts colleges where the following conditions existed.

• A strong sense of community and distinctive organizational culture

• A clear understanding of, and agreement with, institutional goals, values, traditions, celebrations, and rituals

• Wide definition of faculty scholarship with rewards not limited to published research

• An effort to promote participatory leadership

• An intentional focus on teaching and students

• A commitment to momentum: growth, progress, and excellence

• An emphasis on internal collaboration rather than competition, supported by collegiality and a balance of intrinsic and extrinsic rewards and strong ties with the surrounding community

Can deans and other academic leaders find ways to advance these institutional qualities? Of course. The CIC project includes "The Academic Workplace Audit," an instrument that can help deans assess faculty morale in their own institutions and establish a more specific action agenda to improve faculty vitality: not a bad place to begin establishing a high morale faculty.

In such a climate we might also find more high morale deans, deans who do not lose their faculties. Neither deans nor department chairs can make faculty happy (perhaps because, as Abraham Lincoln observed, "Most people are about as happy as they make up their minds to be"), but they do have a duty to support and serve faculty goals and ambitions that also advance the institutional mission. Making judgments about such personal and college congruence of goals takes both wisdom and courage; however, such judgments and commitments help create the kind of climate where faculty vitality and high morale are natural by-products. To do less is to miss an administrator's greatest opportunity and greatest satisfaction.

Because faculty morale is such an illusive concept—hard to define and hard to measure—deans and department chairs need to be both alert and flexible, ready to seize any opportunity that might raise faculty morale. This is often an eye-of-the-beholder phenomenon, and the skillful administrator takes advantage of every opening to shape that perception in a positive direction. Sometimes a departmental meeting or faculty meeting provides an opportunity to commend accomplishments; sometimes the dean or department chair needs only to send a brief "good going" note to tell a faculty member that his or her article, chapter, book, performance, guest lecture, etc. was appreciated by the administrator (or, better yet, someone the administrator recently heard from); sometimes the administrator needs only to delegate with confidence and conviction a responsibility to an individual or group in such a way that the recipients feel the leader's confidence and appreciation. The accumulation of a thousand small acts of confidence and appreciation may do more to raise faculty morale than any formal recognition program, merit-pay system, or tangible reward. Good administrators work on all fronts simultaneously and continuously.

## DETRACTORS IN ADMINISTRATION

Some of your most important detractors will be found not in the faculty but among your administrative colleagues. Perhaps you will find yourself engaged in power struggles—some friendly, some acrimonious—with fellow department chairs or deans. Collegiality may fall victim to competition when resources like money and students are in short supply, and successful administration becomes a contest to secure the biggest slice of the pie. Two relationships with fellow administrators which are of paramount importance for academic leaders who would win over their detractors are the relationships with the person just above and the person just below them in the organizational chart (McDaniel, January 2000; October 2000).

### President-Faculty Relations
Consider this hypothetical situation: You are an academic dean in a college where your president is one of the new-breed leaders, a nonacademic administrator whose expertise is in business management, alumnae affairs, student life, or development. Further, your faculty is a highly organized cohort of professionals who have the security of a tenure system and the strong leadership of a faculty senate. Then you discover that your president, in an effort to establish better communication and rapport with the faculty, is meeting with individual faculty members, academic departments, and the faculty senate. Do you see a dilemma in your future?

The scenario above (or some approximation of it—such as faculty who go around department chairs to meet with the dean) is hardly hypothetical. In fact, it is likely to be the norm in many institutions today. Increasingly, college presidents come from outside the academy; increasingly, faculty members are highly organized and political; increasingly, academic leaders advocate communication and flat or horizontal decision-making mechanisms. These evolutions in management theory and practice put the administrative role of the dean or department chair—the quintessential middle managers—at peril. At least, middle managers need to think about how best to accommodate the increased interaction between faculty and presidents and to make the communication process a positive experience for everyone.

### The Concept of Crisis
We who spend much of our time in the middle know well the challenge of resolving conflicts and dealing with detractors. We also recall that the Chinese symbol for crisis is a combination of the

characters for danger and opportunity. The desire both by presidents and professors to strengthen relations can constitute dangers and opportunities aplenty. Long gone are the days when a dean might recite the dean's dictum: "My job is to keep the president from thinking and the faculty from talking." (Or is it the other way around? I can never remember.) To succeed in an era where presidents and professors seek common ground—with or without the involvement of the dean—deans and department chairs must find ways to minimize dangers and maximize opportunities. Otherwise, they will find life in the middle to be one crisis after another.

In my years as a professor and an administrator, I've had opportunities to assess president-faculty relations and to reflect on the dynamics of such relationships. I seem to be blessed (or cursed) with an ability to sympathize with conflicting points of view, partly because I understand that where you stand depends on where you sit. Because I have sat in many different seats, I can appreciate almost every point of view. That doesn't make solving crises any easier.

### Dean and Department Chair Dilemmas

Middle managers have the difficult task of communicating faculty needs to presidents and boards while communicating institutional policies and priorities from the top administrative positions to faculty and staff. Deans need the help of department chairs in communicating both up and down. Unlike some classical business or military chains of command, colleges have shared decision-making processes which assign distinct spheres of authority to the board, the administration, and the faculty. The middle manager's authority is rarely absolute and is often vaguely defined in college management models and faculty handbooks. In fact, a dean or department chair "rules" the faculty only by the consent of the governed and with the respect and goodwill earned by fair and faithful leadership. One leads the faculty by helping them achieve their best goals, by bringing them together to solve problems and chart new directions, and by skillful consensus building. Part pastor and part policeman, the middle manager is lost without human relation skills.

Dilemmas, then, assail deans and department chairs who fail to listen well, refuse to compromise when good sense and good policy require it, or run roughshod over the sensibilities of individual faculty members. However, middle managers also need to take stands, make decisions, and enforce institutional policies. Presidents can complicate the delicate balances and processes that deans and faculties have worked out over the years to promote a relatively amicable and collegial relationship unique to the academic workplace. The president's laudable intentions can result in an intensified triangulation that creates conflict and confusion. If, say, the president has heard a faculty complaint about another faculty member, does that imply support for the complainant? If the president asks the dean to address the concern, does that require the dean to support the complainant? Are presidents more likely to micro-manage the faculty and faculty to lobby the president for pet projects?

### Solutions for Middle Managers

While I have no simple solutions to offer, I do think deans and chairs can mitigate middle management crises emanating from this triangulation of president, faculty, and dean. Indeed, with some thought, imagination, and planning, a skillful leader can harness the synergy of this triangulation dynamic and turn what looks like a crisis into an opportunity. When a president wants to establish communication or collaboration or connection with the faculty, a dean, for example, might follow one or more of these approaches:

*Reevaluate your relationship with the president.* First of all, be sure that you enjoy the confidence of the president and that your effectiveness with the faculty is not at issue. Next, make sure you and the president have discussed all of the dynamics of triangulation and the ground rules you will follow to avoid end runs, divide and conquer strategies, or other unintended consequences of president-faculty relations. Finally, be sure that you and the president have a common understanding of the goals of such communications and the methods of follow-up.

*Reinvent your role as dean.* Because a dean's authority often is more personal than positional (and vaguely defined), that can give you opportunities to redesign the ways you work with your faculty and president. Perhaps you need to work more closely with department chairs and faculty senate leaders. Perhaps you ought to work more effectively with your president to identify academic needs, issues, and priorities. Perhaps you should arrange more conferences for the president and you with key chairs and faculty in each academic department. A dean's authority is limited, but his or her autonomy is immense.

*Reestablish your reputation for open communications.* Communication is not a zero-sum process. If the president wants more communication with the faculty, that does not mean you should have less. Do you invite open communication by word and deed? Do you get out on campus and into faculty work spaces (including classrooms) with regularity? Do you need to remind yourself that your leadership depends on your availability, your ability to hear and appreciate individual concerns, your responsiveness? The battle scars of deaning can dull our sensitivities and undermine our communication skills. The same may be true for department chairs.

Deans and other middle managers can fall victim to the dangers of president-faculty relations or find the opportunities every crisis or dilemma creates to become more versatile, more creative academic leaders. In the process, they can mitigate the detractor dynamic.

### Dean–Department Chair Relations

One of the major challenges every academic dean faces is developing effective partnerships with department chairs of diverse academic disciplines. There are a number of normal (if not inherent) conundrums and conflicts that almost always complicate dean–department chair relationships. Consider the following short list of factors that show up when deans and department chairs meet.

*Disciplinary differences.* The dean almost surely comes from a particular discipline with all its assumptions, values, and perspectives on curriculum and instruction well-ingrained. Even the most fair-minded deans are conditioned by their particular experiences and training. How does that dean treat all department chairs in an even-handed fashion? What can chairs do to ensure equal treatment?

*Department chair biases.* The department chair will always know the discipline allegiances—real or perceived—of the dean and will act accordingly. That could mean expecting support if discipline interests are congruent and expecting prejudice if they are not. How does the dean overcome such presumptions? How should department chairs deal with their own biases?

*Disparate power.* Role relationships develop within a power context. The dean has the institutional power of office to make certain higher-level decisions while the department chair has the representational power of the department. How does the dean navigate the tricky pathways of power? How does the department chair balance such power differentials?

Now, if you are waiting for great wisdom from me on these problematics of dean–department chair relations, do not hold your breath. I do know, however, that deans need to be vigilant for the signs of dissension and dysfunction that can poison morale and presage problems in the offing. Department chairs need to cooperate to form an effective alliance with the dean. Colleges, like all contemporary workplaces, seem to be venues where venom and violence are on the rise—venues that nurture detractors.

## STRATEGIES THAT SUCCEED

The best deans I know use superior conflict resolution strategies, preventive interventions, and people skills to promote civility, harmony, and goodwill between themselves and their department chairs. Below are a few strategies to think about and evaluate for their value on your campus: There is nothing startlingly new or magical in these concepts and practices, but most are devilishly difficult to implement in the practical world of middle management.

### Put Biases on the Table
It is often helpful to clear away the underbrush of bias at the outset of any discussion, project, or cooperative venture. The dean can tell a department chairman, "Mary, I know where your interests are and what you see as important for your department. I expect you to represent those interests and values vigorously as we work together. Let me tell you where I am coming from so we are clear up front on such matters." Well begun is half done in almost all interactions with department chairs.

### Agree to Find Win-Win Solutions to Problems
In the context of power, relationships between dean and department chair will be less confrontational and more collegial if both power players are working for positive outcomes rather than win-

lose options: The dean might say, "John, I need to save enough money from this departmental project to fund some essential library acquisitions. If you can help me do that, I will make sure that your faculty get the recognition you think they deserve for a job well done." Shared success always leads to more effective partnerships.

### Find Ways to Empower the Department Chair

Effective deaning always involves power sharing. That, of course, is part of the rationale for establishing win-win goals early in the relationship and in goal-setting with the department chair in shared work. There is an art to empowering that goes beyond mere assigning of tasks or cheery encouragement ("Sally, this is your opportunity to shine—I'm counting on you to succeed.") The art starts with skillful listening that shows the dean really understands and values the department chair's ideas and concerns, requires his or her own contribution to the assessment of the issue or project, and culminates with an affirmation of confidence that the department chair is a trusted and competent partner. The department chair who can both initiate and reciprocate will strengthen the partnership immeasurably. By such an art is collegiality built.

As I said, there is no magic here. There are many sophisticated and elaborate practices that conscientious deans and chairs will investigate and (when appropriate) implement: conflict resolution, TQM, strategic planning, mentoring, counseling, cross-functional task forces, communication/collaboration workshops and consultants, faculty morale assessment instruments, team-building models—the list is long. But none of these practices will succeed in the absence of the three fundamental strategies above. No academic administrator can escape some tension and conflict in the workplace. The most successful leaders are those who know how to promote collegiality as they make partners out of department chairs and others to accomplish the shared vision of a leadership team.

## ADDITIONAL STRATEGIES TO WIN OVER DETRACTORS

The experienced dean or department chair knows that (to paraphrase a biblical axiom) "the detractors you will always have with you." The question is simply this: What's an administrator to do?

There is no simple or singular solution, of course, and dealing with your detractors is a test of patience, wisdom, and people skills. Here are a few things to consider.

### Do a Reality Check

Just because these detractors appear to be thorns in your side, do not write them off as inconsequential critics, especially if you find some common themes. Are you unavailable or unapproachable? Are you arbitrary and capricious? Do you play favorites? Do you procrastinate on important projects? These are only a few of the negative barbs that may come your way, and it is important for you to look at yourself honestly and determine what validity may be found.

### Consider the Source

You should know your detractors well enough to know what motivates them and how accurate their complaints might be. Stereotyping can be dangerous, of course, but you should know who might be a pretender to the throne, and who might be a chronic complainer. If you have been honest in your reality check, considering the source of an allegation can help you keep it in perspective.

### Win over Your Detractors

You will note that this short piece of advice can be read in two ways. In some cases, the best strategy may be to confront the detractor in as direct and professional a fashion as possible and lance the boil as expeditiously as you can. But the advice can also mean to bring the detractor over to your side. If the detractors know you value constructive criticism, you have a chance to turn enemies into allies. You never want to miss that opportunity (McDaniel, November 2000).

## CONCLUSION

In many ways, dealing with detractors is ingrained in the art and science of administration. We are, after all, in the people managing business. We who serve as leaders in the academy are charged to work with and through people to accomplish the mission of the department, school, college, or university. Leading people is hard work. Sometimes it requires the power of office to accomplish the mission with only reluctant participation from those you lead; sometimes detractors and others who refuse to contribute to the work of the team to accomplish worthy goals must be disciplined or even expelled from the organization. As Machiavelli noted in *The Prince* (1513), it is more important for the leader to be feared than loved. In some cases, you must take firm action against detractors for the sake of the institution. Winning over your detractors can be wearying work indeed.

More satisfying, and in the long run more rewarding, is winning your detractors over. That requires the personal credibility that is earned by consistent integrity, trust-building behavior, delegation of responsibility, fairness in decision-making, and a genuine sense of service inherent in the term administrator. If those you lead come to know you as one who puts the noble interests of the department and college and the legitimate interests of the followers ahead of self-serving interests, winning detractors over is mission possible, even in the stressful workplace of the academy where bureau-pathology reigns supreme. This mission is not merely to avoid conflict or to avoid provoking people: No mission dedicated to appeasement ever won a war. Effective administrators are always in a campaign to meet strategic goals of the institution and in so doing enlist support from everyone who serves in the same campaign.

Not everyone can be convinced to love the prince, and for a few of your detractors you may hope to achieve no more than grudging respect. You can waste too much time "herding cats" and worrying about your detractors. Be assured that every strong leader will always create some detractors who will remain as thorns in the administrative epidermis. That does not mean you should not continue to go beyond placating your adversaries to transform them into allies. When winning the detractor over is done well, the academic administrator will usually be more loved than feared. And with all due respect to Machiavelli, wouldn't that be better?

## REFERENCES

Adams, S. (1996). *The Dilbert principle*. New York, NY: Harper Collins.

Adams, S. (1997). *Casual day has gone too far.* Kansas City, MO: Andrews & McMeel.

Austin, A. E., Rice, R. E., & Splete, A. P. (1991). *A good place to work: Sourcebook for the academic workplace.* Washington, DC: Council of Independent Colleges.

Bennett, J. B., & Figuli, D. J. (1993). *Enhancing departmental leadership: The roles of the chairperson.* Phoenix, AZ: Oryx.

Higgerson, M. L. (1996). *Communication skills for department chairs.* Bolton, MA: Anker

Leaming, D. R. (1998). *Academic leadership: A practical guide to chairing the department.* Bolton, MA: Anker.

Lucas, A. F. (1994). *Strengthening departmental leadership: A teambuilding guide for chairs in colleges and universities.* San Francisco, CA: Jossey-Bass.

McDaniel, T. R. (1999, November). Faculty morale: A dean's duty? *Academic Leader.*

McDaniel, T. R. (2000, January). President-faculty relations: A dean's dilemma? *Academic Leader.*

McDaniel, T. R. (2000, October). Dilbert on deaning. *Academic Leader.*

McDaniel, T. R. (2000, November). Dean–department chair relations. *Academic Leader.*

McDaniel, T. R. (2001, February). The dean's detractors. *Academic Leader.*

Sax, L. J., Astin, A. W., Korn, W. S., & Gilmartin, S. K. (1999). *The American college teacher.* Los Angeles, CA: Higher Education Research Institute.

Tucker, A. (1993). *Chairing the academic department: Leadership among peers* (3rd ed). Phoenix, AZ: Oryx.

Tucker, A., & Bryan, R. A. (1988). *The academic dean: Dove, dragon, and diplomat.* New York, NY: Macmillan.

Weber, M. (1946). From Max Weber: *Essays in sociology.* H. H. Gerth & C. Wright Mills (Trans.). New York, NY: Oxford University Press.

# Stripping Away Negative Defenses

**7**

*Elliott A. Pood*

> *What started out as an attempt on the part of the department chair to discuss and correct a behavior on the part of one of his or her faculty members has suddenly become a referendum on the skills and qualifications of the chair!*

M anagement scholar Tom Peters in his book *Thriving on Chaos* (1988) makes a bold assertion about management behavior that underlies the whole premise of this chapter. Peters says "Following and administering rules might have been dandy in the placid environments of yesteryear. Not today. Managers must create new worlds, destroy them, and then create anew. Such brave acts of creation must begin with a vision that not only inspires but encourages people to take day-to-day risks involved in testing, adapting, and extending the vision" (pp. 400–401).

Invariably, when chairs and deans create and destroy and recreate, the constant change resulting from such a process creates an atmosphere in which faculty experience uncertainty. Such uncertainty is not necessarily bad. Proponents of System Theory and Information Theory believe systems with significant entropy (uncertainty) also contain much potential. For example, Daft (2001) argues that organizations, as open systems, must constantly get new energy from the environment to survive. He goes on to conclude, "Open systems can be enormously complex . . . . The organization has to find and obtain needed resources, interpret and act on environmental changes, dispose of outputs, and control and coordinate internal activities in the face of environmental disturbances and uncertainty" (p. 14). If they do so, they can potentially maintain themselves indefinitely.

However, one potentially negative by-product of this state of uncertainty is the perception of a threat on the part of many faculty members. The level of threat is related to the perception of the level of risk we must undertake to pursue the transaction. As Myers and

Myers (1982) note, "Much of your interpersonal communication depends on how you define your situation. You appraise how threatening or nonthreatening your interaction with others is in terms of your self-esteem. Your communication with others involves some kind of risk . . . you behave on the basis of how safe you think you are. If you do not feel safe, you will use defensive strategies" (p. 163).

Communication consultant Sharon Ellison (1994) best summarizes the problem with the use of defensive strategies in the organizational setting. In the materials Ellison has developed for her corporate clients, she argues that defensiveness has certain measurable costs, both professionally and personally. Some of the professional costs she articulates include loss of respect, limits on career advancement, reduced optimum team performance, loss of clients, and loss of revenue. Among the personal costs Ellison identifies are a loss of self-esteem, reduced personal growth, loss of intimacy, and a loss of friendship. She concludes, "Defensiveness is pervasive! And it's too expensive—for individuals, families, professional organizations, corporations, and society" (p. 1).

As an observer of human communication behavior, I have ascertained over the years that humans tend to be somewhat predictable creatures of pattern. Myers and Myers (1982) note, "Once defensiveness is aroused, people tend to resort to shallow rituals and protective behavior" (p. 168). One of the best examples of this type of repetitive pattern behavior as it relates to communication can be found in the cyclic pattern of defensive communication.

## THE DEFENSIVENESS CYCLE

The first step in understanding and overcoming negative defenses is to understand the nature and cyclic redundancy of the Defensiveness Cycle (Leonard, 1980). It is helpful to think of the defensive cycle as a steel bank vault. Just prior to the onset of the defensive cycle, the vault door stands open and we may come and go as we choose. The problem occurs when we enter this bank vault and the door slams shut behind us. Once the defensiveness cycle gets started, it is virtually impossible to break out. More on this later.

Defensiveness does not occur in a vacuum. Movement into the bank vault requires a precipitating event. Communication events or environments that suggest a threat to the receiver are what typically bring about defensive communication reactions. This can occur regardless of whether or not a threat was intended. If a communication is received and interpreted by the receiver as an attack of some form, the receiver will undertake action to defend himself or herself. At this point, the receiver has consciously or unconsciously decided to enter that steel vault. He or she moves into the defensiveness cycle at level one of defensiveness—defense by denial.

### Level One: Defense by Denial

Defense by denial is a situation in which it doesn't matter what I am being accused of or whether I did it; my first reaction is to deny involvement or knowledge of any kind. This very denial itself perpetuates and escalates the defensiveness cycle. If you actually did accuse me of something, my denial essentially calls you a liar and encourages me to perceive your reaction as an attack. We then move into the defensiveness cycle at level one of defensiveness, defense by denial, wherein the vault door shuts and we are locked in.

On the other hand, if you did not accuse—or in some other way threaten or attack—me, I am still likely to perceive your denial as an attack on me. Being accused of making an attack is as much a threat as being accused of being a liar. While there are some strategies we might use to break the cycle, we inevitably misuse these strategies, as I will discuss later on. The net effect is the defensiveness cycle spirals inevitably onward.

At level one of the defensiveness, defense by denial, the parties in this locked bank vault make accusations and denials. "Yes you did!" "No I didn't!" "Yes you did!" "No I didn't!" Sooner or later, one participant or the other will begin to perceive that he or she is losing the argument based on the strategy of denial. Will the individual be content to lose? Probably not. Once locked into the defensiveness cycle, a participant who perceives that he or she is losing the argument on the basis of denial is likely to escalate to the second level of defensiveness, known as defense by justification.

### Level Two: Defense by Justification

If I can't deny what I perceive I'm being accused of, I can always try to justify my actions. Here is what a typical example might sound like: "I didn't do it, but even if I did, I had a good reason!"

Once a party escalates to the second level, the other person now perceives that he or she is losing the argument. Will the person be content to lose? Again, probably not. The individual will escalate right along with the first person, and now both will be at the second level of the defensiveness cycle: "I had a good reason!" "There is no good reason!" "Why are you getting upset with me? Everyone does this!" "I'm not talking to everyone, I'm talking to you!" This behavior illustrates justification and counter justification.

### Level Three: Defense by Attack
Sooner or later, one of the participants will perceive that he or she is losing the argument on the basis of justification. Once again, will the person be content to lose? As before, the answer is probably not. The dispute will likely escalate to the third and final level of the defensiveness cycle: defense by attack. If I perceive I cannot effectively deny what you are accusing me of or threatening me with, and if I cannot effectively justify my actions, I can always attack you personally. "I didn't do it, but even if I did I had a very good reason. However, none of this would be happening if you weren't such a rotten department chair." It is not unusual for chairs or deans to find themselves in this situation. What started out as an attempt on the part of the department chair to discuss and correct a faculty member's behavior has suddenly become a referendum on the skills and qualifications of the chair.

When faced with this third and final level of defensiveness, we inevitably fight back: We are now into an attack and counterattack pattern. Depending on the nature of the institution's communication climate and, to some degree, on the past relationship of the parties in the defensiveness cycle, this stage of defensiveness can become quite intense and personal. Parties frequently lose sight of their original goals and objectives and undertake to accomplish one and only one goal: to win. Despite all of our training and intelligence, we define the situation in very personal and specific terms, as one where for one person to win, the other must lose.

To make matters worse, in the intensity of the situation, the parties assign new meaning to the word "win." Through creative redefinition, winning suddenly takes on the meaning of losing less than the other person. Under this new definition, faculty members can win simply by hurting or damaging others more significantly than they themselves are damaged. Under any objective standard, the game has still switched from win-lose to lose-lose, where all parties are damaged by the attacks. The result is a defensive climate that has turned offensive and destructive, hampering effective communication and management. But the process doesn't stop here.

### Defensiveness Recycling

Sooner or later, one or more of the people locked in the vault in this defensiveness cycle will conclude that the other is just meaner and ornerier than themselves and that they are losing on the defensive strategy of attack. Again, they are not likely to simply concede and lose. The question is where to go next? I just stated that defense by attack is the third and final level of defensiveness. The answer lies in the name of the process: the defensiveness cycle. It is a process that is cyclic. When one of the participants perceives that he or she is losing at the level of attack, the person will simply escalate back to the beginning—defense by denial—and continue the cycle. In its most parsimonious manifestation, the defensiveness cycle resembles the following:

"I didn't do it!"

"Even if I did I had a very good reason!"

"None of this would be happening if you weren't such a rotten administrator!"

"But what are you getting upset about? I didn't do anything anyway!"

## STRATEGIES FOR BREAKING THE CYCLE

As I mentioned before, once the defensiveness cycle gets started and the steel bank vault door slams shut, it is virtually impossible for us to break out. There are however, two methods through which we could break the defensiveness cycle, open the vault door, and exit. If these methods were legitimately used to curb the defensiveness cycle, they would provide us with a viable out. Unfortunately, the two methods available to end the cycle are typically used as strategies within the defensiveness cycle, thereby perpetuating rather than ending the situation.

### Consenting to Lose

Specifically, one could theoretically end the cycle once it got started by simply consenting to lose. If at any point in the cyclic escalation, one or more of the parties simply consents to lose, the escalation stops, the door opens, and we are free to leave. This situation describes the legitimate use of this strategy to end the defensiveness cycle. However, far more likely is that we don't really consent to lose, but rather consent to win by losing, a situation frequently described as the "Jewish Mother Syndrome" or the "Jilted Grandparents Syndrome." Rather than consenting to really lose, we consent to being one worse off than the other person. Under the perverse logic of this psychological game, when we are one worse off, we are actually one better off. In the case of the Jilted Grandparents, you can picture them sitting around in the nursing home comparing notes on how neglected they are by their families. The winner is the set of grandparents who are most neglected. The situation becomes one where being worse off than the other person is a badge of honor.

When this strategy is employed in the defensiveness cycle under the guise of an attempt to end the cycle, it merely redirects the cycle to a new line of argument. Now the parties are disputing who is worse off and who the real martyr is in the current situation. The parties are still defending their positions with denial, justification, and attack. The only difference is the focus of the defense has switched to being one of defending who the real loser is, and hence, the real winner. Obviously, the door hasn't opened, and the cycle hasn't ended.

### Ceasing Communication

A second strategy that would work to end the defensiveness cycle—if it were employed legitimately—is to cease communication. This might take several forms, including agreeing to disagree, simply admitting that some subjects are not things we can productively discuss, etc. Keep in mind that the defensiveness cycle is a communication process. It feeds off continued destructive communication. One of the ways to end such a cycle is to remove the energy source off which it is feeding, namely communication. If one or more of the participants would simply agree to cease communication about the topic in a nonpejorative way, the cycle would end, the door would open, and we would be free to leave.

Unfortunately, as with the first strategy, this approach is rarely employed in a legitimate fashion. More likely is the situation where one or more of the parties cease communication as a means of punishing the other party. This is simply another form of attack, albeit a nonverbal form of attack. Another illegitimate way in which we can use the cessation of communication is to agree to cease communication temporarily. In this approach, the individual waits until the other person is not looking and then he or she attacks again. In some ways, the intention is to lull the other individual into a false sense of peace and calm. Rather than opening the door to the vault, this approach simply prolongs the time during which we are locked in the defensiveness cycle and delays the escalation to a presumed more advantageous time for the user.

## UNDERSTANDING THE NATURE OF DEFENSIVENESS

Developing a more effective approach to managing defensiveness requires a better understanding of the nature of defensiveness. The classic essay in this area was published by Jack Gibb (1961). Gibb concluded that defensiveness is fostered by communication that makes people feel uncomfortable. In his essay, Gibb identifies six characteristics of communication leading to defensiveness on the part of the recipient. These include:
1) Evaluative communication
2) Controlling/manipulative communication
3) Strategic communication
4) Neutral communication, lacking concern
5) Superior communication
6) Certain communication

Timm and DeTienne (1995) suggest that faculty who are experiencing a defensive climate will believe they are being subjected to numerous good/bad judgments, manipulation, burdensome and rigid rules and regulations, strategies designed to convey inclusion in decision-making without real inclusion, and administrators who "maintain their status by talking down to the little people" (p. 133).

Conrad and Poole (1998) provide another interpretation of Gibb's categories in their book on strategic organizational communication. They conclude that people become defensive when they are presented with communication which, either in content or in the way it is presented, makes people feel that they are being:

1) Judged (even praise creates discomfort if it is excessively strong or too public)

2) Manipulated or controlled too tightly or inappropriately

3) Tricked, especially into believing that they are having an important impact on decisions or playing an important roles in the organization when they are not

4) Subjected to cold, impersonal, or uncaring treatment

5) Treated as an inferior, relatively useless person

6) Preached at by a smug or know-it-all supervisor

Earlier in this chapter I noted that people generally become defensive when they perceive they are being attacked. We can now refine that definition. Particularly in the working environment, people tend to become defensive when they are confronted with communications that appear to be:

1) Evaluative, personal, or judgmental

2) Controlling or manipulative

3) Tricky or strategically intended

4) Neutral, cold, impersonal, or dehumanizing

5) Treating the recipient as an inferior, less worthy person

6) Overly emphatic, dogmatic, or preachy

Very few of us would have trouble admitting that such communication, when directed at us, causes us to become combative and distrustful. When confronted with such communications, we cannot help but personalize the situation. In fact, much of the contemporary literature on defensiveness defines the concept in terms of a reaction to an attack on the individual's self-concept or self-esteem.

Martin (1980) suggests that defensiveness indicates a motive to protect a central component of the self-concept, or to present oneself in a favorable way. Anderson and Guerrero (1989) define defensiveness as a protective reaction resulting from fear or a threat to one's ego. Stamp, Vangelisti, and Daly (1992) conceptualize defensiveness as related to a perceived self-flaw that the individual refuses to admit and a sensitivity to that flaw. Further, they argue that, in some instances, defensiveness is related to an attack by another person that focuses on an area or issue perceived by the attacker as a flaw in the other. Clearly, perception on the part of both the attacker and the attackee plays a major role in the development of defensive reactions.

Some researchers have argued that defensiveness is caused by a lack of willingness to tolerate differences in others, or of a fear of change in ourselves (Baker, 1980). This research suggests that our desire to maintain the status quo and avoid cognitive imbalance leads us to become defensive in communication with others. Ashforth and Lee (1990) in a study of defensiveness in organizations suggest that defensiveness is a reaction to self-interests. Specifically, they argue that defensive behaviors are designed to avoid action, avoid blame, or avoid change.

If we accept the notion that defensiveness is caused by a desire to protect a person's self-image and self-esteem, and further, if we accept Ashforth and Lee's position that in the organizational setting defensive behaviors are a reaction to self-interest designed to avoid action, blame, or change, then we can begin to understand defensiveness as another element of the organizational politics encountered in every organization. Defensiveness on the part of the faculty member is likely to be a strategic communication designed to further his or her self-interest and frustrate efforts aimed at improved performance and productivity or organizational change. This conceptualization is particularly useful in helping chairs and deans cope with negative defenses.

## COPING WITH NEGATIVE DEFENSES

Negative defenses most typically manifest themselves in communication behaviors. For example, Ashforth and Lee (1990) listed some of the typical manifestations of various defensive reactions. Specifically, they found that defensive efforts designed to avoid action were typically manifested via overconforming, passing the buck, playing dumb, depersonalizing, and stalling, among others. Defensive reactions designed to avoid blame include bluffing, playing it safe, justifying, scapegoating, and escalating commitment. Finally, defensive reactions designed to avoid change include resisting and protecting turf.

Myers and Myers (1982) present a somewhat different view of defensive strategies by noting that the best defense is often a good offense. This analysis helps explain the nature of the defensiveness cycle. In its most simple form, it is a strategy designed to allow the defensive individual to attempt to exercise some control over the situation; in other words, the defensiveness cycle is a good offense.

### Direct Attack

A direct attack upon another person (the chair) may cost a faculty member his or her position or some related perks (such as a desirable teaching schedule). However, the department chair has told the faculty member that some students are complaining about his or her course. The faculty member becomes defensive, assuming the chair thinks he or she is doing a poor job of teaching. Since the faculty member knows that he or she is a superb teacher without flaw and without need of evaluation, review, and revision in his or her approach to this class, the faculty member will become offensive. However, since he or she doesn't want to lose a prime Monday through Thursday teaching schedule with no classes on Friday, the faculty member doesn't want to appear to be directly attacking the chair.

Myers and Myers (1982) suggest if direct attack is too dangerous, faculty members have other alternatives to be on the offense. For example, they can resort to sarcasm and ridicule. They might question the deans' motives or competence to make the judgments they are making. They might find ways to socially and nonverbally exclude the chair from communication with other faculty in the department as a form of punishment. Some faculty members choose to deal with a defensive climate by avoiding putting themselves into a situation where they might be threatened. This reaction to defensiveness helps explain why many faculty members disengage from the day-to-day operation and committee work of the institution and become essentially retired in place.

### Indirect Attacks

Some faculty might choose to go on the offense in more indirect ways, including passive/aggressive behaviors, marginal performance, or even late compliance. As a chair, during a department meeting with senior faculty I was discussing the importance of completing and filing certain paperwork by the printed deadlines. I actually had a colleague say, "We're tenured. What do you really think this institution can do to us for not getting this paperwork in by the deadline?" Even today, every semester there are some faculty members in the college who simply cannot or will not get their grades in by the registrar's deadline. In some instances, the cause is mere absentmindedness or disorganization. Yet in others,

## TABLE **7**.1 DEFENSIVE REACTIONS

1) **Surrender-Treachery:** We betray ourselves when someone treats us poorly, and we give in to it and think it is our own fault.
   **Example:** We might say, "He just treated me rudely because he was in a bad mood. I should have known better than to ask a question just then."

2) **Surrender-Sabotage:** We pretend to agree with someone who is treating us poorly and then get back at the person in some way.
   **Example:** We might talk about the person behind her back, or not follow through on something we told the person we would do.

3) **Withdrawal-Escape:** We avoid talking to someone about something we don't want to discuss.
   **Example:** We might simply not answer, or leave the room, or change the subject.

4) **Withdrawal-Entrapment:** We refuse to respond to someone to draw her into a situation where she may feel uncomfortable or act inappropriately.
   **Example:** We might just stare at the person and not answer a question she asks until she gets embarrassed and drops it or gets angry and says something that makes her look bad.

5) **Counterattack-Defense:** We explain our own behavior or make excuses if someone questions or criticizes us. It is a way to let the person know he is wrong to be upset with us.
   **Example:** We might say, "I would have gotten that done sooner, but I've been really busy," or "I'm doing my best," or "I can't work any faster."

6) **Counterattack-Assault:** We attack the other person's position as a way to defend ourselves.
   **Example:** We might blame the other person for whatever the problem is, saying perhaps, "Why are you in such a bad mood?" or "You are always so critical," or "Do it yourself if you don't like how I am doing it."

*Source: Sharon Ellison web site http://www.pndc.com/summary.htm. Used with permission.*

it is clear that faculty members are responding to some perceived attack with their own personal counterattack.

Ellison (1994) presents us with yet another typology of negative defenses. She says when we are confronted with communication that makes us feel put down, hurt, frustrated, or angry, we often respond with one of the six defensive reactions listed in Table 7.1.

### Summary of Negative Defenses

The litany of negative defenses could go on for several more pages, but I think the point has been made. From the foregoing discussion, we can extract the following major summary points:

1) Defensiveness on the part of faculty members is likely to be a strategic communication designed to further their self-interest and frustrate efforts aimed at improved performance and productivity or organizational change.

2) Negative defenses typically manifest themselves in a variety of communication behaviors. However, regardless of the specific manifestation, the key to understanding and minimizing negative defenses is to recognize them as a pattern of behaviors that are ritualistic and cyclic. This pattern is known as the defensiveness cycle.

3) Once the defensiveness cycle gets fully started and the vault doors shut, it is virtually impossible to break out and end the cycle.

## STRATEGIES FOR AVOIDING THE DEFENSIVENESS CYCLE

The real solution to the defensiveness cycle, and the negative defenses associated with it, is for chairs and deans to find a way to keep the cycle from starting in the first place. There are essentially two ways to accomplish this.

### Don't Get into the Vault

First, as Conrad and Poole (1998) note, relational strategies of leadership must recognize that relationships are two-way streets. In the case of the defensiveness cycle, chairs and deans must recognize that the door to the vault only slams shut and locks after both parties to the communication event have entered the cycle. Consequently, the simplest solution to the defensiveness cycle is for the chair or dean to refuse to engage in responsive communications of a defensive nature. If the chair or dean refuses to allow the faculty member to entice them into the vault of the defensiveness cycle, the cycle never fully starts, and the door remains open.

Because this option is, conceptually at least, entirely within the span of control of the chair or dean, a mechanism exists to theoretically guarantee complete avoidance of the defensiveness cycle. In reality, the constant level of conscious, intrapersonal monitoring, and sheer willpower necessary to achieve this behavioral denial is beyond the ability of most of us to exercise on a daily basis. Given the volume of other administrative demands placed on chairs and deans, it is inevitable that faculty and staff members will confront their chair or dean with a defensive climate in a moment of distraction or weakness. In other words, the simplest, most straightforward solution is not necessarily the easiest solution.

### Use Supportive Communication

When such moments happen, the other alternative for avoiding the defensiveness cycle and its pitfalls is to create a supportive communication climate. As management scholars Paul Timm and Kristen Bell DeTienne (1995) note:

> The supportive environment is differentiated by the absence of the defensive characteristics. Descriptive language replaces evaluative comments and leaders take a problem orientation, that is, not simply calling up the rule or policy to stifle a difficulty, but getting to the root of the issue and seeking out underlying causes. The supportive climate is also marked by spontaneity, empathy for others, a sense of equality and fairness, as well as the replacement of dogmatism with provisionalism—a sense of being not yet certain of the answer but rather engaged in a continuing search for solutions. (pp. 133–134)

### Communication Styles

*Aggressive communication.* Supportiveness requires assertive communication to help reduce defensiveness. Generally, communication scholars recognize three different types of communication styles. The first is an aggressive style of communication, best characterized by the use of the term "you." In aggressive communication, the other individual is likely to experience defensiveness because of statements such as:

"You have a problem."

"You made a mistake."

"You need to do a better job."

"You need to correct this problem."

You-orientated statements are likely to be perceived as an attempt to place blame. Any such attempt is also likely to produce a defensive reaction, even if blame is appropriate.

*Passive communication.* The second style of communication is known as passive communication. Passive communication responses are best characterized by the use of the terms "we" and "they." It is a style of communication that appears to be designed to avoid responsibility. Examples include statements such as, "We decided on this course of action," or "They want it done this way." When the recipient questions who we or they are, the answer is typically along the lines of "You know . . . them. The folks who make these kinds of decisions." Passive communication can be very frustrating and is bound to cause a sense of paranoia. Recipients of passive communication cannot help but wonder who these nebulous groups are who are out to get us. When people start wondering who is out to get them, defensiveness is not far behind.

*Assertive communication.* The third style of communication is assertive communication. The assertive style is most frequently characterized by "I" statements and is designed for the sender to speak about themselves, not about others. Counseling psychologist Alec Gore (2001), relying in his web site on the work of Bolton (1986), suggests six steps to help increase assertive communication and reduce the tendency to defensiveness.

*1) Preparation.* Select an appropriate time to discuss the situation with the other person. Do not pick a time when the other person is likely to be tired, irritable, hungry, etc. Select the location carefully, avoiding confrontation in view or hearing of others. Decide whether it should be on your ground or on the other's.

*2) Sending.* Don't begin the interaction with small talk. Your body language should demonstrate that you mean what you say, that you are not ambivalent about it, and that you expect to get your needs met. But it should simultaneously demonstrate respect for the other person.

*3) Being silent.* The other person's first response is usually defensive. Sometimes he will offer excuses, sometimes attack, sometimes withdraw. Expect the defensive response. The silence allows the other person time to express it, and it needs to be vented before the other person is willing to meet your needs.

4) *Listening.* Instead of reasserting, explaining your assertion, or becoming aggressive in response to the defensive response, it is important to change gears and listen reflectively. This helps diminish the other person's defensiveness. You may receive data in your listening that modifies your need to continue with the assertion. You may discover a strong need of the other person that conflicts with your needs, so you may switch to collaborative problem solving. You may receive a lot of data about how that person views you or your relationship with them.

Because the words are spoken from a defensive standpoint, they may be more extreme than the other person actually feels. Still, they are important and too valuable to ignore. Much of it would have gone unspoken if not for the assertion that you sent.

If you reflect, rather than defend yourself, you will be alerted to many ways the relationship can be improved. Do not respond to the issues raised at this time, apart from listening reflectively. There will be a more appropriate time for that later.

When you engage in assertion, you are likely to be confronted with certain reactions or responses requiring appropriate counter responses. Some of these include:

*Hostile responses.* The finest assertion message is often received as a hostile blow. Instead of really listening to the assertion, most people are searching for a counterblow at the time the assertion is being presented to them. The counterblow contains words designed to put you on the defensive and inflict damage. The other person does not usually deal with the subject matter of your assertion but picks an issue selected for its ability to inflict high damage on you, with relatively low risk to them.

*Dealing with questions.* In addition to showing hostility, some people defend themselves by asking questions. This is a way of derailing assertions in a nonconfrontational way. While they've got you answering the question, you aren't asserting, and the other person is not coming up with solutions about how to vacate your space and meet your needs. Don't answer a question when you are asserting; reply with a reflective response instead. Every question can be converted into a statement and reflected back.

*Sidestepping debates.* Some people respond to assertion by debating. By refusing to engage in a debate and by listening and responding reflectively, you can get your needs met and probably strengthen the relationship at the same time.

*Coping with tears.* For some people, tears are a major coping mechanism when confronted with an assertion. Crying is often a manipulative way to avoid confrontation and to avoid any behavioral change. Do not let tears control you. Recognize that the tears may be real and that the person may be genuinely sad. Reflect the fact that they are sad about being confronted, but then gently and firmly reassert.

*Overcoming withdrawal.* Where the person responds to an assertion with total silence, you may still see a response in the body language that suggests disapproval or despondency. In response, you can provide a lot of silence, reflect on what it appears to you to mean, and then reassert.

In short, the general strategy for dealing with defensive responses is always the same; that is, listen reflectively (especially to the emotions) and reassert.

*5) Recycling the process.* You are ready to begin this process all over again. Because the other person was defensive, he or she will probably have been unable to understand the situation from your point of view. You send the identical message again. Follow it with silence. Then reflect the expected defensive response.

*6) Focusing on the solution.* Do not back the other person into a corner. Allow him or her to retain dignity. Encourage the person to develop solutions of his or her own. Be flexible and open to a broad range of possible options. Finally, don't insist that the other person be cheerful about meeting your needs. All that you can ask is that the other's behavior be changed.

**Minimize defensive reactions.** Sharon Ellison, in her corporate materials on Powerful, Nondefensive Communication (1994), concludes that three simple strategies can be used to minimize defensive reactions.

*1) Ask questions.* Be curious, open, and sincere.

*Purpose:* To gather thorough information in order to understand accurately what the other person means by what she is saying.

*Example:* You may be doing a task when someone says, in a tone that sounds judgmental, "There is a better way to do that." You can ask the person directly, "Do you feel critical of how I am doing this?"

*Avoid:* Using a question to transmit information or to entrap others.

2) *Make position statements.* Say what you hear, see, and experience.

*Purpose:* To express and clarify your thoughts, feelings, and beliefs about the other person's reactions as well as your own.

*Example:* If someone says in an irritated tone that he was too busy to do something he had previously agreed to do, you might say: "I hear you saying you were to busy to do it." "I see that you are acting upset with me for expecting you to have gotten it done even though you had agreed to do it." "I feel frustrated when you don't do your part because it makes it hard for me and the others. I would really appreciate it if you would get it done."

*Avoid:* Using a position statement as fact or to convince others.

3) *Predict consequences.* Set your own boundaries without trying to control the other person's choices.

*Purpose:* To create security by telling another person ahead of time how you will react to the different choices she might make.

*Example:* If someone keeps interrupting you or putting down your ideas, instead of trying to convince the person to listen, you can set a limit using an "If/then" sentence. One possibility is: "If you don't want to hear my idea, then I won't try to make you." "If you do want to hear it, then I will be glad to tell you."

*Avoid:* Using a consequence prediction to punish or to falsely threaten others.

According to Ellison (1994, p. 2), "When you ask questions, make position statements, and predict consequences in an open and sincere way without trying to control how other people respond, you are using nondefensive communication. People are more likely to respect you, and you can strengthen personal and professional relationships."

Paul Timm and Kristen Bell DeTienne (1995) summarize the overall value of developing a supportive climate and supportive communication style when attempting to overcome negative defenses. They note, "In the supportive climate, individual members have a sense of participation without threat to their ego or sense of self worth . . . The degree of supportiveness present is a key dimension in communication climate. Without supportiveness, communication becomes a contest of power plays rather than a search for common understandings. The waste of human resources in such an organization can be enormous."

## THE LEADER'S GOAL: MINIMIZE OCCURRENCE
## AND EFFECT OF DEFENSIVENESS

On a final note, communication scholars have long accepted the fact that human communication will probably never be perfect. The same is true of your attempts to overcome negative defenses on the part of faculty and staff. No matter how hard you work at it, some faculty and staff will still become defensive. There are times when, in spite of your best self-control efforts, you will find yourself feeling and reacting defensively. In some instances, both for faculty and ourselves, the defensive reactions will feel good because of the negative effect they are having on others. In still other instances, the defensive reaction will just be an instinctive or habitual response. Whatever the cause, you will never totally eliminate defensive reactions. Just bear in mind that elimination is not the goal. The goal is to minimize the occurrence and effect of defensiveness to the point where it is manageable and nonthreatening.

## REFERENCES

Anderson, P. A., & Guerrero, L. K. (1989, February). *Avoiding communication: Verbal and nonverbal dimensions of defensiveness.* Paper presented at the meeting of the Western Speech Communication Association, Spokane, WA.

Ashforth, B. E., & Lee, R. T. (1990). Defensive behavior in organizations: A preliminary model. *Human Relations, 43* (7), 621–648.

Baker, W. H. (1980). Defensiveness in communication: Its causes, effects, and cures. *Journal of Business Communication, 17* (3), 33–43.

Bolton, R. (1986). *People skills.* New York, NY: Touchstone.

Conrad, C. (1985). *Strategic organizational communication: Cultures, situations, and adaptations.* New York, NY: Holt, Rinehart, and Winston.

Conrad, C., & Poole, M. S. (1998). *Strategic organizational communication: Into the twenty–first century* (4th ed.). Fort Worth, TX: Harcourt Brace.

Daft, R. L. (2001). *Organization theory and design* (7th ed.). Cincinnati, OH: Southwestern.

Ellison, S. (1994). Powerful, nondefensive communication home page. [online]. Available: http://www.pndc.com/summary.htm.

Gibb, J. (1961). Defensive communication. *Journal of Communication, 11* (3), 141–148.

Gore, A. (2001). Alec Gore web site. [online]. Available: http://www.theroad.com.hk/skills/assert3.html.

Leonard, R. (1980). *The defensiveness cycle.* Symposium conducted at the North Carolina Public Manager's Program, Raleigh, NC.

Martin, R. P. (1980, September). *Cognitive factors in consultee defensiveness.* Paper presented at the meeting of the American Psychological Association, Montreal, Quebec, Canada.

Myers, M. T., & Myers, G. E. (1982). *Managing by communication: An organizational approach.* New York, NY: McGraw-Hill.

Peters, T. (1988). *Thriving on chaos: Handbook for a management revolution.* New York, NY: Harper and Row.

Stamp, G. H., Vangelisti, A. L., & Daly, J. A. (1992). Social interaction: The creation of defensiveness. *Communication Quarterly, 40* (2), 177–190.

Timm, P. R., & DeTienne, K. B. (1995). *Managerial communication: A finger on the pulse* (3rd ed.). Upper Saddle River, NJ: Prentice Hall.

# Handling Conflict With Difficult Faculty

**8**

*Ben Bissell*

> *Down inside each of us is an anger bucket.*
> *Every time one feels angry a drop goes into the*
> *bucket. When the bucket is full and someone*
> *drops another drop, we do not give a drop back;*
> *we give them the whole bucket!*

No college, university, or department is free of difficult people, and, as a result, conflict is inevitable. The choice for an administrator is not whether we will deal with difficult people but how we will deal with them. As individuals, we have each developed our own preferred method of handling difficult people. As administrators, we need some new options and new models in order to deal successfully with difficult people.

## UNPRODUCTIVE CONFLICT STYLES

First, it is important to examine some styles that difficult people use to get their way. I'll briefly describe six common styles.

### The Bully
The most popular style for those with the most power is to simply be a bully. If they cannot solve the conflict through shouting ("Give him what he wants if it will shut him up!"), then there are always threats and intimidation upon which to draw. From the bully's perspective, "might makes right." The sad truth is that they often get their way even when that way resulted in poor productivity and low morale.

### The Complainer
Complainers present themselves as weak victims, unable to solve problems because of others. They make it clear that they are inundated with problems and doing better than anyone has a right to

expect. They hope that someone will rescue them by taking on the conflict.

### The Procrastinator
The procrastinator simply puts any problem on a back burner. Their motto is "Let sleeping dogs lie." Unfortunately, they can see only sleeping dogs.

### The Guerrilla Fighter
Guerrilla fighters use an insidious sarcasm and criticism to browbeat their "enemies" into feeling that they were stupid to even have raised the issue. They "shoot" from trees and bushes, attacking with no warning and catching the unarmed colleague unaware. Guerrilla fighters insult others in public, demeaning them in an attempt to disarm them. They might use remarks such as the following:
    "Mr. Negative will now speak."
    "How's that black cloud over your head?"
    "Not having a good day, are you?"
    "Watch out! You're about to agree with someone!"
    The guerrilla fighter believes that he can feel smart if he makes you feel dumb.

### The Expert
A most frustrating style is the expert. Often bright and often right, these people refuse to ever be wrong. They will wear you down with data, credentials, and at times long, involved arguments. They will believe whoever knows the most is the winner. Getting your ideas heard by them is almost impossible.

### The Icicle
The most difficult style to manage that I have found is the icicle. The icicles freeze up at the first sign of conflict. When asked what they thought, they would say nothing. When confronted about where they stood, they replied, "Not sure yet." When asked if anything was wrong, they said, "Not now. Everything is fine . . . just fine." The icicle believes that whoever is the quietest wins: If you say nothing, you cannot be attacked.
    This short list of six difficult people is only the beginning and reveals one common theme: Difficult people are poor problem

solvers and hope to steer any responsibility away from themselves. We need a new model to deal with difficult people, in which problems get solved and individuals accept responsibility for their part in conflict management. After examining and teaching these observations in dozens of study groups in colleges, universities, businesses, and hospitals, I realized that a major barrier to developing a healthy model for managing conflict is that most of us have never seen or experienced a healthy model. In fact, during the majority of conflict encounters shared by group participants from their experiences, someone was hurt, the problem was not solved, and blaming was rampant.

## A PROFILE OF THE DIFFICULT PERSON

Difficult people share certain characteristics.

1)    They have a predictable abrasive style of behavior. You can count on them! If they complain on Monday and you miss it, don't worry because they'll do it again on Tuesday.

2)    Nearly everyone finds them difficult—not just you.

3)    They are certain to keep all blame outside themselves. It is never their fault.

4)    They rob you of time and energy. A minute with a difficult person is like an hour with anyone else. Furthermore, they do not even have to be present to affect you. Someone can just mention their names and you immediately become tense.

5)    Their behavior is almost always out of proportion to the problem. Like Henny Penny, they get hit in the head with an acorn and assume the sky is falling.

6)    They are terrible problem solvers. This has nothing to do with their intelligence, skills, or abilities. Many difficult people are very skilled and bright and yet do not know how to work through differences with others. Difficult people are only difficult when they are not getting their way. From their perspective, they know best and are blind to the positive possibilities in other options or the negative consequences of their own plans.

## A NEW MODEL

The goal of this chapter is to present a healthy model of dealing with difficult people, one gleaned from the experiences shared by seminar participants as well as from my own discoveries through personal struggle in dealing with difficult people. The model must conform to the goal so that no one gets hurt and problems get solved.

At the root of the model is finding a new way to deal with an old emotion—anger. Anger fuels conflict and prevents conflict management. Difficult people trigger our anger to such a degree that we cannot think clearly. For me, the first ray of hope came when I learned that it is possible to separate feelings from behavior. It is not angry feelings that cause the damage during conflict; it is the way those feelings are expressed. You will recall as a child that you were not punished for your feelings but rather for your actions—slamming doors, talking back, or kicking the cat. Yet somehow as time went by, most of us began to believe that just feeling angry was bad. Not only did we believe the behavior was unacceptable but so was the emotion. If a new model is to work, we need to accept our angry feelings and give them healthy expression. It may help to say, "I will never again apologize for my anger (my feelings). However, I may need to apologize for my behavior (expression)."

Anger signals that things are not right. Angry feelings tell us that there are issues that need attention. Anger is a good warning that matters of importance are at risk. The angry feeling is a call for a response or action to protect us, to defend our ideas, and to resolve a problem. That action must come only after examining and learning that what the feeling is trying to inform us is wrong. When we are angry and conflict is present, it is crucial to clarify the issue before taking any action. (For an overview of the ways men and women differ in their views of anger, see Sargent, 1983, pp. 26–35.)

However, it is not enough to simply accept our feelings; they must also be released. While it is important to reflect on and learn from anger, it should not be stored as it can build to explosive and irrational behavior. To avoid the unhealthy release of negative behavior, it is vital to stay in touch with just how intense our feelings are.

I find it helpful to reflect as follows: Down inside each of us is an anger bucket. Every time I feel angry, a drop goes into the bucket. When the bucket is full—100% full—and someone adds another drop, I do not give a drop back; I give them the whole bucket! Difficult people tend to fill our buckets rather quickly.

Therefore, the first step is to accept and to examine the message of the angry feeling.

The good news is that almost everyone was taught to think before they act: Count to 10 before reacting. Unfortunately, we were not told what to do after we had counted to 10. The class bully would count to 10 and punch us. Others of us counted to 10 and then internalized our anger until we had either a headache or stomachache. Thus, there is a need for the model to include guidelines for reflection before expression. Reflecting on and answering the following four questions clarifies the conflict and the appropriate behavior required. The four questions of reflection before action or response to the difficult person are:

1) What triggered my anger?

2) What/who is the target?

3) How full is my bucket?

4) What do I want?

A personal and simple example happened when I drove home from the airport one evening. As I stopped at the last traffic light before turning into my subdivision, a car lined up behind me. When the light turned green, I moved my foot from the brake to the gas pedal as fast as I could. However, it was not fast enough for the driver behind me, and I heard "BEEP! BEEP!" I became angry and then instead of continuing to drive home at a normal speed, I took my good and easy time. What happened in that moment? I needed to use the four reflections-before-action questions to analyze the situation:

1) What triggered my anger? *the beep of the other driver's horn*

2) Who was the target? *the driver of the car behind me*

3) How full was my anger bucket? *very full (and probably the other driver's was, too)*

4) What did I want? *to get home*

Notice that no one is keeping me from getting home but myself. Before the driver blew his horn, I could not wait to get home. After he blew it, I did not care if I ever got home. By analyzing my anger, I see I am only defeating myself. If I wanted to get home, then I should not have driven slowly (and possibly risk being shot from road rage) or too fast and possibly be stopped and given a ticket for speeding. I should have driven at the legal speed limit and avoided letting another person's behavior control mine. Often we keep ourselves from getting what we want. Our anger blocks our thinking. After analyzing the situation, it is possible to clarify and respond appropriately.

The second step is to avoid sitting on the anger too long. It is vital to keep in mind that as anger mounts, thought diminishes. Avoid letting the anger build until it explodes in damaging, irrational ways.

The four questions of reflection help to get the anger out on the table in a healthy way. The question now becomes: If I am angry with a colleague, how can I confront in such a manner that my concerns can be heard? For example, what do I want? What does my colleague want? I want to present the problem so that the other person is less likely to be defensive and the problem can be both heard and understood.

The following guidelines for working with difficult people to resolve conflict are derived from seminars and study groups.

### Stand Up

Once an acceptable emotional climate has been established and the anger is down to an acceptable level, be certain to stand up. By that term I do not mean physically stand, though sometimes that can be important. By standing up, I mean presenting yourself in such a fashion that you avoid body language that says either "I am here to fight" or "I am here to be trampled." The healthy message is "I am not here either to fight or run away. Rather, I am here to be taken seriously and to solve a problem." Too often our very stance makes conflict resolution impossible.

To get body language correct, find an answer to the question, "How do other people experience me?" It is not only how you see yourself that matters, but how other people see you. All of us have an idealized self-image. We see ourselves in a certain way, but nobody else sees us like that. Have you ever heard yourself on a tape recorder? Does that sound like you? Not to you, but it does to others. Have you ever seen yourself on videotape? That's painful. The point is that I see myself one way and others see me differently. The same is true for everyone.

It has been my experience that most people are either fighters or flighters. In my early training, I went to a large hospital to do patient and family counseling. My job involved special reports that were to be completed and returned to me on a regular basis. I had great difficulty in getting certain staff members to return the reports on time. It seemed that nobody took me seriously when I said that I really had to have the reports. My goal became to discover what I was doing wrong. I wanted to know how I was presenting myself. To learn this it was necessary to ask someone— to find someone to tell me how I was being perceived. Of course, the odds of getting a straight answer were small, but I asked some coworkers anyway. Sure enough, at first they were very reluctant to level with me. One afternoon around the lunch table, I asked a group of colleagues, "Okay, guys, tell me how you experience me."

One of them said, "I have a question for you first. Ben, how do you see yourself?" No one had ever asked me that question before. Here is how I responded: "I think I am polite, kind, considerate, thoughtful, generous, and gentle. I have a good sense of humor. Overall, I would say that I am a very nice person." One of my colleagues answered, "I don't see you that way at all." "You must be kidding! You don't think I'm nice?" I replied. "No, you aren't nice," he quickly responded. That really made me angry. "If I'm not nice, then what am I?" I asked.

"You're not nice. You're passive," he said emphatically. Passive. What a different way to define nice! He then continued, "Let me show you what I mean. Let me act out for you how you ask for your reports. I may exaggerate a little," he said, "but not much. Ben, you tend to say to people, 'Excuse me. I hate to bother you. I know you're very busy, but I've got 20 or 30 reports that I need to have done. If you could do two or three in the next 10 or 15 years, I surely would appreciate it. Take your time. I'll check back later.'"

Somewhat taken aback, I did get the point and made an important discovery. I saw myself as nice; others saw me as passive. What I was doing was presenting myself in a very nice, pleasant way that was perceived as weak and wimpish.

The next thing my colleague told me was "Bissell, you need to know something else. You smile when you're angry." I asked him to explain. He said it happened when I was told, "No, Dr. Bissell, your reports are not ready." Then I would say while all the time smiling, "Well, I'll be back." Why did I smile? I was furious with that person. Unbeknownst to me, here is what people were saying, "If you have more reports than you have time to do, put Bissell's on the bottom." "Why? Because when he comes back and you haven't finished them, it makes him happy!"

Who taught them that? I did. And if I taught them that, I could teach them something else—how to take me seriously. Notice: The very thing I did to get what I wanted was the very reason I did not get what I wanted. It was also the reason I could not resolve the conflict.

Then I said to my colleagues, "I don't even know how to be different. What do I need to do to change?" "First," they said, "put your shoulders back. You have a tendency to bend over." (They called it "apologetic shoulders"). I was using an "Excuse me, can I breathe now?" leaning-back stance that I am sure you have seen in other people.

"Next," they said, "raise your chin about half an inch." You may also wish to try what they suggested. Stand in front of a mirror and raise your chin about half an inch. Do not stick your chin up in the air or down toward your chest. Level it. That will change every muscle in your face. People will begin to take you seriously.

I did what they told me to do. I went back, and I stood up. Guess how the people responsible for the reports responded? Negatively! They were mad! They did not say, "This is great." They said in a rough tone, "Here are your reports!" The good news is I got my reports on time, I was taken seriously, and my conflict was resolved. (Notice that I got what I wanted.)

You may say, "Folks will not like me if I stand up." The truth is those people did not like me to begin with. What they liked was being able to postpone doing my reports. They liked my wimpishness—my passivity. But they did not like me. I could not get respect or be taken seriously until I stood up. I have little control over whether people like me, but I have enormous control over whether they take me seriously.

Here is the challenge: Where can you get honest feedback in order to establish your stand-up stance? Your spouse may be good if you want to risk your marriage. Whom else could you ask? Your boss, a friend, coworkers, colleagues. Ask several people because you want to get an overall picture. Think of places where you are not taken seriously. Then think of someone you trust who sees you in that situation. For starters, ask them.

Eventually, you can learn how to stand up, but here is a word of warning. If you have been a lean back-er (or flighter) for most of your life, when you stand up during conflict, it will feel as if you are leaning into (fighting). If you have been a lean into-er and you stand up during conflict, it will feel as if you are leaning back. Standing up will be tough, but it is critical in getting others to take you seriously and in resolving differences.

I have been asked if it is really possible to change. Nobody understands fully how personality develops or how we change, but I do believe that behavior can be changed. I have learned that I can stop people from running over me. Still, because of the way I was raised, even now when I stand up, I often feel a little guilty. All I have done is taken care of myself. My sense of guilt is neurotic. It will probably be with me forever. In dealing with the everyday world, I need to be aware that I cannot always change the way I feel, but I can change the way I behave. The good news is that the more I change my behavior, the more other people's behavior changes. I begin to feel different about who I am and best of all I gain more respect.

### Talk Straight

Once the body language is correct, it is necessary to confront in an appropriate place—if possible, in private. Never embarrass anyone anywhere. Add to this an appropriate time so that the issue can be considered and discussed thoroughly.

Once you identify the appropriate place and time, then talk straight. Be clear about what you want and what the issue is. Keep your concerns short and to the point. When you are angry, you are not getting what you want. Therefore, state clearly your wants and needs. Have you noticed, however, that it is not so much what people say but the way they say it that affects others? Talking straight means that your words, tone of voice, and body language all send the same message; they are congruent. When they are not, they send a mixed or double message, a common phenomenon of conflict. For example, suppose you ask a coworker to do something for you. "Hey, Bob, would you mind picking up the new catalog for me when you go across the street?"

Bob responds in a sarcastic tone with a snarl on his face, "No, I don't mind. I'll do it, for goodness sakes. I'll be glad to do it. I'm going that way. I'll do it!" He said he would do it. Do you believe that he wants to? No! His tone of voice and body language proclaim otherwise. The words sound fine. But the tone of voice and body language sent me through the roof. If he had said, "I'll pick it up, though it's not really on my way," I could have handled it because it would have been straight talk. His words, tone, and behavior would have fit, and the message would have been consistent. During conflict, people often do not talk straight. They send mixed messages. Unfortunately, the heat under your collar may make you send one back to them instead of talking straight.

*Use "I" messages.* Recently during a meeting I was leading, a participant stood up and said very straight, "I disagree with you." I flinched a little bit but not nearly as much as I would have if he had said "You are wrong!" During conflict, it is important to use "I" messages, which leave room for discussion of the situation and consequences of actions.

*Acknowledge consequences.* Consequences are not and must not be threats or intimidation. Rather, consequences are the results—positive or negative—of the behavior. If there are no consequences, do not expect any positive behavior. For example, an employee comes in on Monday at 8:05 a.m. and nothing is said about his being five minutes late. So, on the next day he arrives at 8:10 a.m. Again, nothing is said. Difficult people will keep adding on time until consequences kick in. The key is to set limits, be fair, and mean them. Do not promise what you cannot deliver; otherwise, difficult people will not take you seriously.

*Be specific.* Avoid saying, "I want it done well." Instead, spell out exactly what you want. You say, "I want you here early tomorrow." What does early mean? When you say, "I want you here at 8:00," you are being specific.

### Listen

After you have presented your concerns, stop and listen to the other person's response. Our usual impulse is to talk or get away, but listening is one of the most powerful ways of changing behavior. The flip side is also true: One of the least effective ways to change someone's behavior is to talk. But what do we usually do in conflict? We talk. We do what is least effective. We do need a two-way conversation, but the challenge is to set the example by listening first and then clarifying the conflict. Send it out and then check it out.

*Listen between the lines.* Another key point is to listen between the lines. Do not assume that you know what the other person means. Always check out the meaning. When you hear a double message in the midst of conflict, do not assume you know what the speaker means. Frequently, something else is happening, and it is important to know what. A lot of miscommunication and hostility get transmitted that have nothing to do with the person who receives the message. Quite often the hostility originates somewhere else entirely.

I have trouble listening to people I do not like. Furthermore, I have trouble listening when I am angry. In fact, the angrier I become, the more difficult it is for me to listen. Note the correlation: I do not like someone; they anger me. At this point what are the odds of my listening? Almost zero. Yet, I must listen because it is the only way to know how the other person sees the problem so that we can move to resolution. You do not necessarily need to agree with the person, but you must listen in order to understand. The good news is that people would rather be heard and understood than agreed with. No doubt you have had people agree with you, but you felt angry anyway. You have had other people disagree with you, but you came away feeling heard and understood. Listening can change negative behavior when it includes understanding. Explaining to people how listening to you will benefit them is important and is especially necessary when dealing with a difficult person.

### Avoid Triangles

Up to this point, I have emphasized three points: stand up, talk straight, and listen. Before proceeding with the next step, it is important to mention triangling. Avoid asking someone to express your problem to another person for you. Triangling occurs when a third person gets involved in a conflict between two other people. In a triangle, there are three players—a persecutor, a victim, and a rescuer. We will call the persecutor Harold, the victim Sue, and you will be the rescuer.

Here is the scenario: Harold bullies Sue. Sue feels inadequate to deal with Harold, so she rushes over to you to be her rescuer. She wants you to take care of her situation with Harold. After listening to Sue's pleas, you decide to play the triangle game. You confront Harold on Sue's behalf. The moment you do that, how does Harold feel about you? He hates you; you can mark him off. However, we will say in this case that Harold promises to cooperate. You seem to have succeeded, but you have lost Harold. Furthermore, when you tell Sue, "I have saved you. I have rescued you," you have now angered her as well. While she may thank you profusely, she is now more angry with you than she is with Harold. Why? You have taught her two things. First, you taught her that she is inadequate, weak, and incapable of handling Harold. Secondly, you taught her that any time she has a conflict with someone she can come to you. You have now created a dependency relationship; Sue is dependent upon you. And all dependency relationships breed hostility. The more someone depends upon you, the greater the hostility.

Rather than making Sue dependent, we have to help her in a positive, healthy way to learn how to deal with the Harold's of the world. Sue must learn to stand up, talk straight, and listen. We must teach her how to take care of herself so that she can handle conflict situations on her own. It might be helpful to practice with her as she role-plays her interaction with Harold. Help her attain the skills and confidence she needs to deal with Harold by herself.

Here are a few rules for staying out of triangles:

1) Never do for anyone what that person can do for himself or herself.

2) Always separate your problems from the victim's problem. Sue's problem was with Harold. Your problem is with Sue. You must deal with Sue, not with Harold.

What it boils down to is this: Any time you rescue someone, that someone perceives you as a persecutor and will attempt to make you a victim.

Why do we get involved in triangles? First, we are trying to help someone. Most of us enjoy helping people. It feels good when someone asks us to take care of his or her problems. We get hooked on helping. Second, we are good at solving problems. Third, we also feel a little superior to the person who is playing the persecutor's role. And finally, many of us have been taught that we are supposed to be rescuers. We think rescuing people is part of the job of a manager.

The goal, however, should be to make sure that others take care of themselves. We do not want to write them off, but we do want to train them, work with them, encourage them; we will not do whatever it is they want us to do for them when it is their responsibility.

One footnote about triangles: Suppose two workers are in conflict and ask you to solve the problem. Here is what I have found: One of the workers will complain that you favor one side over the other, and you will unless you are a Solomon from biblical times. In addition, almost inevitably the two will end up liking each other and hating you. It is almost impossible to win. You say to them, "The two of you have a problem. Work it out between you."

Can you remove yourself from a triangle once you are involved in one? You can, but not without scars. Once you have gotten involved and then start to pull back, the others in the triangle will become hostile because they have become dependent. Avoid triangles. (For more information on triangles, see Satir, pp. 149ff.)

## SOLVE THE PROBLEM

There are nine basic steps to solving a problem.

### Identify the Emotional Climate

First, assess how angry the individual is. If he or she is very angry, then he or she is not very likely to be rational or even able to hear what I say. Neither is the person likely to hear or think straight until some of the anger has been drained. Therefore, I allow a few minutes for a cooling-off time. I spend a minute or two listening, trying to understand the problem. The worse thing I can say is, "Calm down. Just calm down!" This only makes the person angrier. As anger goes up, listening goes down. As anger rises, thinking falls. So, cool off!

Some people are what I call "flooders." A flooder floods you with anger and will talk forever. People like this must be stopped. Here is what I suggest: If after a few minutes the person has not slowed down, call his name—twice. Calling it once will not work because he will not even hear it. You say, "Harold. Harold." This is a powerful tool. If you stand in the middle of a busy airport with hundreds of people coming and going and yell, "Harold. Harold," 85 people will stop and turn around even though none of them is named Harold. Another technique is to give a time-out signal with your hands. After I call Harold's name, he may snarl, "WHAT?" Now I know I have his attention. I have interrupted the flooding.

The moment I do that, I have a couple of options. One is to offer an emotional listening response that reflects feelings. For example, I might say, "You really sound mad (upset, frustrated, or disappointed)." A second option is to ask, "What do you need from me?" This question moves to problem solving.

### Identify the Problem

After you have stopped the flooding, then identify the problem from the other's perspective. This includes the person's frame of reference as well as his feelings about the issue. Here is the question I ask, "I wonder what the problem is as you see it? Tell me in a sentence or two." Why do I add in a sentence or two? Time is important, and without that limitation, people will talk forever. By asking the question and defining the length of their answer, I bounce the ball into their court. This forces them to think. Have you ever tried to stay angry and think at the same time? It cannot be done.

### Stay Focused on the Problem

Once the problem has been identified, stay on it. Watch for the person's looping to other issues. I call it "looping" because the person presents you with a problem and then hops about like a Mexican jumping bean. When this happens, the person will leave your office half an hour later and you still will not know why he came to see you.

Looping happens a lot. In a staff meeting, the department head presents a simple problem and says, "We are here to design a form that gets better information on students." Then someone says, "What size paper should we use?" Someone else responds, "Is that going to be on red or blue paper this time?" The next person asks, "Will it be ready by Christmas?" It ends with someone asking, "Speaking of Christmas, just who's having the party this year?"

Have you been in meetings something like this? When you leave the meeting and someone not present asks, "What's the new form going to look like?" you respond, "I don't know, but we're going to have a great Christmas party!"

Some people are masterful loopers. When they start to loop, we have to say, "That's another problem. Let's stay with this one." Everyone has many problems and can go in many directions. Your goal is to be keenly aware of the present problem and not wander from it.

### Resist Placing Blame

The fourth step in problem solving is to resist blaming once the process has begun. It is easy during conflict to turn to blaming. The conversation becomes, "Not my fault. I know who did it. I can tell you exactly who did it!" It is possible to know who did it and still not solve the problem. It is even possible to fire someone and not solve the problem.

This is another behavior learned during childhood. You are familiar with the scenario. Mother rushes into the kitchen and sees a shattered cookie jar with cookie crumbs scattered everywhere. Four little angelic faces are looking at Mother. Then Mother asks a ridiculous question, "Who did this?" When no one confesses, Mother makes another ridiculous statement. "Well, I am not leaving this kitchen until I know who did it." She will die there. She will never get out.

Instead of trying to find out who broke the cookie jar, Mother might have said, "We've got a mess here. I want all of you to clean it up. I'll be back in about 10 minutes. If it is not cleaned up, there will be no more cookies for a while."

The goal is to move to problem solving. Remember, even if you discover who created the problem, the problem still must be fixed. It may well be essential to identifying the creator of problems. But to solve a problem, the major focus must be on fixing it.

### Avoid Name-Calling

The fifth step in moving toward problem solving is to avoid put-downs, discounts, and name-calling. A part of you will want to say, "You are at fault . . . irresponsible . . . unconcerned . . . stupid . . . or incompetent. That approach is pointless. Instead, tell the person what those words mean. Instead of telling an employee he or she is slow, say, "I want all six reports by 3:00 p.m." In place of saying, "You're irresponsible." Say, "I want the material filed alphabetically rather than chronologically and I want it completed by 4:00 p.m. today."

If you are working with someone over whom you have no direct authority, what kind of consequences can you hold up for nonperformance? In this case, you will need to show the employee that it is more to the employee's advantage to work with you than against you. If your difficult colleague sees no such advantage, then he sees no reason to work with you. Remember that people work with you because they believe that it is to their advantage to do so, and they resist you if they believe that it is to their advantage not to do so. If you have a resistant colleague, you must show the benefits of cooperation. Demonstrate the positive aspects of working with you.

Always focus on the behavior. General terms only get in the way. Telling someone that he or she is a slow worker is not helpful. Be specific about what the person is doing or what you want accomplished. General complaints cause further conflict. If you cannot measure it, you cannot manage it.

### Develop Alternatives

The sixth step in problem solving is a big one and very important: Ask the person to list possible alternative solutions to the problem. Avoid suggesting alternatives yourself. If you propose a solution and it does not work, the person will blame you. If your proposal does work, then that person will continue to expect solutions from you. When it is his or her problem, it is critical that the person supply the alternatives to the problem.

You may be asking, "But how do we keep this person from doing something counterproductive?" The answer becomes step seven.

### Evaluate the Alternatives and Select One

Evaluate the alternatives with the person in light of their costs. Now what kind of costs might there be? Money, time, personnel, and public relations are only a few, but all are important. When you ask the person "What would it cost?", you are not saying the idea is bad; rather, you are asking for an evaluation as to its cost and chance of success.

The angry person may say, "Burn the place down and fire everyone in it." This is when you swallow your impulse to call names and say, "What would it cost if you did that?" Being a basically intelligent person, he would say, "I'd probably go to jail."

You could respond, "Then it is too costly and way too expensive." You did not use name-calling. You just said that the proposed solution was not cost-effective. That approach will avoid a lot of conflict. Discuss alternatives until a cost-effective one is discovered.

If the proposal causes more problems than it solves, you have a right to say that it is not acceptable. In discovering a solution to the problem, the person must present an alternative that will be effective and at a price that both of you are willing to pay.

### Be Clear about Procedure

Before concluding the conversation, discuss the procedure in detail. Make sure that the person fully understands what specific steps will solve or alleviate the problem. State how you understand the alternative will be handled. Who will be responsible, what is the time frame, how are you going to measure the results? Unless the person understands and accepts all these points, the plan will never happen.

### Evaluate the Success

The last step is to have some way to evaluate the proposed solution. The proposal will be difficult to manage if it cannot be measured. Remember, if you cannot measure it, you cannot manage it. You can ask directly, "How can we measure if we achieved what we wanted?" Always check out how the other person understood both how things will be done (the procedure) and what it will look like if successful (measurement).

### CONCLUSION

To review, there are five goals one should hope to achieve during conflict. They are
1) Stand up
2) Talk straight
3) Listen
4) Avoid triangles
5) Move to problem solving

Stating the goals is, obviously, a lot easier than achieving them when working with difficult people. But when you stand up, talk straight, listen, avoid triangles, and model problem solving, you are teaching people how to handle conflict situations. Before too long, even difficult people realize there is no reason to get you to solve their problems because what they do in your office, they can do for themselves. (For additional information on personality types, see Bissell, 1989.)

### The Backup Plan

In some conflicts, we are not going to get what we want. In fact, there will be times when we will get nothing at all. The backup plan is what you are going to do if you do not get what you want. Never go into a conflict situation without being clear just how you will react to a "no" or rejection; otherwise, you will leave more angry than when you started. Such frustration usually leads to irrational behavior. Therefore, have clear in your mind what your options are if you cannot get what you feel you need or what needs to be done. Be ready with a second or even third option.

Furthermore, never let a person leave your presence without a backup plan if you have rejected his plans and needs. Sometimes you must say no. In such cases, ask the person whose request you are turning down, "Now that you did not get what you wanted, how are you going to handle the situation?" Talk about the back-up plan right then and there, not later. The rule is never let anyone leave your presence feeling helpless. Discuss alternatives, consequences, cost, and multiple options even if they are just temporary. The individual may not get what is wanted, but at least he can leave with constructive directions and a sense that something can be done. Also, he will feel that he has been heard and understood. People must always feel that they have a way out even if it is not a perfect or satisfactory one. Conflict, while inevitable, is not the problem. The problem and solution is the manner in which conflict is managed. Whichever style you may use, keep in mind: Everyone is entitled to be treated with respect and dignity. That includes you!

## REFERENCES

Bissell, B. (1989). *Dealing with difficult people* (video). Richmond, VA: W. R. Shirah.

Rogers, C. (1989). *On being a person: A therapist's view of psychotherapy.* Boston, MA: Houghton Mifflin.

Sargent, A. (1983). *The androgynous manager.* New York, NY: AMACOM.

Satir, V. (1972). *People making.* Palo Alto, CA: Science and Behavior Books.

# Dealing With Troubled Faculty

# 9

*Howard B. Altman*

> *Let me be clear here. The vast majority of faculty members in American colleges and universities are not "troubled," at least to the extent that visibly impacts their job performance or their relationships.*

## SOME SCENARIOS

Dr. Donald Prendergast had been an excellent colleague for 20 years. He participated actively in all departmental faculty meetings, he volunteered for committee service on a regular basis, he was at all times highly engaged in the life of the department. But over the last year something had happened. Shirley Thompson, department chair, was at a loss to explain why Prendergast's attitudes toward everything seemed to have changed for the worse. Where once he had been outgoing and enthusiastic, he was now sullen, aloof, and disconnected. He refused all opportunities for departmental involvement with a curt "No, I have no interest in that." He spent as little time in his office as possible. Students complained they couldn't find him, and when they did, he seemed uninterested in what they had to say. "What can I do about this?" Dr. Thompson mused.

The laboratory was where one could always find Dr. Kathryn Robinson. Her research in regional ecology was a magnet for the department's students; small hordes showed up each day to "do science" with the personable young professor. But last year, Dr. Robinson's fifth year in the department as an assistant professor, students began to complain to the department chair, Sam Hillman, that the ecology lab was often closed to them, and that Dr. Robinson no longer wanted to direct student ecology projects. Once the most popular teacher in the department, Dr. Robinson seemed preoccupied, and would no longer spend hours each day in the lab developing the research skills of her undergraduates. Dr. Hillman wondered whether this was a temporary phenomenon, or whether he needed to get involved in some way.

Dr. Joe Mitchell had joined the department last year as a new beginning assistant professor. A husband and father of three children, Dr. Mitchell bought a house in an upscale neighborhood so that his children could walk to the excellent private school nearby. At first he seemed very happy to have this new position and enjoyed spending time interacting with his colleagues in the departmental lounge. But within six months of his arrival, Dr. Mitchell had changed. He seemed to resent his move to this institution, and his erstwhile cheerful demeanor, which had so impressed his colleagues, had evaporated. Now he never had a good word to say about anything, and he was always gone from campus the minute his teaching duties were over. One of his colleagues spotted him driving a cab last weekend. "Did we make a mistake in hiring Joe?" the department chair wondered.

Donald Prendergast, Kathryn Robinson, and Joe Mitchell exist under a variety of names in countless departments at the majority of colleges and universities in the United States (and quite possibly in other countries as well). They are troubled faculty. One or more of their scenarios will certainly sound familiar to most readers of this volume.

"Troubled faculty" may be defined as those whose job performance and/or relationships with students and colleagues have deteriorated from their normal pattern as a result of emotional stress. In the absence of some kind of intervention or of a change in circumstance, troubled faculty may remain troubled for a long time.

Chances are, especially in large departments at large institutions, troubled faculty may not be perceived as troubled; rather, they may be labeled by their colleagues (behind their backs, of course) as oddballs, or deadwood, or misfits in some way. After all, we all know that every department has its share of academic kooks, right? So unless they do something really egregious—for example, stop teaching their classes, physically threaten their colleagues, etc.—why should anyone else be concerned?

Let me be clear here. The vast majority of faculty members in American colleges and universities are not troubled, at least to an extent that visibly affects their job performance or their relationships with students or colleagues. Indeed, in the recently issued report, *The American Faculty Poll*, published by TIAA-CREF and the National Opinion Research Center (NORC) (2000), over 90% of faculty surveyed claim to be satisfied or very satisfied with their current positions, and 63% would definitely (and another 24% would probably) pursue an academic career again if they could begin their careers anew. These data suggest a strong endorsement for academic life by its major players.

So why this attention to troubled faculty? Some demographic data may be a good place to start. According to the NORC-TIAA report, 51% of the faculty are at least 50 years of age (p. 6). In this 1999 study, 62% of the faculty have tenure (p. 8), and given the relative scarcity of senior-level openings, most are likely to remain at their current institution until retirement. Some 66% of the faculty polled have worked in higher education for more than 10 years; indeed, almost 37% have been academics for more than 20 years. Close to a third of the faculty have never been employed in academe except at their current institution (p. 11).

If even 5% of faculty members are troubled to the extent that job performance or relationships with students or colleagues are negatively affected—and 8.2% of faculty surveyed in the NORC TIAA poll claimed to be "not very satisfied" or "not at all satisfied" with their current position (p. 16)—then we are talking about a not-insignificant number of individuals. Some simplistic arithmetic demonstrates this: Given about 800,000 faculty members in this country (Finnegan, Webster, & Gamson, 1996, p. 3), 5% of that number would be 40,000 faculty! Most academics (and academic administrators) can point to one or more faculty members on their campus whose job performance and/or relationships with others have changed for the worse. In this sense, while a comprehensive definition of troubled faculty may be hard to pin down, most of us assume we know one when we see one.

## PROFESSIONAL VERSUS PERSONAL TROUBLE

Professors may become troubled by events in their personal or professional lives. Academics are not immune to the kinds of life-changing events that affect the rest of the population: midlife crises, drug or alcohol dependency, gambling addiction, physical and/or psychological health problems, marital, family, and relationship issues, death of a loved one, financial worries. In some cases, faculty members may successfully conceal the source of the problem from their colleagues and even from close friends. Some refuse to recognize that they have a problem until they are confronted with the changes in their behavior.

In this chapter I indicate some of the ways higher education institutions are attempting to assist faculty whose problems are nonacademic in origin.

We have far more data on faculty who become troubled as a result of issues in their professional lives. The junior faculty member who discovers he or she has set unrealistically high goals for publication in the first few years, the junior faculty member who has gone through a bruising and unsuccessful tenure battle, the midcareer professor who discovers he no longer cares about his research agenda, the senior faculty member who feels overlooked by her younger colleagues in departmental planning, the faculty member who is constantly at loggerheads with the department chair or dean, the professor who is bothered by consistently poor teaching evaluations but has no idea how to teach any differently— these are but a sample of professionally troubled faculty in our departments. Whether the trouble is transitory or becomes permanent may depend upon whether and what kind of institutional intervention is offered. Below is a list of suggestions for institutional interventions for troubles arising out of a faculty member's professional life.

## THE SIGNS OF TROUBLE

Whether the etiology of a troubled faculty member is professional or personal, there are often telltale signs. In the manual *Employee Assistance Program: Supervisor's Guidebook*, published by the Hershey Foods Corporation (n.d.), there is a list of "patterns of deteriorating job performance," which, while describing employees in nonacademic situations, may also be valid for troubled faculty members. These patterns (and my examples from faculty life) include:

### Excessive and Increased Absenteeism
A troubled faculty member may repeatedly fail to show up for his or her classes, or to keep scheduled appointments. This pattern may include excessive tardiness for classes and appointments,

consistently letting classes out early, taking three- and four-day weekends, and providing unusual and improbable excuses for absences when asked.

### Absenteeism on the Job

Increased forgetfulness of appointments, commitments, class meeting times and locations, etc. may be symptoms of a troubled faculty member. (These may also, of course, be symptoms of a medical problem.) Walking around in a daze, repeated failure to provide students with needed materials, or a change for the worse in hygiene habits may all signal a troubled faculty member.

### High Accident Rate and Resulting Accident Claims

This may be especially applicable for faculty in areas of science and technology where there is a greater chance of laboratory accidents.

### Difficulty Concentrating

A troubled faculty member may experience increased frustration at an inability to carry out teaching or research responsibilities as easily as before. Everything seems to take much more time, and it is harder to concentrate on the task at hand.

### Confusion

An increased level of difficulty in recalling instructions, assignments given to students, memoranda from the chair or dean, deadlines for projects, etc. may also be symptomatic of troubled faculty.

### Spasmodic Work Patterns

A troubled faculty member may alternate between periods of very high and very low productivity over short intervals. There may also be periods where no productivity at all is visible.

### Difficulty Making Changes

Faculty are called upon to make changes in their way of doing things more and more often. A troubled faculty member may feel especially threatened by mandated changes in institutional policies, for example. (One might speculate that drastic or frequent changes in institutional policies governing faculty life may contribute to the number of troubled faculty on campus.)

### Lower Job Efficiency
Faculty who are troubled are more likely to miss deadlines, do sloppier work, prepare less well for teaching duties, receive more complaints from students, and make more excuses about their diminished job performance.

### Poor Relations with Others
Relations with students, colleagues, staff, and institutional administrators may be strained. Troubled faculty may overreact to criticism, both real and imagined. Students may perceive them as unfriendly or uncaring; colleagues may find them resentful and unreasonable. Troubled faculty may hold grudges against their colleagues for perceived slights; because of this perception they may attempt to avoid their colleagues entirely.

### Stress and Burnout
Troubled faculty are more likely to exhibit symptoms of job stress and more likely to burn out in the workplace. They may cease to see any value or meaning in their work; they may feel alienated or discriminated against; they may believe that "nobody around here cares what I think." They may derive little if any satisfaction from their academic duties. They are apt to feel stuck in their career, in a rut, with no way out.

## CAUSES OF FACULTY BURNOUT

While not all troubled faculty burn out, all cases of faculty burnout in academe signal troubled faculty in some way. Thus, let us explore faculty burnout in more depth. There are three major causes of faculty burnout: disillusionment, boredom, and stress.

### Disillusionment
Faculty, like other professionals, can experience disillusionment with the progress or direction of their own work. They may conclude that their research is of little value, that their teaching is unappreciated by their students, or that their reputation among their disciplinary peers has become tarnished or insignificant. They may become disillusioned with the policies of their institution, or with the direction in which their institution—or disciplinary profession—is moving. Faculty who have made one institution

their home for many years and have lived through constant policy changes in recent years may be especially susceptible to this form of disillusionment. These faculty may feel alienated from their colleagues, unrespected by students or administrators, and no longer in control of their professional environment. They may show signs of physical or emotional exhaustion, low self-esteem or morale, and depression.

### Boredom

Faculty may experience boredom when their duties remain constant year after year. Academe provides few incentives or opportunities for faculty to grow—faculty are expected to make their own such opportunities—and even fewer opportunities to do something different at their same institution. Once one has completed the hurdles to a tenured full professorship—and roughly 35% of the faculty are at the full professor rank, the largest percentage of any rank in the academy (TIAA-CREF/NORC, p. 6)—there are few externally recognized goals to shoot for in colleges and universities. Most faculty are not interested in becoming deans or provosts, and in any case only a very small percentage of faculty will be able to become academic administrators. Thus, unless a faculty member is sufficiently self-motivated to continue to grow, he or she is likely to settle into a routine which may become boring. Faculty become bored from the lack of a perceived challenge and a lack of meaningful incentives to grow. While many faculty continue to challenge themselves and provide their own incentives for development throughout their career, others may become complacent with the status quo, blasé, too comfortable. They stop growing, lose their vitality, begin to perform like automatons, mechanically carrying out their duties with little if any interest or conviction.

### Stress

Stress is pandemic in faculty life. Work-related stress is the major health problem in the United States today in adults between 20 and 65. Women in the workplace (including academe) suffer as much stress as men, often without the same degree of family or collegial support. Some have argued that up to 80% of all illness in this country can be related to mismanaged stress.

UCLA's Higher Education Research Institute's 1995–96 Faculty Survey studied sources of faculty stress (see Table 9.1). It is interesting to note that too many tasks in too little time is the largest single stressor for both male and female faculty members. Other major stressors include teaching load, institutional procedures and red tape, students, and the need to manage household responsibilities while simultaneously attending to one's duties as a faculty member.

## TABLE 9.1 SOURCES OF FACULTY STRESS

|  | Total | Men | Women |
|---|---|---|---|
| Managing household responsibilities | 68.6% | 64.7% | 76.4% |
| Child care | 32.3% | 32.0% | 32.9% |
| Care of elderly parent | 27.4% | 25.3% | 31.7% |
| Physical health | 43.2% | 41.1% | 47.5% |
| Review/promotion process | 44.7% | 42.0% | 50.1% |
| Subtle discrimination (predjudice, racism, sexism) | 23.8% | 18.4% | 34.4% |
| Personal finances | 58.7% | 58.3% | 59.7% |
| Committe work | 55.7% | 53.5% | 60.0% |
| Faculty meetings | 50.2% | 48.2% | 54.2% |
| Colleagues | 55.8% | 54.0% | 59.4% |
| Students | 60.8% | 58.8% | 66.2% |
| Research or publishing demands | 49.3% | 50.2% | 47.5% |
| Institutional procedures and red tape | 69.0% | 69.3% | 68.4% |
| Teaching load | 63.0% | 59.5% | 69.8% |
| Children's problems | 32.3% | 32.7% | 31.6% |
| Marital friction | 24.8% | 25.6% | 23.3% |
| Time pressures | 85.7% | 82.6% | 92.0% |
| Lack of personal time | 81.0% | 76.5% | 90.0% |

Source: *The American College Teacher: Norms for the 1995-96 H.E.R.I. Faculty Survey.* Published by the UCLA Higher Education Research Institute. Data based on a sample of 33,986 faculty who spent part of their time teaching undergraduates.

The causes of faculty stress today seem to fall into eight major categories. Faculty exposure to harmful levels of stress in these categories differs based on rank, disciplinary affiliation, tenure status, institutional type, and degree of personal and institutional support available.

1) Perceived inadequate or unfair reward structure of one's institution

2) Unrealized and/or unrealistic goals and expectations

3) Too much to do in too little time

4) Perceived lack of acceptance from students, colleagues, or administrators

5) Intrusion of problems in one's personal life

6) Difficulty of balancing one's professional and personal life

7) Decreased mobility and job opportunities

8) Job insecurity caused by internal or external pressures

## FINDING SOLUTIONS

At the beginning of this chapter, I defined troubled faculty as professors whose job performance and/or relationships with others (students, colleagues, staff, administrators) have deteriorated from their normal pattern as a result of emotional stress. The question is, what can be done about this? How can a troubled faculty member be revitalized, be returned to his or her normal (pre-trouble) pattern of performance and/or academic relationships?

### Faculty Vitality

The excellent literature on faculty vitality (e.g., Baldwin, 1985; Baldwin, 1989; Bland & Bergquist, 1997; Bland & Schmitz, 1988; Clark & Lewis, 1985) is a good place to start. Numerous studies conclude that there is no such thing as the vital faculty member; that is, there is no one definition of, or formula for, faculty vitality which can be applied universally throughout the academy. Faculty vitality is both contextual and situational; its meaning varies in different institutional settings and likely varies in different intra-institutional settings as well: arts and sciences, engineering, medicine, social work. The differences in vitality exist across disciplines and from one individual faculty member to the next.

Despite the conventional wisdom, faculty vitality does not necessarily decrease with age; just as most deans can sadly point to senior faculty who show symptoms of burnout, so, too, can most deans proudly point to senior faculty who are more productive and more engaged in their work today than they were a decade earlier. Vitality in academe is probably linked with a sense of personal or professional purpose and satisfaction; those lacking this sense—that is, troubled faculty—are likely to exhibit diminished vitality.

As part of a small unpublished study I conducted some years ago at a mid-size public research university, I asked two questions of campus deans and of faculty members who had won institutional awards for teaching or research: What institutional policies and practices in your view detract from faculty vitality? What institutional policies and practices in your view enhance faculty vitality? The answers I received were as different as the individuals who provided them. I include here a sample in Tables 9.2 and 9.3 below.

## PROVIDING HELP FOR TROUBLED FACULTY

### Employee Assistance Programs

Many colleges and universities have established Employee Assistance Programs (EAPs) to offer counseling and support to faculty and staff who suffer from alcohol dependency, drug abuse, gambling addiction, and other special health problems that negatively affect an employee's job performance and that are viewed as treatable. EAPs rely on proven therapies, and participation is confidential, though referral to an EAP may be by one's supervisor (e.g., department chair or dean), by family members, by colleagues in one's department, or by self-referral.

### Campus Wellness Programs

There are techniques that faculty themselves can employ to reduce the effects of stress. Many of these are taught in campus wellness programs, which have mushroomed on American campuses over the past decade. An institutional investment in faculty and staff wellness can reduce absenteeism caused by physical or psychological ailments. In wellness programs, faculty and staff are taught to reduce stress in their lives through such techniques as deep breathing, progressive relaxation, visualization, meditation, biofeedback,

## TABLE 9.2
### INSTITUTIONAL POLICIES AND PRACTICES THAT DETRACT FROM FACULTY VITALITY

"Committee work and frequent meetings."

"Teaching effectiveness is measured (by the administration) in quantitative (rather than qualitative) terms."

"My teaching load is too heavy for me to do the level of research expected at a first-rate institution."

"The personnel policy pits colleague against colleague for promotions and available resources."

"There's too much pressure right now, especially pressure to bring in outside grant money."

"The university policy is much too rigid in regard to the way it expects faculty members to spend their time. Individual differences among faculty are not taken into account."

physical exercise, and proper nutrition. An institution wishing to make a commitment to faculty wellness may sponsor support groups or provide on-campus counseling or short-term psychotherapy at little or no cost to participants.

### Faculty Development
For faculty whose job performance and relationships with others on campus have deteriorated because of professional disillusionment or burnout, deans and department chairs need to look at faculty development opportunities as a way of fostering revitalization. Unfortunately, most deans and chairs have had no training in

---

## TABLE 9.3
## INSTITUTIONAL POLICIES AND PRACTICES THAT ENHANCE FACULTY VITALITY

"Availability of financial support for research."

"The presence of a small core of supportive colleagues."

"I am pretty much left to do what I want."

"I think vitality is augmented when institutions give clear messages to faculty that they are worthwhile, first-class people."

"We try to find ways of saying 'yes.' If someone has an idea, we try to help him or her put it into effect."

"In this unit we have very few policies or procedures that are written, and I think that has a lot to do with maintaining vitality . . . We do not treat faculty members as a standardized commodity."

---

clinical psychology or human resource management. Many deans and chairs are also unaware of the extensive faculty development literature which exists today. Thus, coming up with an effective plan to revitalize a professionally troubled faculty member may well be a team effort, with input from the faculty member himself or herself, the chair or dean, the institution's faculty development specialist, and possibly the institution's director of mental health.

It is essential as part of any revitalization effort to ascertain why a faculty member has become professionally disillusioned or burned out. Is the faculty member simply bored with repetitive duties over many years? Does he or she feel stuck in a rut? Has the pace of change on the campus overwhelmed this professor? Is there ongoing conflict with colleagues or the department chair which has caused depression? Has the faculty member's scholarly reputation in the discipline been a source of concern? Does the faculty member feel unappreciated, alienated, unrespected?

### Ten Faculty Development Options

The following list of faculty development options may prove helpful for revitalizing professionally burned-out faculty. The choice of option needs to be explored collaboratively between the faculty member concerned and his or her chair or dean, and the troubled faculty member must commit to making a serious effort or there is no chance of success. It is a truism that no faculty member can become revitalized if he or she refuses to allow change to happen.

*Networking.* Professors, even burned-out professors, have things they care about, activities that interest them, people they enjoy spending time with. What is it in the institution that makes a faculty member's pulse race? Getting a disillusioned professor together with others who are interested in those academic issues that he or she cares about may rekindle a spark. The issues may have little or nothing to do with the faculty member's own department, but a faculty member who rediscovers the excitement of involvement in one area of the institution may be able to transfer this excitement to other areas.

*Direction of a project.* Similar to networking, direction of a project builds on academically related interests—perhaps long latent—that still ignite a spark in the faculty member who is experiencing professional burnout. The professor who has long felt he or she would like to revamp the college's admissions procedures, or reexamine the priorities of the college library, or advise the provost's office on ways of improving morale, might be allowed to direct a project in this area. Clearly, as with all other institutional projects, there must be guidelines and outcomes expectations; this is not meant as busy work, but rather is a way of reviving and channeling the suppressed enthusiasm of a faculty member in a professionally useful direction. Some projects may be within the faculty member's own department: running a conference, planning for and hosting a series of important visitors, gathering data from students who are majors in the department, developing a new curriculum for undergraduates, etc.

*Mentoring of junior colleagues.* It may seem counterproductive to ask professionally burned-out faculty members to serve as mentors to young colleagues in their department or institution.

Isn't there a chance that the disillusionment or hostility to the institution will rub off on others? Clearly, not all professionally troubled faculty would make good mentors, but some might, and possibly thrive in the process. Most professors enjoy sharing the wisdom of their experience with others, and we need to remember that the collective experience of a troubled faculty member is not all negative. Much has been written about ways of mentoring junior faculty, the selection and training of appropriate mentors, and the pairing of mentors and protégés (e.g., Boice, 1990; Wunsch, 1994).

*Service as an institution-wide teaching consultant.* Those faculty whose sense of burnout emanates from a frustrated desire to have a greater impact on the instructional programs of the institution, or from a sense that teaching is not being sufficiently valued at the institution, might be given an opportunity to work with their colleagues to create a more positive climate for teaching on the campus. Institution-wide teaching consultants might be assigned to a centralized faculty development office where, under the direction of the institution's faculty development specialist, they would assist other faculty to teach or to deliver instruction more effectively. They might also serve as advisers to the provost in the area of appropriate ways of rewarding teaching.

*Intra-institutional visiting professorship.* Some faculty become burned out because their disciplinary area has lost favor with students, or because over the years their own scholarly interests have moved into the domain of another discipline which the territoriality of the departmental structure prevents them from teaching. A faculty member with solid research credentials in more than one discipline might be offered a chance to serve as an intra-institutional visiting professor and to teach and lead seminars (for students and faculty) across the institution.

*Retraining for a new academic or occupational area.* For faculty who have lost interest in their original discipline, or whose original discipline is no longer a priority at the institution, retraining for a new academic area or a new nonacademic position within the institution may be a way of salvaging an otherwise productive and loyal institutional citizen. There are numerous examples of faculty who have thrived professionally as a result of joining different disciplinary units in the institution—for example, the psychologist from an arts and sciences college who joins a management department in a school of business; the science educator from a school of education who joins a chemistry department in arts and sciences; the philosopher from arts and sciences who becomes an ethicist on a medical school faculty; etc. Some faculty may be revitalized by joining the institution's administrative staff in some capacity: service as a special assistant to the dean or provost, liaison with the library or the campus bookstore, working in public or external relations for the institution, etc.

*Faculty development sabbatical.* Traditionally, sabbatical leaves are awarded to productive faculty for scholarly or major curriculum projects which could not be easily accomplished without release from other duties. They are one of the most highly coveted perks of a faculty career. Perhaps it also makes sense for institutional leaders to think of the sabbatical as a tool for revitalizing the less productive members of the faculty, as an opportunity for faculty to learn how to be more effective in the classroom or laboratory. If the sabbatical is successful, the provision of salary for a semester's sabbatical leave may bring forth a professor who will (again) be an asset to the institution's programs for many years to come.

*Faculty exchange.* The opportunity to live and teach elsewhere for a semester or a year may serve to reinvigorate a burned-out faculty member. At a new institution, a faculty member does not necessarily have the emotional baggage (or unpleasant relationships) left behind. There are potentially positive outcomes from a faculty exchange program:

• The faculty member realizes that life at his or her home campus wasn't so bad after all (compared to this new place), and returns home after the experience a more contented professor

• The faculty member realizes that the grass really is greener elsewhere and makes the decision not to return to his or her original campus.

In the former case, the home institution gains a revitalized faculty member; in the latter case, the home institution loses a disgruntled one. The National Faculty Exchange brokers dozens of faculty exchanges between member institutions annually. (For further information on faculty exchanges, contact the National Faculty Exchange, 4656 B. Jefferson Blvd., Suite 140, Ft. Wayne, IN 46804.)

*Temporary outplacement into business or industry.* It may be mutually advantageous for higher education institutions to be able to contract with local business and industry to place one or more interested faculty members in an industrial setting for a period of time. Similar to the case with faculty exchanges, the participant gets to try his or her wings in a new (in this case nonacademic) environment, while the sponsoring company—which provides the faculty member's salary and benefits for the duration of the outplacement—gets a chance to benefit from the faculty member's expertise and problem-solving skills. Again similar to exchange programs, the faculty member may return to his or her campus with a renewed appreciation of the higher education environment, or may thrive in the industrial milieu and relinquish his or her academic position entirely.

*Phased buyouts and early retirement options.* For the disgruntled faculty member for whom all other institutional efforts at revitalization have proven ineffective, an opportunity gracefully to sever one's connection with the college either immediately or in stages may be to the advantage of both parties. Institutions ought to provide appropriate kinds of counseling—both fiscal and psychological—for faculty who contemplate accepting a buyout or an early retirement option. It is a wise administration that finds ways of ceremonializing and thanking retiring faculty, even troubled ones, for their many years of service, as any university development officer can attest.

## FINAL WORDS

None of the 10 faculty development techniques outlined above can guarantee revitalization of a troubled faculty member. For these solutions to work, they must be offered and implemented humanely and with great deference for the needs and values of individual faculty participants. Faculty are highly educated and justly proud professionals who will likely reject overt attempts to fix them. Faculty development must therefore be presented by deans and chairs, and perceived by the faculty concerned, as a positive opportunity for growth and stimulation, not as an attempt to cure anyone.

A dedicated and skillful faculty is the greatest asset any higher education institution can have. Finding ways to renew this dedication when it wanes, and to enhance these skills when they atrophy, is among the most gratifying responsibilities of academic administration.

## REFERENCES

Baldwin, R. J. (Ed.). (1985) *Incentives for faculty vitality.* San Francisco, CA: Jossey-Bass.

Baldwin, R. J. (1989). Super highway or scenic route: What is the best path to faculty vitality? In H. B. Altman (Ed.), *Faculty vitality in Kentucky: Proceedings of the fourth annual conference on faculty development in Kentucky higher education.* Louisville, KY: University of Louisville Center for Faculty and Staff Development.

Bland, C. J., & Bergquist, W. H. (1997). *The vitality of senior faculty members.* Washington, DC: George Washington University, (ASHE-ERIC Higher Education Report 25:7).

Bland, C. J., & Schmitz, C. C. (1988). Faculty vitality on review. *Journal of Higher Education, 59* (2), 190–224.

Boice, R. (1990). Mentoring new faculty: A program for implementation. *Journal of Staff, Program, and Organization Development, 8* (3), 143–260.

Clark, S. M., & Lewis, D. R. (Ed.). (1985). *Faculty vitality and institutional productivity: Critical perspectives for higher education.* New York, NY: Teachers College Press.

*Employee assistance program: Supervisor's guidebook* (n.d.). Hershey, PA: Hershey Foods Corp.

Finnegan, D. E., Webster, D., & Gamson, Z. F. (Ed.). (1996). *Faculty and faculty issues in colleges and universities* (2nd ed.). Needham Heights, MA: Simon & Schuster.

*The American Faculty Poll* (2000).Chicago, IL : TIAA-CREF, and New York, NY: National Opinion Research Center.

Wunsch, M. A. (Ed.). (1994) *Mentoring revisited: Making an impact on individuals and institutions.* San Francisco, CA: Jossey-Bass.

# Improving the Odds of Hiring the Right Person

**10**

*Baron Perlman & Lee I. McCann*

*Department chairs and deans must balance pressures from above and below. Achieving this balance during the recruitment of new faculty is best accomplished through the use of productive communication, in conjunction with a responsible use of power, authority, and control.*

The need to do a good job in recruiting new faculty is more important than ever. Aside from some rapid growth areas, the number of faculty has been relatively stable for the last decade or two. Permission to hire additional faculty has been relatively rare, although in many disciplines replacement of those leaving remained common. It was a buyer's market. Now the cohort of faculty hired during academic expansion in the 1960s and 1970s is retiring, and large numbers of the professoriate will do so in the next few years. There will be many faculty to replace. Many institutions will be hiring simultaneously, more than ever competing for faculty. In many disciplines, it will be a seller's market.

In addition to hiring the right person, good recruiting must include professional treatment of all applicants. It is important that even those who do not make the cut as semifinalists or who are invited for a campus visit but not offered a position, speak highly of their experience with your institution, college, and department. They, their peers, and their graduate students may seek positions at your institution in the years ahead, so treat them well as part of an efficient, effective, and ethical search.

The roles that department chairs and deans play in recruitment depend on institutional policy and history and often on the size of the unit in question. In a large doctoral department, the search committee usually has a faculty chair. In a small department, it is not unusual for the chairperson of the department to chair the search committee, and in some institutions, the dean may chair a search committee or be very involved. Depending on institutional processes and departmental problems, the dean may pay close attention to searches. Regardless of their specific role, there is much that a department chair or dean can do to facilitate the recruitment process. For example, receiving written material on rules and processes is beneficial for any recruitment committee.

Recruiting faculty can be a difficult, time-consuming, and thankless job for department chairs and college deans. If the hiring process is successful, everyone is thankful (but typically not to the chair or dean) and moves on to other matters. If the search process fails for reasons that can—rightfully or not—be attributed to the chair or dean, or if rancor and ill feelings arise during the process, or if disagreement about who should be or was hired occurs, the department chair or college dean may be in for some strong words from faculty closest to the search.

We will emphasize the recruitment of full-time faculty, recognizing that local searches for ad hoc faculty and emergency searches are also important and time-consuming activities. We discuss chairs and deans getting their house in order, planning, training, the organizational place of the department chair and dean, ethical searches, the failed search, use of technology, campus visits, a letter of offer, and retention.

## GET YOUR HOUSE IN ORDER

Department chairs and deans need to know a lot about recruitment. They should talk with other chairs or deans who have overseen searches and ask questions and borrow good ideas. Reading a good book on the process will be helpful. Even if a chair or dean has experience with recruitment, getting some new ideas is important.

### Examine Your Procedures
Take a close look at the bureaucracy and procedures in place and determine if they can be updated, streamlined, or changed to better assist search committees. In what ways are they cumbersome or inappropriately intrusive? Obtain feedback from faculty about how they were treated when recruited by your institution and at others. Learn what they are thinking and feeling about their department, college, and the institution. Get a sense of their job

satisfaction and what issues and events are important to them, and how the strengths and weaknesses of their department or the institution affect them. They may have good ideas for you.

### Develop a Recruitment Handbook

Every institution needs a recruiting handbook. The issues discussed in this chapter are a good place to start when planning the handbook's content areas. Other important information can be added such as hiring part-time instructional staff, clerical staff employment policies and procedures, and the like.

## PLANNING

There are two types of planning. One focuses on departmental (or college or institutional) self study and needs, the other the nuts and bolts of a recruitment.

### Unit Self Study and Needs: Assessing Your Needs and Advertising the Position

Some of the most important work in faculty recruiting occurs before a job description is written and published. If a department chair or dean anticipates faculty vacancies or expanding a unit, systematic planning can pay enormous dividends. While such planning sometimes takes place as part of periodic department program review, it is more powerful when specifically oriented toward recruitment when a department can voluntarily focus on issues it defines as important, such as curricular change and resultant future staffing needs. Deans may also provide workshops for their department chairs to encourage consideration of future trends and options, and to develop a coherent vision of an achievable future. Some recruitment-related questions that should be asked during planning include:

• What is the identity of the department? What is the department trying to accomplish with its existing undergraduate and graduate programs, research programs and laboratories and studios, and community outreach programs?

• What are the strengths of a department, its weaknesses, the threats and opportunities it faces?

• Can new faculty realistically develop and thrive in the institution or department? Why or why not? What must be done to help such faculty thrive?

• Where does the department want to go in the years ahead, and what will be the consequences for curriculum and staffing? What staffing profiles would it like to have in five or ten years?

As a department chair or dean, be prepared to support reasonable solutions to problems identified in the planning process or to explain clearly why you cannot.

*Know your staffing needs.* Department chairs and deans can be helpful by ensuring that the processes departments or interest groups must go through to gain permission to search are standardized, fair, well understood, and timely. Departments make a strong argument for a new or replacement position when they have planned well. Such departments might be asked to provide the dean with:

• A full position description including how the position is consistent with its long-term planning. Recent program reviews or planning sessions will be helpful in addressing such requests as they often evaluate curricular and faculty needs.

• A description of the advantages of filling the position, consequences of not doing so, and current and projected faculty (and nontenure-line full- or part-time staff) workloads.

• What additional resources (e.g., equipment, space) will be needed if the position is approved and filled.

• Whether the request reflects departmental consensus.

If a department has not determined what its staffing needs are, it will be difficult to identify the candidate who best fits its needs. It is also important for a department to have a sense of its identity and direction and to be able to share these with position applicants.

Chairs and deans must work with departments to avoid the common mistake of thinking of a search as filling a vacancy. True, the successful candidate may replace colleague X and teach some of the same courses, but it is far better to acknowledge that hiring someone is a very long-term commitment and that the new hire will have to help move the department into the future. No search should ever begin unless the department has analyzed what it has on hand, what it really needs, and what just might be possible if an enthusiastic young teacher and scholar in a brand-new subdiscipline was hired.

*Make sure it is an acceptable fit.* Make sure there is a discussion on issues of fit. The issue of fit between what a department needs and what a new faculty brings is important. Some criteria for a good fit are acceptable (e.g., specialty area, past success in obtaining grants, amount of teaching experience). For example, it is becoming harder to obtain extramural grants of all types. Rojstaczer (1999), a faculty member at Duke University, has an interesting discussion of the effect of reduced grant availability. The university life after the Golden Age may affect expectations for new faculty and position descriptions. It will affect their work once hired if grant monies are to help support their salary, laboratories, or graduate students.

An acceptable fit implies the individual's qualifications best fit the department's defined needs, the candidate's research complements that of colleagues, and the applicant's teaching will be of high quality.

When the planning is completed and the needs to be filled are well defined and match recent department program reviews and college initiatives, writing a position description becomes an easy task since departmental needs and expectations for teaching, scholarship, and grant writing are clearly defined. A department can move forward with a solid foundation for its recruitment.

*Handling disagreements.* Even with good planning processes in place, two or more departments or warring factions within a department may both covet a tenure-line position. In such a situation, a chair's or dean's goal is to be fair. In some colleges, faculty committees advise deans on the priorities of new position requests. This committee's goal is also an equitable decision. In the best case, where the competing factions have done excellent planning, a demonstrable need may exist for a new faculty position in several units. Someone will have to wait until next year (if next year ever arrives). Good data, established criteria, a reputation for hearing people out, and measured, thoughtful decisions are a chair's, dean's, or faculty committee's ally in such a no-win situation.

Sometimes there is disagreement between a department and its chairperson or dean about the specialization and affiliation of the new faculty to be hired. The chair's or dean's perspective may be different from that of the department faculty on what exactly is needed. Sometimes new positions can only be justified if they are shared between departments or support multiple programs.

*Closing the package deal.* Sometimes a perfect candidate can be recruited only if employment can be found for a spouse or significant other. This fact needs to be discovered early in a search process if it is to be addressed successfully. Realistically, there is only so much any department chair or dean can do to help the second career person in the family. Good contacts with the business community and awareness of openings in departments in other institutions in the geographical area are helpful, but at most institutions deans cannot create new positions in the same or another department to recruit someone they want. The issue of dual-career hiring should be addressed during department or recruitment chair training. Knowing what is possible makes losing an ideal candidate in such a situation understandable, not a bitter pill to swallow.

### Nuts and Bolts Planning Issues
The second type of planning focuses on the nuts and bolts of a successful search. While a dean or department chair may closely oversee some of this planning, the recruitment committee should have the freedom to manage it. Some of these important planning details are as follows:

*Expectations, goals, responsibilities, and membership for the search committee.* Are junior faculty typically appointed both for their perspective and to introduce younger colleagues to this type of service? Is it important that a woman, faculty of color, affirmative action representative, or other faculty serve on the search committee?

*Applicant pool.* The applicant pool is everything. If candidates do not apply, they cannot be considered. Everything possible must be done to reach and encourage candidates to make application.

*Selection criteria.* The selection criteria to be used should be identified.

*Affirmative action and equal employment opportunity.* Committees should understand what is permissible and what is not.

*Open meeting laws.* State or institutional open meeting laws must be explained.

*Scope and limits of the search.* This (usually national or international) should be determined.

*Timeline for the search.* All ads should be published and disseminated within the normal timeline for the discipline (typically no later than November) and a closing date set at two to two-and-a-half months after the ad will appear in the most widely read publications in the discipline. A deadline set too early may preclude excellent candidates from making application (e.g., at our institution, candidates who submit materials after the posted deadline cannot be considered). A deadline set too late may push the search back too far; good candidates may have already been interviewed and made decisions.

*Search process.* Know which search processes you will use (e. g., bringing candidates to campus, screening at conventions). Some departments and colleges find convention screening insufficient and it should never be a substitute for campus interviews and visits of finalists.

*Financial support.* Decide who can and will give financial support for the search (e.g., who pays for the ads, how often and where can and must they be published, number of candidates to be brought to campus as finalists).

*Preparation of the search committee.* Providing the committee with a list of initial tasks (see Perlman & McCann, 1996, p. 105) can identify areas where a chair or dean can be helpful, and potential areas for training.

*Record keeping.* The committee must keep thorough records. While record creation is time-consuming, it is much more arduous if done after the recruitment is complete.

*Treatment of files.* Always treat files of applicants in a confidential manner.

*Use of summary forms.* When reading candidates' credentials, use summary forms. Then discuss and evaluate them. Such forms emphasize important candidate characteristics, not summarizing the résumé, and may have an overall rating for each candidate (see Perlman & McCann, 1996, p. 124 for an example of such a rating form).

*Letters of recommendation.* Asking candidates for letters of recommendation often yields boilerplate letters that can be useful for preliminary work. But consider having candidates supply names and asking recommenders specific questions relevant to your specific search. It is slightly more work but is often worth the effort. Topics for such letters range from whether a candidate would be happy at an institution such as yours to specific questions on teaching, scholarship, and service.

*Telephone calls.* Calling one or all authors of letters of recommendation can be extremely useful. Provide faculty who are recruiting with a list of what types of questions can and cannot be asked.

*Campus visits.* A reasonable number of candidates should be brought to campus. We recommend two to three. Campus visits should be carefully planned. Candidates and recruitment committee members should know who will discuss salary (benefits and moving expenses) with the candidate during campus visits and if an offer will be made before the candidate leaves campus. Candidates are often anxious about both, and it is useful for them to know in advance when both discussions (salary and a decision on offering a position) will occur. It also is helpful for the search committee to understand what topics they should, and should not, address.

*Start-up funds.* Can successful candidates expect an office, computer, or laboratory or studio space? Who will decide on amount and how soon it must be spent? Oftentimes start-up funds cannot be defined in advance and are a point of negotiation during the recruitment process.

*Salary range or limitations.* These should be discussed in advance.

*Assessment of teaching.* Teaching can be assessed in more ways than through a colloquium presenting a candidate's scholarship. Candidates can be asked to write teaching statements or finalists to submit modified teaching portfolios. Once on campus for visits, candidates can teach a class, answer questions about teaching, and be engaged in pedagogical discussions. There are many teaching questions useful in assessing candidates' thought, preparation, and experience (Perlman & McCann, 1996).

*Assessment of scholarship.* Scholarship also can be assessed in ways that complement a colloquium. Candidates can be asked to write scholarship statements, to describe how they would work collaboratively with undergraduate or graduate students, to explain their philosophy about laboratories (or artistic or musical studios), and to identify their future research plans. Extended conversations with mentors at doctoral programs and post-doctoral laboratories can be held.

*Notifying candidates who are not selected.* Such notification must be completed in a timely manner. Semifinalists and finalists have earned the courtesy of a phone call followed by a formal letter.

*Role of the committee when it is finished.* After it makes recommendations, the committee should know what will happen next and their role in it.

*Transition and mentoring.* Responsibilities should be assigned for assisting the new hire in transition to the department and for mentoring the new faculty member.

## THE COMMITTEE CHARGE

Both types of planning issues (self study and nuts and bolts) are often discussed when a dean or department chair meets with a search committee or writes a committee charge (Marchese & Lawrence, 1989). The purpose of the charge is to avoid ambiguities and oversights, and to build a common understanding before the search process begins. The department chair or dean may also help the search committee by providing information, ideas, and expertise.

## TRAINING

Planning and recruitment training often overlap. Chairs and deans must decide if recruitment training is needed, especially in-depth or refresher workshops on procedures and affirmative action, and if so, the best time for it. Such training brings together faculty and chairs from across a large department, or from many departments in the institution. These workshops can provide factual information, build a sense of shared commitment, reduce isolation for faculty who will be serving on search committees, and generate many good ideas. The training need not be extensive: Often two or three hours are sufficient to greatly improve the quality of searches, and decrease the time a chair or dean will spend dealing with common questions and mistakes. We recommend that such training be done annually for those who will be recruiting in the coming year.

### Recruitment Committees

Recruitment committees need to know process, and all parties to the search should be clear about the mechanics of the search (e.g., job description, time line, the decision process). Deans should consider publishing a document containing recruitment protocols (rules and practices) which would be distributed to departments and available on the college web site. Such a document helps ensure a stable recruitment process that will be perceived as fair. The rules generally are available, but many faculty are not familiar with them. In terms of what is expected by and acceptable to the institution and the law, there is no room for creativity. Affirmative action forms and files must be complete and accurate, and no irrelevant considerations can be allowed to affect the outcome of a search. When a choice is made, either positive or negative, the committee and department must be able to provide a persuasive rationale. No one can be disenfranchised from the selection, confidentiality must be maintained, and communication must be proper.

Do not forget to include teaching considerations in a training session, including the fact that a heavy teaching load results from the number of different course preparations as much as the number of credits taught each semester. Departments should avoid saddling new faculty with too many course preparations their first year or two. Class size and course level also affect the amount and type of work new faculty will be doing. Keep in mind faculty teaching responsibilities outside the classroom (e.g., advising, independent study, or collaborative scholarship) because they influence the type of person the department may want to hire and the amount and type of work a faculty member will be doing once on board.

## THE ORGANIZATIONAL PLACE OF THE DEPARTMENT CHAIR AND DEAN

Department chairs and deans must balance pressures from above and below. Achieving this balance during the recruitment of new faculty is best accomplished through the use of productive communication in conjunction with a responsible use of power, authority, and control. Certain requests by the dean may be more palatable (e.g., need for more women faculty or faculty of color) if the reasons are clearly stated and discussion is allowed. On occasion a tenure-line position may be swept up and not returned to a department, or for good reasons, become adjunct staff. The latter offers funding flexibility and is becoming more and more common. But the loss of a tenure-line position is a grievous one, and chairs and deans will need to clearly explain the rationale for such a decision.

## Communication

A chair or dean's communication with the department and search committee must be crystal clear, open in both directions, and understood. In addition, chairs and deans must understand what those to whom they report (e.g., dean, provost) expect regarding the hiring of new faculty, as well as the institutional goals and mission such recruitments are intended to meet. To that end:

*Meet with everyone involved in the search.* A dean or department chair should seriously consider meeting with both the department and search committee chair before the search begins. The department chair must meet with both.

*Be readily available.* Communication during the search to answer questions and solve problems should reflect an open door policy. Be available.

*Get a summary on the search.* After the search is over, consider meeting briefly with the search committee again, or at least ask for a brief report from its chair after the committee has been polled. Learning the rationale for why candidates were invited to campus as finalists and why offers were made provides valuable information on whether the committee followed through on earlier training and conversations about what types of new faculty were most valuable and needed. Suggestions on what could improve the next search, observations on what worked well, and general comments can only be helpful in the years that follow.

## Authority and Power

A second major concern is the use of authority and power. A chair or dean's goal should be to facilitate search committee and department activities, to help in any way possible to increase the probabilities that searches will be successful. For example, does a chair or dean want to review the letters the search committee sends to candidates? Perhaps a chair or dean can save the committee work by suggesting generic models for use at all stages of the search and published in the dean's written recruitment materials. Such material allows a dean to positively influence the professionalism and ethics of the search while serving as a helpful resource (a win-win situation). While chairs and deans may be tempted to require all committees to use standard content, they should be flexible enough to consider changes that reflect individual department and discipline needs.

Obviously departments and interest groups within large departments cannot conduct a search however they wish or hire whomever they like with whatever specialty strikes their fancy.

*Set parameters.* The parameters for many important elements of a position (e.g., tenure line, teaching and scholarly expectations, subdiscipline area and expertise) should be set as it is being structured. These deliberations and decisions must be managed carefully and the reasons communicated clearly so that department faculty do not become unnecessarily upset.

*Articulate moral and legal responsibilities.* Chairs and deans have legal and moral responsibilities for recruitment. Realistically, departments need to know and understand why deans must be able to say no to applicants whom a committee recommends for campus visits or positions.

*Be careful about job announcements.* Even publishing job announcements can become contentious. Publishing job announcements can be costly, and they may not appear everywhere or run as long as faculty would like. This is simply reality. Providing a budget limit for such expenditures and asking for recommendations on how best to spend it, may provide for more feelings of faculty control.

### Hiring with Advanced Rank or Tenure

The department or dean may have good reasons to advertise a position with possibilities of associate professor or professor status, and/or tenure. Depending on institutional rules and needs, it is the chair or dean who may have to stand firm for or against such requests. Generally, hiring someone with tenure can be difficult as this involves an entirely different level of commitment and review than probationary appointments. But sometimes, because of too frequent turnover or competition for expertise, someone must be hired with tenure if he or she is to be hired at all. The classic example is the troubled department in which a tenured chairperson is to be recruited. Sometimes this strategy is a superb way to hire truly excellent faculty. A department may push to hire someone whose previous work (in academia or not) will count toward rank or tenure. Such conditions of hiring may be risky, as the candidate has fewer years to build credentials on campus for these personnel decisions

### Salary

The issue of salary can also be delicate, and deans usually try to work within a departmental compensation structure. Two scenarios can be problematic. The first involves the high salary. Chairs and deans may not be popular for advocating high (but realistic) salaries for new faculty or tenured hires to provide new program and department leadership. Some faculty argue that encouraging the dean to offer a high initial salary is a good idea because it will provide an objective argument for raising the salaries of others in the unit. While this sounds logical, in practice it often means hard feelings, failed pleas for equity, and salary compression.

If a relatively high, but reasonable, salary is needed to attract a good candidate, other faculty may grumble, even though salary compression and inversion are common in academia. Their feelings must be addressed. Even though it is true that the dollars used for a new colleague's salary are typically not available to existing faculty for salary or support, the issue can rankle, and faculty may need to discuss the issue and gripe a little before they see this as preferable to hiring a less capable person, or no one at all.

The second area of concern is the low salary. Department faculty often worry that offering too low a salary may jeopardize the search or leave a new colleague with bad feelings about compression. Often, however, what a dean is offering is not out of line with other institutions' compensation schedules. Moreover, it is what faculty and administrators do and say to candidates that makes them want to come. Recently hired faculty report that their impression of colleagues, the chair or dean, or how they were treated during recruitment were often much more important in their decision than the salary offered. Candidates also often strongly value the potential in a new position: a chance to grow as a teacher and scholar and to work with superb colleagues.

## CONTROL

Chairs and deans need to decide how much control they will exercise over a given search. With the large number of faculty retirements now taking place, an average-sized college may conduct many searches in an academic year. To best accommodate so much ongoing recruitment work, we recommend what Peters and Waterman's *In Search of Excellence* (1982) called "loose-tight" control. The concept implies simultaneous control and empowerment .

Briefly, a department chair or dean must first decide what parts of the search and the search process are nonnegotiable (e.g., tight). For example, an ethical search in which everyone is treated equitably should be expected. At a research university, a candidate's potential for successful grant writing would be expected. By clearly communicating certain standards and givens, department chairs and deans are identifying the institution's, college's, or department's core values.

Everything else in the search can be decided and overseen by the search committee in any fashion it chooses (loose). In other words, as long as the search committee meets the department and college givens (e.g., institutional criteria for rank, advertising restrictions—some institutions cannot say that women and minorities will be given preference—hiring based on criteria that appear on recruitment solicitations), it can proceed in ways it deems best, knowing that a department chairperson, dean, or external officer such as a university's affirmative action officer will approve reasonable action. The caveat is that the search committee also must keep the committee charge clearly in mind; empowerment is not permission to make mischief.

Simultaneous loose-tight processes necessitate planning and clear communication by deans and department chairs so that everyone is on the same page before a search begins. This approach allows search committees the confidence to move forward in a timely manner without need to always check in, which serves to develop their skills and feelings of efficacy and control. The clearly stated expectations that a chair or dean provide mean that as the process begins, everyone knows those things that *must* be done.

## ETHICAL SEARCHES

Ethical recruiting implies acting fairly, responsibly, professionally, and legally. There is no substitute for treating people fairly and justly. Whether those who work in higher education like it or not, one of their responsibilities is to serve as role models for others. Moreover, integrity is the bedrock on which trust, confidence, and relationships are based. Candidates for positions need employment and have dreams, hopes, and prospects for the future, sometimes fragilely constructed. Those involved in recruitment often wield more power than they imagine when searching for new colleagues. Also, many candidates rightfully judge the desirability of working in a department and institution by how they are treated during the search process. They need to be treated fairly. Unethical searches are likely to lead to difficult and time consuming (yet predictable) outcomes.

### Ethical Principles
Ethics are a guide for how to behave during the entire search process. Six ethical principles (Perlman & McCann, 1996) provide the basis for a well-run search.

*Equal treatment.* All candidates should receive the same information, have their materials treated with confidentiality, and be given the same courtesies. Someone known to a recruitment committee or departmental faculty should not be given undue consideration.

*Maintain clarity and stability of criteria and procedures.* Processes and criteria in recruitment should be consistent, objective, and clearly stated.

*Maintain confidentiality.* Confidentiality cannot be breached (Council of Colleges of Arts & Sciences, 1992). For example, aside from those who need to know (e.g., recruitment committee members, departmental chair, or dean) the names of applicants or specifics of their application materials should not be discussed until necessary (e.g., a departmental meeting with presentation of semi-finalists with the goal of choosing finalists and campus visitors.

*Maintain honesty and integrity in communication.* Avoid misleading even by omission, provide accurate information, and be honest in response to candidates' questions.

*Keep promises to candidates and institution.* Once a charge for a recruitment committee is agreed on, the committee, in essence, makes a promise to its chairperson and dean to hire to meet these goals. To preserve credibility, anything promised to candidates must be delivered.

*Do no harm.* Respect the welfare of others. Throughout the search recruitment committee members, chairs, and deans must treat others in a professional and respectful manner.

## THE FAILED SEARCH

Searches fail for many reasons, and often the failure comes when the wrong person is hired for the right job. Picking a candidate who is a poor fit or who has a poor chance of contributing to the institution, college, and department, or of gaining tenure may be more of a failure than not filling the position. On the other hand, some departments may not find someone to hire because they find new faculty threatening, are acting out against a dean, or have poor departmental chemistry. Sometimes the institution is a strong one, and it is the right position, but current colleagues (at times, just one) are so unpleasant that no reasonable candidate is willing to come. Department chairs and deans need to listen carefully to what the departmental decision-makers are saying. "Envy and prejudice do far more than sloth in producing failed searches" (T. Herzing, personal communication, June 25, 2000).

In many successful searches, a department hires someone who was not the first choice or was a compromise in some way. Looking for the perfect candidate has great risk: If such a person cannot be found, permission to hire again for the next year may depend on local circumstances which are unpredictable. Obviously, departments that demonstrate they are incapable of conducting a good search will need closer oversight before they recruit again. If a reasonable search failed, readvertising the position in the same form, or modified after thought and study, can be a good solution.

## THE ROLE OF RECRUITING

### Technology
The growing sophistication of technology contributes to what we call the new age of recruiting. Technology, if properly used, can

increase the competitive edge for a department or institution over other institutions and may be especially useful for foreign candidates. Check with your personnel office and affirmative action officer before the search proceeds. For example, requesting videotapes of finalists' teaching allows the committee to know their ethnicity, gender, and handicap status. The following is a list of ideas on how technology may be beneficial to a department or college in its recruitment efforts.

*Fax.* Applicants can send materials at the last moment.

*Email.* Email can be used for nonconfidential communication such as notification that materials have arrived or that more information is needed.

*World Wide Web.* Use of the World Wide Web allows communication of information via institutional and departmental web sites (e.g., full job description, departmental or college materials, personnel materials including department's tenure and renewal policy). Links to local communities, chambers of commerce, and so forth can be very helpful.

*Online video.* Depending on budget and sophistication, candidates could put videos of their teaching online for anyone to access and view at departments where they are making application. Conversely, departments could have tours of department facilities, or their college or university campus, for applicants to view.

*Spreadsheets.* Spreadsheets can be used to keep track of applicants' status, material in-hand or needed, and any important information the search committee wants instantly available and organized.

*Distance education sites.* Distance education studios can be used to talk face-to-face with candidates or to see them teach before bringing them to campus.

### Campus Visits

Campus visits are an important part of recruitment. They typically occur in early or mid-spring, before the semester ends. In emergencies or when the search simply runs late, there may be no choice but to interview during an intersession, although some colleges simply do not allow campus visits during the summer.

Chairs and deans can play a helpful role in assisting search committees with campus visits. Campus visits must be carefully organized and provide both candidates and departments with information that is useful for the decision-making. Give candidates as much information as possible so they can make informed decisions and understand what is expected of them if they accept an offer.

A department chair or dean may suggest who the candidate should meet (e.g., university grant officer, director of the teaching and learning center, personnel, department secretary, purchasing). They also can provide materials to candidates via a web site or in paper copy before the visit takes place. We have developed a list of such materials (Perlman & McCann, 1996, p. 159) that ranges from institutional catalog to a copy of the itinerary and all paperwork to be completed for reimbursement. If the campus is notoriously slow in reimbursing candidates, department chairs and deans may want to see if this process can be speeded up. Our campus reimburses within one week, and candidates are often impressed with such efficiency.

Chairs and deans may be able to assist departments with campus visits in which a significant other comes with a candidate. Such individuals are not involved with the formal interview process, but the decision to accept or decline an offer often hinges as much or more on nonwork issues as on the position itself. Housing, recreation, school systems, and the like are critical considerations for many candidates. If specific requests are made of a search committee, a department chair or dean may know how to meet such a request.

Chairs and deans should be enthusiastic and open in answering candidates' questions. The meetings they schedule with candidates should be long enough to get to know each other and discuss issues of importance to each.

A prior discussion on the major points a department and the dean will be making with candidates lets everyone know that they are on the same page. Such questions may include careful and in-depth exploration of degree completion, ensuring the department has been open about a changing curricula, and so forth. Conflicting messages may leave a candidate confused.

On occasion, and despite the best recruitment committee efforts, it is apparent after only a short while that a finalist will not be offered a position (e.g., competence or personality issues not apparent prior to face-to-face interactions). Regardless, the campus visitor needs to be treated with respect. Their colloquium, teaching, and meetings are all chances for them to get practice in seeking a position. They may be a good fit and well liked on another campus. Or perhaps someone will want to tell the candidate the truth, and not take up more of his time or raise her hopes unrealistically.

### A Letter of Offer

Once candidates have been offered and have accepted a position, they receive a letter of offer, often from a dean or provost. The search committee should be informed of what is included in such an offer as it is a contractual promise between the institution and the candidate about conditions of employment. Suggestions for the content of such a letter (Perlman & McCann, 1996, p. 177) include:

*Terms of employment.* (e.g., rank, tenure-track, credit toward tenure, length of probationary period, salary and benefits, and so forth)

*Other content.* (title, need for a physical exam, form of formal acceptance, information on who must approve the appointment such as a board of trustees)

*Special situations.* (e.g., evidence of employment eligibility, expectations for completion of doctoral degree, definition of completion, consequences if doctoral degree not completed, temporary appointments)

A well-crafted and complete letter of offer can prevent later problems and misunderstandings.

### Retention

A successful recruitment includes all efforts necessary to ensure that the newly hired faculty member will stay and prosper. Retention efforts should be considered part of a successful recruitment, not a process that begins at a later date. Recruiting has often been compared to a romantic relationship, and what a department or institution wants to avoid is the seduce-and-abandon phenomenon. This process occurs when finalists for a position receive a great deal of attention and support when being recruited but are left largely to their own devices or ignored once they accept an offer.

Department chairs and deans can be extremely helpful to new faculty in need of assistance over the summer when they are moving and settling in. Some of the most important people on campus are outside the formal academic circle, yet good relationships with staff in purchasing, technology, or the student bookstore can make all the difference in the world. Cultivate such relationships. They are especially valuable in serving new colleagues. Know someone at the chamber of commerce; find individuals knowledgeable about housing, schools, and the like; and find students who might want to earn some money helping a new faculty move.

New hires should expect to be treated as the professionals they are. Office and laboratory space should be available as promised, their faculty name should be on the door, with the phone hooked up, the computer purchased and ready to be installed or already installed, the office furniture in place, and so forth. Departmental program assistants (secretaries) serve a crucial function in imparting information and dealing with the requests new faculty make.

Department chairs and deans are in excellent positions to begin or improve mentoring programs that may involve mentors from within a department, outside the department, or both. They also can ensure that the campus teaching center devotes programs and energy to new faculty. Many campuses have both an orientation for new faculty including teaching and ongoing seminars on pedagogy. Similar processes could be implemented for scholarship or other responsibilities of new faculty, depending on the department and institution's expectations and needs.

## CONCLUSION

Recruiting is an extremely important part of academic work. Those who are hired are critical to a college and department, collaborating collegially (one hopes) with colleagues and providing quality teaching, scholarship, and service to all levels of the institution. New faculty serve the mission and goals of an institution and contribute to its reputation, either positively or negatively. They provide an opportunity to maintain or improve programs and departments, and to assist them in moving forward with their missions and identities. There is a lot at stake; they are our future.

The hiring of faculty who will contribute to the quality of education students receive and the reputation of a college or university is an important responsibility of a department chair and dean. There are many areas in which expertise is needed including planning, training, communicating, clearly using power and authority equitably, behaving ethically, dealing with the failed search, using technology, organizing campus visits, developing a letter of offer, and retaining new hires. We hope that this chapter increases your recruitment skills in one or more of these areas and that capable faculty join your institution in the years ahead.

When the hiring is completed, do not forget your established faculty and the hard work they have put in when working on recruitment efforts. Remember to praise search committees now and later for effort and for success. A note to the committee chair that brought this year's successful tenure candidate to campus costs nothing and will be greatly appreciated. Good luck and happy hunting.

## REFERENCES

Council of Colleges of Arts and Sciences. (1992). *The ethics of recruitment and faculty appointment.* Columbus, OH: The Ohio State University.

Marchese, T. J., & Lawrence, J. F. (1989). *The search committee handbook: A guide to recruiting administrators.* Washington, DC: American Association for Higher Education.

Perlman, B., & McCann, L. I. (1996). *Recruiting good college faculty: Practical advice for a successful search.* Bolton, MA: Anker.

Peters, T. J., & Waterman, R. H., Jr. (1982). *In search of excellence: Lessons from America's best-run companies.* New York, NY: Harper & Row.

Rojstaczer, S. (1999). *Gone for good: Tales of university life after the golden age.* New York, NY: Oxford University Press.

# Using Evaluation to Enhance Faculty Performance and Satisfaction

**11**

*Nancy Van Note Chism*

> *It doesn't seem to matter whether the occasion (evaluation) calls for formative evaluation (for improvement) or summative evaluation (for making personnel judgments)—the thought of engaging in either type brings on stalling tactics and avoidance in most of us.*

It's that time of year again. The folders are trickling in, telling tales of tremendous accomplishments and extraordinary dedication. Well, one faculty member admits that maybe the student ratings aren't what they should be, but that was a bad class. Another rails at the narrow-minded reviewers at the National Science Foundation (NSF) who didn't see the merits of his proposal but promises that with a little tweaking and different reviewers, it will fly next year. You've flipped through the first few, and suddenly, looking over this month's office supply expenditures seems more inviting. The dread of annual review leads to procrastination once more.

## REASONS FOR AVOIDING FACULTY EVALUATIONS

For most chairs and deans, faculty evaluation is a necessary, but not eagerly anticipated, part of the job (Licata, 2000). It doesn't seem to matter whether the occasion calls for formative evaluation (for improvement) or summative evaluation (for making personnel judgments)—the thought of engaging in either type brings on stalling tactics and avoidance in most of us. There are five reasons why this is so:

1) Most academic settings are characterized by a norm of privacy. Teaching, in particular, is viewed as personal; classrooms or office interactions are rarely open to outsiders without special

permission. Faculty often find it hard to separate personal from professional in receiving evaluative comments.

2) Another key faculty value is autonomy. Faculty often maintain that this freedom to explore and to arrange their schedules and activities with a fair amount of choice is a key feature that draws them to their profession. Evaluation can be seen as a threat to this autonomy.

3) Faculty are very suspicious of systems that elevate some over others. The ambiguous position of the chair as colleague yet administrator puts the chair in a role that is very difficult with respect to evaluation.

4) Evaluation, done well, is quite time-consuming, and other administrative pressures on the chair and deans can overshadow the need for evaluation.

5) Many deans and chairs feel that they do not have the skills they need to set up good evaluation systems and counsel faculty (Licata, 2000). They also may feel that their choice of approach is constrained by a campus-wide system that they might feel ambivalent about, such as a mandatory student ratings system.

## CHANGING THE PERCEPTION OF EVALUATION

A key to surmounting all these difficulties lies in changing the way in which evaluation is perceived, a change that Higgerson (1999) calls a "climate" change, one that relies on shared perceptions. "Faculty rely on the department chair and other academic administrators to interpret campus policy and practice. Consequently, administrators can help shape faculty perceptions of teaching evaluation as a constructive process that is essential for teaching improvement and quality instruction" (p. 199). A similar observation can be made for evaluation of other types of faculty work. Tierney and Rhoads (1994) speak of the importance of "faculty socialization as a cultural process."

As a dean or chair, you can take several steps toward promoting climate change with respect to evaluation of faculty performance:

• Recognize the fundamental value of feedback.

• Infuse feedback into departmental faculty personnel practices from hiring through annual, pretenure/contract renewal, and post-tenure/contract renewal reviews.

• Learn how to give constructive feedback.

- Throughout the process, locate others who can assist you with evaluation.

## THE FUNDAMENTAL VALUE OF FEEDBACK

An essential part of evaluation is feedback, the conveying of information and judgments to the receiver. While it seems obvious that feedback is important for improvement of performance, not every kind of feedback is inherently useful. Centra (1993) specifies four characteristics of evaluative feedback that are important for promoting change.

1) It must provide new knowledge. Perceptions or information that are different from those already held by the receiver are essential for challenging existing beliefs.

2) Faculty must feel that the information is valuable. They must respect the source of the information as knowledgeable and credible.

3) The information must provide helpful advice on how to change. Recommendations for action and identification of helpful strategies and resources make it more likely that improvement will occur.

4) The feedback must tie into faculty intrinsic or extrinsic motivation by being aligned with faculty perceptions about the meaningfulness of their work, their professional responsibilities, or the reward system that is in place.

In addition to supporting Centra's claims about perceived value and helpful information, Menges and Associates (1999) make an additional observation about feedback: It should be early and continuous and detailed rather than general. Menges and Rando (1989) promote feedback that is characterized by relevance (faculty perceive it as important to their work), manageability (proposed changes are feasible), and accuracy (it comes from an unbiased source or method).

The usefulness of feedback is also enhanced when it is descriptive, rather than judgmental in tone; when multiple communication channels—print, dialogue, demonstration—are used for conveying feedback; and when consultation with a peer, a consultant, or an administrator is part of the feedback (Braskamp & Ory, 1994; Brinko 1993).

It's worth taking some time to think about the usefulness of feedback in your own growth and development. A good deal of the strength of your work as a chair arises from the extent to which you are a true believer yourself. You must be authentic in your convictions that evaluation is worthwhile and necessary and that the feedback component, in particular, is essential for learning and growth. You can begin by thinking about the feedback you have received in the past—have the most helpful instances exemplified the characteristics cited above? Are there others you would add? Next, try searching for inner sources of doubt and resistance: To what extent do you believe that student ratings are merely a popularity contest? How convinced are you, based on your own experience, that peer observers are very discriminating? Then, take some time to examine the arguments and evidence that scholars have advanced.

### Resources on Faculty Evaluation
Several authors have written particularly rich and comprehensive books on faculty evaluation (see, for example, Arreola, 2000; Braskamp & Ory, 1994; Centra, 1993; and Seldin & Associates, 1999). This literature should have a place on your bookshelf. It provides the kind of expertise you should have on hand—advice on which claims about bias in student rating systems are likely to be unfounded, recommendations for judging the contents of teaching portfolios, cautions on the timing of feedback for new faculty. As you feel more knowledgeable, you will strengthen your inner conviction and confidence, creating the motivation and energy you need for enacting structural changes, which is a key administrator's approach in this situation.

### Infusing Feedback into College, School, or Departmental Practice
Models of experiential learning, professional development, and continuous quality improvement all situate good data collection and feedback at the heart of effective individual and organizational functioning. How does a chair or dean create an environment characterized by this spirit of inquiry and improvement? The answer lies in infusing the work of each academic unit with evaluative processes that promote the collection of good information and the provision of constructive feedback, beginning with the hiring process and extending through post-tenure review.

## EVALUATING CANDIDATES

### During the Hiring Process

For both existing faculty and candidates for new positions, the hiring process is an important occasion for displaying performance expectations. (See also Chapters 9 and 10.) We can use these opportunities to both affirm and communicate department, college, and institutional values and standards through the way in which we evaluate the candidate. As part of the interview process, Shulman (1993), Hutchings (1996), and others have argued for the pedagogical colloquium, sessions during which the candidates discuss their philosophy of teaching, teaching methods, and scholarship of teaching. Added to traditional parts of the candidate visit, such as the research presentation, discussion of past professional service, and possibly teaching an actual class, the pedagogical colloquium rounds out the process by which we assess the fit of candidates for faculty positions. When these aspects of the candidate visit are assessed systematically, both existing faculty and potential new faculty gain information about expectations.

Instead of using the usual short open-ended forms or informal discussion to assess faculty opinion on candidates for hire, you might work with a faculty group to put together a clear list of attributes the department values in candidates' performances on each of the tasks we set for them. Such a form (see Figure 11.1) arises out of dialogue within the hiring unit and thus establishes or reinforces expectations of existing faculty. If it is also shared with candidates, it communicates those expectations to them as well. Bensimon, Ward, and Sanders (2000) argue, "We view the recruitment and selection phase as the first stage of a prospective colleague's initiation into the culture of the department and institution" (p. 2). Having faculty use a clearly defined and consensus-driven process to evaluate candidates is also helpful in paving the way for the introduction of a similar process for peer review of existing faculty into department or college practice.

## TRANSITION FROM CANDIDATE TO NEW FACULTY

Since most letters of offer are general, it can be very helpful to develop more detailed documentation of what is expected of the

## Figure 11.1
## Form For Evaluation of Candidate's Pedagogical Colloquium

A. To what extent did the candidate address the following values of our academic unit and institution?

*Listed here would be the values from your mission statements and planning documents. They might include, for example:*

|  | To a great extent |  |  |  | Not at all |
|---|---|---|---|---|---|
| Serving the special needs of an urban student population | 5 | 4 | 3 | 2 | 1 |
| Promoting service to the community | 5 | 4 | 3 | 2 | 1 |
| Developing critical thinking | 5 | 4 | 3 | 2 | 1 |

B. To what extent was the candidate's approach characterized by the following qualities that we value in teaching?

*Listed here would be the values articulated by your faculty. They might include, for example:*

|  | To a great extent |  |  |  | Not at all |
|---|---|---|---|---|---|
| Reflectiveness | 5 | 4 | 3 | 2 | 1 |
| Student-centeredness | 5 | 4 | 3 | 2 | 1 |
| Ability to articulate rationale for specific practices | 5 | 4 | 3 | 2 | 1 |
| Concern for currency and accuracy of course information | 5 | 4 | 3 | 2 | 1 |

*C), D), etc. Additional items might deal with the fit of the candidate's expertise within the curriculum you offer, the flexibility and citizenship attributes demonstrated, or other concerns of your unit.*

faculty member. Perlman and McCann (1996) and Bensimon, Ward, and Sanders (2000) offer convenient lists of items to consider for such a document, whether it be in a letter or a statement developed later. Bensimon, Ward, and Sanders (2000) provide a sample letter of offer that is helpful in tone, as well as clear in expectations.

### New Faculty Roles and Expectations

A pervasive theme in the literature on new faculty is the stress they experience (Boice, 1992; Menges & Associates, 1999; Rice, Sorcinelli, & Austin, 2000; Sorcinelli, 1992 and 1995). A key source of this stress is their anxiety about lack of information on expectations. ". . . Across these studies [of new and junior faculty] there is remarkable agreement. The picture one gets is of junior faculty working all the time with fairly high anxiety, not knowing how much is enough, not being comfortable with teaching or seeking help with it from their colleagues. As a result they may not teach very well and may not produce much useful scholarship" (Sorcinelli, 1995, p. 125).

*Be clear about responsibilities.* Documenting results of a conversation about responsibilities is a key way for establishing a reference point. It's important to first establish clarity about the roles that the faculty member will play and the relative emphasis on each. Bess (2000), Brand (2000), and Wergin (1994) discuss the notion of differentiated staffing, whereby assignments are negotiated regularly and can change, depending on the needs of the department and faculty interests and ability. Every faculty member, then, might have a different emphasis within the department, but their assignments complement each other's to accomplish the work of the unit. If percentages or weightings can be used, numbers of courses or publications spelled out or estimated, or nature of campus and professional service defined, all the better. The goal is to produce a document that allows for some flexibility, but also focuses effort and eliminates confusion. Arreola (2000) situates the work of determining these emphases as primary to a good evaluation system.

While clarity can be enhanced through good hiring and contracting processes, it is important to continue to provide information for new faculty as they begin their careers. Bensimon, Ward, and Sanders (2000) caution, "Clarity of expectations smoothes the new faculty member's transition to campus and prevents later allegations of unfairness" (p. 25). They list the uncertainties that new faculty typically have, such as when they should list graduate students' names on publications, how important it is for them to seek external funding, and how they can begin making contacts for letters of review that they will later need (p. 55). The authors especially recommend that expectations with respect to service are clear: "Good citizenship is highly subjective and is often used against scholars who do not conform to the expectations of senior faculty or who question the way things are done. Chairs can help circumvent this ambiguity by clearly articulating service expectations for the first year" (p. 42).

*Emphasize expectations.* Experts recommend that the early emphasis with new faculty be on expectations rather than on formal evaluation (Boice, 1992; Sorcinelli, 1995). You might find yourself having to repair damage done when new faculty hear an administrator at an orientation cautioning them not to buy a house until they have two publications, or to correct perceptions conveyed through the departmental rumor mill about what it takes to get tenure. The message should be characterized by confidence within the context of good information. When faculty feel support and have clarity, they are less likely to work defensively and over-cautiously and more likely to feel secure enough to seek out help when they need it.

*Provide resources.* In order to help faculty understand expectations, you can provide them (even before they are on campus, given the availability of electronic and print mail options) with a variety of resources—policy and dossier requirements for promotion and tenure at all levels; statements describing annual review procedures, use of student ratings, lists of journals that are valued in your field, URLs of helpful resource people or offices on your campus. Better still, you can establish, with the permission of the authors, a resource file of exemplary grant proposals, teaching evaluation summaries, syllabi, journal articles, CVs, and other artifacts for the use of both new and experienced faculty. You might commission a small faculty task group to prepare an orientation packet or resource file. Taking time at a department or college meeting or at an occasional lunch meeting to discuss expectations helps junior faculty in particular, but is also important for more experienced members of the unit.

*Give feedback.* Feedback should begin as expectations become clear. At first, this feedback might well be gentle and private. Often, self-assessment is a point of entry. New faculty can be encouraged to keep a journal on their work or to make monthly annotations on their list of responsibilities. If they are teaching, they should be collecting student feedback early in the term through use of classroom assessment techniques (Angelo & Cross, 1993), short course comment questionnaires, a student course committee, or the like. You can help them by letting them know about resources for using course feedback methods, such as the campus teaching center or the name of a faculty member who uses these well. Many teaching centers offer a helpful service called small group instructional diagnosis (Clark & Bekey, 1979; Lenze, 1997) that involves having a consultant collect information from students and summarize this for the faculty member.

## ESTABLISHING MENTORING RELATIONSHIPS

Establishing mentoring relationships through which support, but also constructive feedback, can be provided is also important as faculty begin their careers. Gmelch (1995) highlights, as one of the key responsibilities of chairs, the importance of helping faculty network with others. This fostering of collegiality early on not only helps to create a healthier department (Massy et al., 1994), but also helps to address the fear of inspection, defensiveness, and loneliness that is harmful in faculty life. It should be clear to the new faculty member that asking a colleague to read a draft of a manuscript, look over a course exam, or advise them on how to participate on a college committee are all smart things to do, rather than signs of inadequacy or tentativeness.

### Recommending Mentors
Deciding whom to recommend as mentors can be difficult. Several scholars advise that those who mentor faculty should not also be involved in personnel decisions about these same faculty, yet in smaller departments, this situation is hard to avoid. One possibility to consider is the use of mentors at other institutions (especially for scholarship) or in other academic units (for teaching or service). Some campuses have centers for teaching or service that will provide consultants who are either professional staff or faculty

with special responsibilities to help mentor others. Campuses with teaching academies, or more informal groups of faculty who have won teaching awards or been acknowledged in some way for their teaching expertise, can also offer interdisciplinary teaching mentoring opportunities. Rather than attempting to suggest one mentor for the new faculty member, it might be more helpful to think in terms of a network of expertise, with different coaches for different aspects of the faculty role.

## CONTINUING FEEDBACK AND EVALUATION THROUGH TENURE OR CONTRACT RENEWAL

While the importance of formative evaluation continues through the faculty career, summative evaluation looms larger as the new faculty member becomes established and it continues to be a major consideration through the post-tenure years. The role of the dean or chair in setting up a timeline and procedures for the evaluation cycle may be somewhat constrained by institutional requirements or union agreements, but there is almost always some latitude for local modifications or additions to these requirements. Working within the institutional framework, you can enhance the climate for good practice in your academic unit by involving faculty in constructing and using a comprehensive evaluation system. The work includes articulating a timeline of events, developing processes, and maintaining oversight for use and periodic examination and revision.

### The Timeline of Events
Whether faculty are tenure-track or not, there are decision points throughout the career dealing with such issues as contract renewal and merit pay. Increasingly, for tenure track faculty, the third- and fourth-year annual reviews are becoming more summative than formative, involving senior faculty in making a recommendation about continuing the faculty member or recommending their dismissal. You can help faculty by articulating this timeline of evaluation events, including both formative and summative aspects. Figure 11.2 shows such a timeline. In constructing this timeline, it is important to engage faculty in a conversation about the desirability and regularity of activities. Once again, this conversation in itself is an occasion for communication of expectations as well as buy-in by the faculty. It can be used by faculty at all levels.

## FIGURE 11.2
## TIMELINE OF EVALUATION EVENTS

Candidacy
- Preliminary screening: examination of materials, reference calls*
- Interview: seminar on scholarship, pedagogical colloquium, sample class teaching, sessions with various constituencies*

Offer
- Clarity on expectations through letter/contract, official policy state ments or documents

First Year
- Establishment of coaching network
- Collection of student feedback at mid-term and end-of-term for each course*
- Class observations and reviews of course materials with mentors*
- Sharing of scholarly writing with others–works in progress
- Discussions of service and citizenship performance with chair and mentors

Annual Reviews (each year, with special reviews at year a, b, and c)
- Setting of performance goals for each year*
- Coaching sessions with chair or mentors at months x and y
- Systematic collection of student and peer feedback on teaching*
- Systematic review of scholarly products and processes*
- Self-assessment and documentation of performance*
- Review and salary and role discussion, followed by documentation

Tenure/Contract Renewal/Promotion Decisions (years d and e)
- Submission of accumulated evidence*
- Judgment by chair, deans, and peers

Post-tenure Review (years f and g)
- Continuing articulation of performance goals*
- Coaching sessions as appropriate intervals
- Continuing collection of systematic evidence on all aspects of faculty work from students and peers*
- Regular self-evaluation and reflection on goals*
- Triggered or regular post-tenure review sessions*
- Decisions on roles and development activities

*Details can be listed or additional documents can be used to communicate these, such as required student rating forms, list of dossier contents, or procedures for peer review

## Developing Processes

The main roles of the administrator in developing processes for evaluation of faculty are articulating the importance of the work, choosing good people to draft procedures, providing resources, and monitoring implementation of the system. Determining things such as how often classroom visits occur, who does them, and what format their ratings and feedback take is best left to faculty within the department or school, yet the chair or dean has the responsibility for ensuring that the group is informed. Part of the work lies in choosing faculty who are reasonable, practical, and respected by their colleagues. You can also take efforts to pass along good literature on the topic, put the faculty group in touch with experts, either on the campus or from other campuses, and offer your assistance in helping the group gain the cooperation of their colleagues in responding to requests for suggestions or help.

There are several volumes that can help faculty as they outline recommendations for evaluation processes. Books by Arreola (2000), Braskamp & Ory (1994), Centra (1993), Chism (1999), Leaming (1998), Richlin & Manning (1995), and Seldin & Associates (1999) all contain actual forms that can be adapted and modified, as well as recommendations for policy statements and procedures. Highlights of the literature are outlined below.

*The importance of the annual plan* (Gmelch & Miskin, 1995) by which faculty spell out their goals for the year. This plan serves as the reference point for evaluation and can be especially helpful in stimulating faculty to articulate their goals and for you to judge fit with the larger mission. Bensimon, Ward, and Sanders (2000) provide an example of such a plan.

*The need to attend to both formative and summative processes.* Procedures that call for faculty to be reflective and to receive detailed information for improvement continuously are perhaps more important than a carefully constructed summative process, since the former serves to help prepare faculty for success when personnel decisions are made. Reflective memos, coaching sessions, mid-course evaluations, and portfolios are good vehicles for stimulating growth and change in faculty.

*The necessity of any plan to call for multiple sources and multiple kinds of evaluation information and multiple occasions for information collection.* Experts point out the importance of including information from self, peers, students, and administrators; of using a wide variety of methods, including ratings forms, review of teaching materials, citation indices, classroom observation, and documentation of service; and of distributing occasions for collection of this information over time, rather than succumbing to the usual mad scramble right before a decision point. Braskamp and Ory (1994) provide convenient tables of evidence that can be collected to document and assess work in teaching, research, and service. Bringle (1999) offers specific insights into judging service, often a most difficult and mysterious activity.

*The wisdom of considering context in developing processes.* Bland and Bergquist (1997, p. 54) provide a convenient chart that applies development theory to faculty careers, showing that faculty are likely to need different kinds of challenge and support at different phases. Similarly, institutional context should be considered in weighting different forms of accomplishment and in adapting processes from other locations.

*Ensuring that the system is aligned with institutional values.* Altman (2000) rightly points out that the chair is the key to communicating departmental evaluation and expectations documents to the dean, chief academic office, and other campus-level faculty oversight committees, explaining any unusual parts so that there is clarity and acceptance at these levels.

### Maintaining and Revising the System
Unfortunately, many academic units have good processes on paper but not in action. The same factors that work against faculty evaluation in general are primary factors in failure to implement a system—respect for faculty privacy and autonomy, time pressures, and perceived lack of competence as evaluators. Setting up a system that is characterized by faculty authorship and support goes a long way toward countering the normative pressures. As faculty engage in periodic dialogue, supported by your leadership, commitment, and resources, the climate for evaluation becomes more open and the work more respected. Time is not an easy issue to deal with overall, yet you can help maintain faculty priorities on the work of evaluation by ensuring that processes are as efficient as possible and by serving as a role model by committing appropriate amounts of your own time to the work of evaluation. The problem of competency is more easily handled. Clear guidelines for evaluation procedures, forms that will be used in rating or reporting judg-

ments or feedback, and sessions devoted to a discussion of how to serve as an evaluator all help.

## GIVING CONSTRUCTIVE FEEDBACK

Braskamp and Ory (1994) work from the root word of assessment, which means "to sit beside" to articulate a developmental stance for evaluation activity:

> Assessment as "sitting beside" promotes a developmental perspective. It is not a single snapshot but rather a continuous view. It facilitates development rather than classifying and ranking the faculty by some predetermined measurement such as a student rating item or number of publications. . . . The focus is on understanding the colleague's perspective and achievements, which means the focus is on real-world performance. (p. 14)

Glassick, Huber, and Maeroff (1997) underscore this notion: "In a good system of evaluation, colleagues stay in touch with the scholar throughout the process" (p. 57).

At the same time, an important group of organizations looking particularly at the tenure and promotion process observe that candor is especially important: "Most flawed academic evaluations tend to be excessively positive. A sugar-coated review is easiest for the chair to dispense and for the candidate to swallow. But over the long run, it can prove harmful to everyone" (American Council on Education et al., 2000, p. 17). Higgerson (1996) uses the term "performance counseling" to describe the chair's role in presenting feedback openly, emphasizing the coaching aspects as a way of reducing the natural fear of confrontation or reluctance to criticize that bothers most chairs.

### Coaching

Depending on the size of your academic unit, you may or may not be the most likely person to do extensive one-on-one counseling with each faculty member. It is easy to understand the dismay of a department chair in a unit of 50 faculty when faced with a campus policy dictating full annual review by the chair of each faculty member. This is not an appropriate expectation. Nor is it feasible to expect a dean to personally coach the 30 junior faculty in the school or college unit. In situations where numbers preclude a great deal of personal involvement by the dean or chair, the main work is providing leadership and resources for system construction and maintenance, as well as becoming directly involved at key decision points on the timeline, such as the writing of promotion and tenure recommendation letters. The work of coaching will be best accomplished by those closest to the faculty member's group—the coordinator of the large course or program area in which the person teaches, the chairs of committees on which the person serves, or peers in the person's area of scholarship. If the chair has helped the faculty member to identify these people, they will be the actual coaches.

Whether you are in a small unit and can do the coaching yourself, or in a larger unit and will need to rely on others, there are several principles that can inform this work. A classic list was generated by Bergquist and Phillips and appears in their revised *Handbook of Faculty Development* (1995), but others have affirmed or added to this advice. The list below reflects observations and suggestions by Braskamp and Ory (1994), Brinko (1993), Hecht, Higgerson, Gmelch, and Tucker (1999), and Marincovich (1999).

• Cultivate good personal relationships with faculty members through frequently relating to them on a human level through talk about leisure activity interests and the like. You will then have a good basis for communications.

• Time feedback for improvement so that it is prompt and continuous. It is better to have a short conversation close to a performance information collection activity than to say nothing while you wait for an occasion when a larger amount of time is available.

• Be careful to draw upon data that have been collected for the purpose at hand (either formative or summative), that come from multiple sources, that are reliable and credible, and that are consistent.

• If multiple reviewers have information on the faculty member, make sure that you look at all the information and clarify contradictions or confusing statements in advance.

• Encourage the faculty member to do the problem posing. Consultants who use videotape of classroom performance, for example, find it most helpful to ask faculty members themselves to identify parts of their tapes that they feel display problems. Asking faculty to prepare for a feedback or evaluation session by writing a reflective memo in advance or coming with a list of observed strengths and weaknesses in their scholarly records will help to create ownership and collegiality.

• Work to have the faculty member do the problem solving. Although you may have many helpful suggestions, it is best to first facilitate the process through which the faculty member can troubleshoot and generate alternative solutions. Doing so helps them to cultivate a reflective practitioner stance.

• Rather than dealing with all of the observed problems with performance, start with a few that can be corrected quite easily. Work with other issues at subsequent times when the faculty member is more ready.

• Help the faculty member to take a global view of the information that has been collected, rather than focusing inordinate attention on the comments of one disgruntled student or one feisty journal editor. Assist the faculty member in seeing the larger picture.

• Offer specific information that focuses on behavior rather than personal attributes. For example, simply convey your observation that the faculty member calls on males much more frequently than females, rather than assuming that sexism is one of his or her characteristics.

• Be as data-based as you can in providing feedback. Draw upon student or faculty comments, examples from the piece of writing or performance under discussion, or the professional literature in the field to reinforce observations.

• Focus the faculty member on contributions to the missions of the academic unit, institution, community, or profession rather than solely on his or her own academic interests, trying to help articulate the fit and encouraging a broadening of the perspective when needed.

• Consider the context within which the feedback is being given. At times, faculty need more support than challenge—they may be going through a hard personal situation or working in unfamiliar areas. At other times, they need challenge—they may be coasting along on past success or not being sensitive to shortcomings in their work perceived by others. Try to frame your feedback accordingly.

- Consider using what Braskamp and Ory (1994) call "a variety of channels of communication," such as telephone calls and notes as well as face-to-face meetings. Faculty will be more comfortable with some channels over others, but your message will be reinforced by use of multiple methods.
- Be as forward looking as you can, focusing on what can be improved over what went wrong.
- Suggest print resources or consultation with people whom you have found to be helpful as a follow up to your conversation.
- Check to make sure that the faculty member has heard what you intended to say by asking him or her to summarize the conversation.
- Follow up conversations by summarizing observations and suggestions in writing for your future reference as well as that of the faculty member.

## HELPING STRUGGLING FACULTY MEMBERS

In most academic units, faculty generally perform to expectations and are pleased with their work and the progress of their careers. Some individuals, however, are engaged in a continual struggle to perform as well as they should, while most of us have at least a short period during our career span when we, too, struggle. There are several potential situations in which evaluation, particularly the feedback it provides, can be extremely useful. There are some other times, such as periods of health and personal problems, when information is not the problem. Let's explore some different situations.

### Goal Disorientation
Given the complexity and busyness of faculty life, it is easy to become unfocused. The classic case is the new faculty member described by Boice (1992) who obsesses about teaching preparation while neglecting to engage in any writing. Feelings of insecurity about content and the immediacy of having to provide regular learning facilitation for groups of students motivate faculty to delay attention to other responsibilities. Unfortunately, as Boice points out, these delays often become habitual and prevent faculty from adopting more balanced work patterns.

The reverse case, of course, also happens: A research-oriented faculty member operating in a teaching-oriented context may shortchange teaching or shirk service responsibilities or think of them as a bother that distracts from research.

In either case, the annual process of goal setting and checking of goals against performance is the part of the evaluation process that provides the focus for improvement. With struggling faculty, you might increase the frequency of such checks. Candid conversations about the fit of goals to institutional mission will be required. If the tone of these is constructive, the attention is on the lack of fit as a problem, rather than on personal inadequacies. Some faculty may see that there is not a good match with the institution and may seek other opportunities; others may rechannel their efforts in the desired direction.

To help those who want to focus more clearly on their goals, you might ask them to reflect on the amount and kind of effort they are putting into various tasks. Ask them to keep a log of time use for a period of a week or more and to analyze their time use by categories. Often, this is quite revealing and provides a stimulus to change. Or, you might suggest that they list their major accomplishments over a specified period of time under each goal statement. As the areas of weak performance are identified, specific plans for addressing these can be generated. Using timelines, journals, frequent reporting memos, or other tools may help to focus the faculty member.

### Inadequate Quality of Performance

When the problem is not lack of focus but rather poor performance in one or more specific areas, evaluation provides the feedback that diagnoses the nature of the problem and suggests corrective activity. Often, evaluative information is global in nature and thus not specific enough to lead to change. It may also be confusing or hard to interpret. General information does not necessarily provide motivation for change and can call forth defensive reactions or projection of the cause to others. When a faculty member is struggling in some area but the diagnostic information base is not specific enough, your role is to suggest other information-gathering strategies that will help. It is also important to make sure that you, or another coach, help the person to interpret and accept this information and use it constructively.

Again, the literature on faculty work can be quite helpful. In the area of teaching, for example, once a problem, such as poor course design skills, has been identified, there are many helpful books that can be recommended. Pairing the faculty member with a mentor who excels in the area in which the faculty member is experiencing poor performance is also useful. Increasing the frequency of checkpoints, encouraging regular collection of feedback and reflection on these data, and providing encouragement and rewards for improvement all enhance the possibility of progress.

### Malaise or Disengagement

Particularly in the case of more experienced faculty, struggles arising from boredom or dissatisfaction with their assignments, colleagues, or other working conditions can occur. In many instances of dissatisfaction, the focus will have to be on changing the offending condition or in getting the faculty member and others to agree to compromise. When the problem is boredom or lack of interest where there previously was a commitment, however, chairs can help faculty to problematize their work. Assigning the person to a new situation or set of responsibilities is a good solution, but not always possible.

When the existing situation has to be seen in a more intrinsically interesting light, it often helps to tap into the faculty member's sense of curiosity and creativity. On a small scale, you might encourage the person to conduct some inquiries in their area of underperformance or disinterest. If teaching is the problem, classroom research might identify interesting areas for exploration and lead indirectly to ideas for improvement of practice. For example, you might suggest that the faculty member analyze the relationship between student performance and class attendance or participation for a presentation at a department meeting on attendance policy. You might ask him or her to collect and display information on the range of committees staffed by departmental faculty. These inquiries provide evaluative data that stimulate interest and allow the person to see himself or herself in relation to others.

## When Results Indicate Poor Fit

Despite the availability of the best evaluation systems and forms of feedback, there will be instances in which faculty motivation is lacking or the fit of individuals to the faculty career in general or to the mission of your academic unit or institution will be poor. Irreconcilable differences occur in departments as well as in marriages. The best approach, once again, is to avoid blame and accusations of personal inadequacies. These are instances in which career counseling and placement become important. Linking the faculty member with someone within or outside the institution who can help to suggest direction and serve as a resource for career change is the most helpful action.

In cases where failure to achieve tenure or contract renewal occurs, you can help the faculty member to progress and alleviate feelings of anxiety and resentment among other departmental faculty through several practices recommended in a new publication, *Good Practice in Tenure Evaluation* (American Council on Education et al., 2000). Among those on the convenient checklist they provide are reducing social isolation by continuing to interact with the person, providing funds for the person to travel to conferences or subscriptions to periodicals that will be useful in a job search, and providing release time, if the person desires it.

## Legal Considerations

In order to be able to demonstrate that you made expectations clear and that you offered repeated opportunities for feedback and development to each faculty member throughout their career, it is important to document meetings and agreements. While the model of continuous feedback advocated here does not lend itself to formal documentation, periodic memos to the file can be inserted into the records along with documents filed at formal occasions, such as annual review. These informal memos can document times when you suggested that a certain course of action be taken (or avoided), asked a faculty member to take on a specific task that was not specifically mentioned at the time of the annual goal setting, or explained the reasoning behind a decision. Whatever the format, Higgerson (1996) suggests some helpful attributes of this documentation: accurately reflect content of interactions; avoid giving mixed signals; be specific in summarizing evaluative comments; reiterate specific suggestions for improvement; and write with third-person clarity, by which she means write in such a way that a person who was not part of the interaction can understand what happened.

## SUMMARY

Among the roles of the chair and dean listed in the literature, none is stressed so highly as that of people developer. Many reasons are given for this emphasis. Leaming (1998) emphasizes responsibilities to individual faculty, their students, and faculty colleagues as well as to the building of the departmental reputation. In addition to these responsibilities, Tierney and Rhoads (1993) and Gmelch (1995) advance an economic argument, pointing out that personnel account for the greatest share of an academic unit's budget. Whatever the rationale, it is clear that in the role of developer, the administrator has a fundamental need for performance information. Seeing that a good evaluation system is set up and that faculty get the feedback they need to grow and excel is an essential part of this important work.

## REFERENCES

Altman, H. B. (2000). The departmental voice in the faculty reward system. In A. F. Lucas and Associates, *Leading academic change: Essential roles for department chairs* (pp. 138–157) . San Francisco, CA: Jossey-Bass.

American Council on Education, American Association of University Professors, & United Educators Insurance Risk Retention Group. (2000). *Good practice in tenure evaluation*. World Wide Web: http://acenet.edu/bookstore/.

Angelo, T., & Cross, K. P. (1993). *Classroom assessment techniques*. (2nd ed.). San Francisco, CA: Jossey-Bass.

Arreola, R. A. (2000). *Developing a comprehensive faculty evaluation system: A handbook for college faculty and administrators on designing and operating a comprehensive faculty evaluation system*. (2nd ed.). Bolton, MA: Anker.

Bensimon, E. M., Ward, K., & Sanders, K. (2000). *The department chair's role in developing new faculty into teachers and scholars.* Bolton, MA: Anker.

Bergquist, W., & Phillips, S. (1995). *Developing human and organizational resources: A comprehensive manual.* Point Arena, CA: Peter Magnussen Press.

Bess, J. (2000). *Teaching alone, teaching together.* San Francisco, CA: Jossey-Bass.

Bland, C. J., & Bergquist, W. H. (1997). *The vitality of senior faculty members: Snow on the roof—fire in the furnace.* ASHE-ERIC Higher Education Report, 25–7. Washington, DC: Graduate School of Education and Human Development, George Washington University.

Boice, R. (1992). *The new faculty member.* San Francisco, CA: Jossey-Bass.

Brand, M. (2000, November/December). Changing faculty roles in research universities: Using the Pathways strategy. *Change, 32* (6), 42–45.

Braskamp, L. A., & Ory, J. C. (1994). *Assessing faculty work: Enhancing individual and institutional performance.* San Francisco, CA: Jossey-Bass.

Bringle, R. (1999). *Service at Indiana University: Defining, documenting, and evaluating.* Indianapolis, IN: Center for Public Service and Leadership.

Brinko, K. T. (1993). The practice of giving feedback to improve instruction: What is effective? *Journal of Higher Education, 64* (5), 54-68.

Centra, J. A. (1993). *Reflective faculty evaluation: Enhancing teaching and determining faculty effectiveness.* San Francisco, CA: Jossey-Bass.

Chism, N. V. N. (1999). *Peer review of teaching: A sourcebook.* Bolton, MA: Anker.

Clark, D. J., & Bekey, J. (1979). Use of small groups in instructional evaluation. *POD Quarterly, 1,* 87–95.

Glassick, C. E., Huber, M. T., & Maeroff, G. I. (1997) *Scholarship assessed: Evaluation of the professoriate.* San Francisco, CA: Jossey-Bass.

Gmelch, W. H. (1995). The department chair's role in improving teaching. In P. Seldin & Associates, *Improving college teaching.* Bolton, MA: Anker.

Gmelch, W. H., & Miskin, V. D. (1995). *Chairing the academic department.* Thousand Oaks, CA: Sage.

Hecht, I. W., Higgerson, M. L., Gmelch, W. H., & Tucker, A. (1999). *The department chair as academic leader.* Phoenix, AZ: Oryx.

Higgerson, M. L. (1996). *Communication skills for department chairs.* Bolton, MA: Anker.

Higgerson, M. L. (1999). Building a climate conducive to effective teaching evaluation. In P. Seldin & Associates, *Changing practices in evaluating teaching: A practical guide to improved faculty performance and promotion/tenure decisions* (pp. 194–212). Bolton, MA: Anker.

Hutchings, P. (1996, November). The pedagogical colloquium: Focusing on teaching in the hiring process. *AAHE Bulletin, 49* (3), 3–6.

Leaming, D. R. (1998). *Academic leadership: A practical guide to chairing the department.* Bolton, MA: Anker.

Lenze, L. F. (1997). Small group instructional diagnosis (SGID). In K. T. Brinko and R. J. Menges, (Eds.), *Practically speaking: A sourcebook for instructional consultants in higher education* (pp. 143–146). Stillwater, OK: New Forums Press.

Licata, C. (2000). Post-tenure review. In A. F. Lucas and Associates, *Leading academic change: Essential roles for department chairs* (pp. 107–137). San Francisco, CA: Jossey-Bass.

Marincovich, M. (1999). Using student feedback to improve teaching. In P. Seldin and Associates, *Changing practices in evaluating teaching: A practical guide to improved faculty performance and promotion/tenure decisions* (pp. 45–69). Bolton, MA: Anker.

Massy, W. F., Wilger, A. K., & Colbeck, C. (1994, July/August). Overcoming "hollowed collegiality," *Change, 26* (4), 10–20.

Menges, R. J. (1999). Dilemmas of newly hired faculty. In R. J. Menges & Associates, *Faculty in new jobs: A guide to settling in, becoming established, and building institutional support* (pp. 19–38). San Francisco, CA: Jossey-Bass.

Menges, R. J., & Associates. (1999). *Faculty in new jobs: A guide to settling in, becoming established, and building institutional support.* San Francisco, CA: Jossey-Bass.

Menges, R. J., & Rando, W. (1989). What are your assumptions? *College Teaching, 37* (2), 54–60.

Perlman, B., & McCann, L. I. (1996). *Recruiting good college faculty: Practical advice for a successful search.* Bolton, MA: Anker.

Rice, R. E., Sorcinelli, M. D., & Austin, A. E. (2000). Heeding new voices: Academic careers for a new generation. *New Pathways Working Paper Series, 7.* Washington, DC: American Association for Higher Education.

Richlin, L., & Manning, B. (1995). *Improving a college/university teaching evaluation system: A comprehensive, developmental curriculum for faculty and administrators.* (2nd ed.). Pittsburgh, PA: Alliance Publishers.

Seldin, P., & Associates. (1999). *Changing practices in evaluating teaching: A practical guide to improved faculty performance and promotion/tenure decisions.* Bolton, MA: Anker.

Shulman, L. (1993, November/December). Teaching as community property: Putting an end to pedagogical solitude. *Change, 25* (6), 6–7.

Sorcinelli, M. D. (1992). New and junior faculty stress: Research and responses (pp. 27–37). In M. D. Sorcinelli & A. E. Austin, (Eds.), *Developing new and junior faculty. New Directions in Teaching and Learning,* No. 50. San Francisco, CA: Jossey-Bass.

Sorcinelli, M. D. (1995). How mentoring programs can improve teaching. In P. Seldin & Associates, *Improving college teaching* (pp. 125–136). Bolton, MA: Anker.

Tierney, W. G., & Rhoads, R. A. (1994). Faculty socialization as cultural process: A mirror of institutional commitment. *ASHE-ERIC Higher Education Report*, 6. Washington, DC: School of Education and Human Development, George Washington University.

Wergin, J. F. (1994). *Analyzing faculty workload.* New Directions for Institutional Research, No. 83. San Francisco, CA: Jossey-Bass.

# Building and Maintaining Morale

## 12

*Deryl R. Leaming*

> *The erosion of working conditions and the public's dissatisfaction with higher education factor into the morale equation. As we know, the public is demanding greater accountability, they complain about our workload, and they have little faith in the tenure system.*

As Thomas McDaniel points out in Chapter 6, faculty morale is hard to define. However, we can gauge when faculty are unhappy or disgruntled. If asked, they will quickly tell us how they feel about their jobs and working environment. If they're dissatisfied, we must first find out precisely what is bothering them. There are a number of ways to do this, but the best approach, in my judgment, is to simply ask faculty how satisfied they are in their job. If they are unhappy, we need to ask them what influences or causes these feelings.

While low faculty morale can do great damage to a department, it is seldom something that chairpersons deal with systematically or formally. One reason for this is that morale is a vague and complex concept. Moreover, many administrators believe there is nothing they can do about morale—even if it is bad and getting worse. In this chapter we will examine ways of assessing and talking about faculty morale and look at ways of dealing with it.

Johnsrud (1996, p. 1) defines morale as "the level of well-being that an individual or group is experiencing in reference to their worklife." She makes several other observations relative to the meaning of morale and our attempts to assess and deal with it. She says:

• The factors that administrative staff and faculty perceive as having an effect on morale can be measured.

• Morale exists in individuals and groups.

• Morale matters. This is based on the evidence that demonstrates that morale affects performance (pp. 4–5).

## CAUSES OF LOW MORALE

The causes of low morale are virtually unlimited, and some are beyond your control. We know, for example, that personal or family problems can lower morale. However, those that are strictly work related include the following:

### Salary and Related Matters
Given the reduced level of support for higher education in the United States in recent years, salary increases seldom exceed increases in the cost of living. Faculty members are understandably concerned over this. Johnsrud (p. 31) points out that "salaries that are perceived as being unfair lead to long-term dissatisfaction and can have a great effect on the faculty members' morale and effectiveness." But salary by itself is not the only issue: Fringe and retirement benefits matter. Faculty members expect support for professional development.

### Leadership
Many faculty members do not have good feelings about their university's leadership. Johnsrud (p. 34) says that "The confidence the faculty have in their leaders decreases with the distance the leaders are from the faculty (i.e., they have the most confidence in their chairs, less in their deans, even less in vice presidents and presidents, etc.)." Indeed, most studies show a definite decrease in confidence from chairs through boards of trustees.

### Collegial Relations with Department
Morale is influenced by the faculty member's relationship with the chair as well as their intellectual and social fit within the department. Faculty members who are difficult to get along with and who are themselves unhappy can create low morale for the entire department.

### Professional Worklife
Teaching, advising, and committee load bear on faculty members' assessment of their professional worklife. So does the level of support—whether clerical or technical—they receive. Even the parking situation can make a difference in a faculty member's professional worklife well-being.

### Faculty Governance
Faculty members want and expect to have some input both at the department level and the college and university levels. They want some say about budgets and personnel matters. They also expect protection of their academic freedom.

### Reward and Evaluation System
Faculty members look for rewards in their productivity in teaching and research. They also want clearly stated promotion and tenure expectations. Those who are not praised for doing a good job or who feel that tenure guidelines are ambiguous are likely to have low morale. Rosner (1997, p. 3) notes that, "[D]epartments with a good annual review system are also departments that run well and have much higher morale than those that don't."

### Quality of Students
Students at all levels who have ability and a strong work ethic make a difference in the way faculty members feel about their professional worklife.

### Support Service
A good library provides support for faculty as do the offices of research, faculty development, and computing. Even duplicating/printing facilities make a difference in the way faculty members assess their morale.

### Public Dissatisfaction
The erosion of working conditions and the public's dissatisfaction with higher education factor into the morale equation. As we know, the public wants greater accountability, a justification of our workload, and dissolution of tenure. Many believe that faculty members are arrogant and out-of-touch and that we don't deserve higher salaries or additional support. Moreover, many of those outside the academy—including our elected representatives—believe we are not doing a good job of educating students.

Tenure is under attack. The relevance of our research is being questioned. We also are being criticized for expanding programs and increasing tuition, and many states have developed policies intended to reduce program duplication. We look for support from some of those legislators who have been there for us in the past, but they are listening to their constituents. Unfortunately, many of their constituents are angry taxpayers who are insisting that taxes be lowered. Moreover, legislators have found that diverting higher education funds to other areas such as building prisons, maintaining roads, and fighting drug abuse does not raise too many objections from their constituents.

Whether justified or not, many nonacademics—including a fair number of legislators—perceive higher education as 1) having a watered-down curriculum, 2) being administration-heavy, 3) wasting taxpayers' dollars, 4) lacking a work ethic (in other words, having a soft job), and 5) getting paid too much for the hours we work.

Kerlin and Dunlap (1993, p. 58) found that:

> Retrenchment activities in higher education learning institutions in the U.S. has seriously undermined the morale of faculty members. There has been a notable deterioration in both education quality and faculty morale as a result of austerity measures initiated by administrative officials of educational institutions. Retrenchment and reorganization measures have also increased the incidence of occupation-related stress and overall job dissatisfaction among faculty members.

## IMPROVING FACULTY MORALE

Despite the many factors that seem to be conspiring to produce widespread low morale among faculty, there are many strategies administrators can employ to bolster morale.

### Communicate, Communicate, Communicate

Faculty members want to know what's going on and to feel a part of things. When you don't share information with them, they don't feel included.

Faculty members should know how money is allocated to the department and how it is spent. Keeping faculty members in the dark regarding budget matters contributes to their low morale.

Having regular faculty meetings and communicating in other ways on a regular basis helps morale.

### Let Faculty Members Know that They Are Appreciated

As a chairperson, you must be ever alert for the accomplishments of faculty so that you can congratulate them and let them know how much you appreciate their efforts. If faculty members do an especially good job supervising a project or chairing a committee, tell them how much you appreciate the time and effort they have given.

### Involve Faculty Members in Department Governance

All major policy decisions made at the department level should have faculty involvement. For example, if the department is expected to have a merit salary plan, faculty members should help to develop one. Likewise, departmental promotion and tenure guidelines should grow out of faculty committee work. Any way you can involve faculty in the major affairs of the department, the better off you will be.

Budget decisions should be made public, and department members should be asked for their input regarding academic program priorities and how funds should be spent. Most faculty members are aware that difficult choices have to be made, but they most resent not being included in the decision-making process.

### Establish a Tone of Cooperation

If all faculty members work to cooperate with each other, department morale will be enhanced. As chairperson, let faculty know that you expect cooperation. When a faculty member is ill or must be away from campus, do other faculty members willingly cover his or her classes. Are they willing to share equipment?

### Address the Issue of Starting Salaries

Very often these days, salary increases are small and mandated, which leaves you with little say or flexibility regarding salary increases. However, when you hire a new faculty member, you often have some latitude with their starting salary. I believe that you should stretch this to the limit by providing the best beginning salary possible. If you do this, however, you will want the support of current faculty. If you create inequities and do not bring them out into the open, you will create morale problems.

The topic of starting salaries needs to be addressed annually with faculty members during a regular faculty meeting. Discuss university policies on the topic and explain your position regarding exceptions to the beginning salaries at the various professorial ranks. Most universities have some mechanism that allows you to negotiate the starting salaries of all those you hire. During this general discussion with faculty members, provide those present with the rationale used by your university for establishing starting salaries and what, if anything, the president, provost, or dean has cited as valid reasons for exceptions to those figures.

For example, our provost has said repeatedly that when we are trying to hire new faculty members, our salary offer must be competitive with institutions comparable to ours. I establish ahead of time the kind of institutions the provost considers comparable. Then, if a search committee's first-choice candidate for a new associate professor comes to campus for an interview and reports that he or she has just received a job offer of $65,000 from one of these institutions, I am ready to act. I know that the candidate's other offer is $4,000 above our starting salary. At this point, I meet with each associate professor whose salary is lower than the offer the candidate has received. I inform them of the situation and discuss it with them. I even request that those individuals write me a memo in which they state they know about and support the salary offer we will extend to the candidate. Some faculty will certainly raise the question of fairness, and you must be prepared to explain and/or justify the circumstances that result in inequity. Some faculty will question why they, too, are not receiving that salary. You will need to further discuss this issue with them, but that is an issue separate from the situation at hand: the offer you want to extend to the candidate. You may need to meet with these faculty at a later point to discuss their own situations. The most important thing to secure now is their knowledge of what is happening and, if possible, their support. If you don't address the issue of starting salaries head on, you will most certainly encounter morale problems. In addition, should the candidate accept your offer, he or she could be shunned by disgruntled colleagues.

### Don't Permit Small Amounts of Money for Merit Raises to Divide Your Faculty

A small salary increase has been approved, and you are asked whether you want to provide across-the-board salary increases or merit increases. If the amount is small and you have a choice, I believe you ought to favor across-the-board increases. The problems inherent in giving merit increases simply are not worth the struggle when the dollars are less than the cost-of-living increases.

### Establish Clear Policies and Distribute Them Widely
Faculty have every right to be upset and dissatisfied with their professional worklife when policies are unclear and shifting. Whether these policies have to do with promotion and tenure or travel funds, faculty members need to know what the ground rules are. Moreover, it is especially important to be consistent with policy application and interpretation.

### Treat Faculty Members Fairly, without Favoritism, and with Respect
There always will be the temptation to reward some faculty members and punish others. This, of course, is permissible providing we reward and punish within acceptable and known policies. We shouldn't be governed by ad hoc policies.

You will find that you can have a positive influence on morale of faculty in your department if you treat all faculty members with respect and as professionals. Faculty members need to be told precisely what is expected of them and then trusted to do their jobs as long as they fulfill expectations.

No one likes to have another person looking over his or her shoulder, and most faculty members do not need excessive supervision; generally they will work more efficiently and productively if they are treated as professionals.

### Look for Consulting Opportunities for Faculty Members
In your position as chairperson, you often are called to recommend faculty for consulting positions. By recommending your faculty on the basis of their competence rather than how you feel about them personally, and by spreading these opportunities around, you can help with faculty morale.

### Work to Develop Positive Relations with Members of the Community
If you can develop a special tie to the local community, this special relationship will enrich the lives of individual faculty members. Involve community members in planning and decisions that might affect the community, do some outreach, educate the community

about what you do; part of the reason the public is so critical is that they feel we in higher education have been secretive.

### Assign Work Evenly
There is a temptation to assign work to those you know will do the work well and get it done on time. In doing so, however, you penalize the good workers and reward the slackers. This contributes to an unhealthy work environment that can produce low morale. We should make certain that all faculty members know they are expected to do their fair share of departmental work.

### Avoid the Unilateral Contract
Partin (1991) makes a good point that the unilateral contract can be one of the most insidious causes of low faculty morale. He says that a unilateral contract is "an unwritten, unspoken agreement between two parties—only one of whom is aware of its existence" (p. 1). Most chairpersons have had to deal with this problem at one time or another. We've all had faculty members who will take on most any assignment in the department. They are on virtually all department committees, they teach those night classes that must be covered, and they work hard at recruiting students. But they are not doing research or publishing—the things they must do for promotion. When they are not promoted, they want to know why you have not lived up to your end of the bargain.

We must make certain that faculty members are doing those things that will get them promotion and tenure and that they are not spending an inordinate amount of time on other assignments. Counsel those who are not making appropriate progress toward promotion and tenure.

### Create a Supportive Culture
Listening to faculty and being willing to discuss their concerns without judging goes far in creating a supportive culture. Also, going out of your way to find funds for faculty travel, covering for them when they are ill, or hearing what they say about their research projects help creative a supportive culture.

You need to do what you can to provide an environment and structure that adequately satisfies the human needs of your faculty. It should encourage new ideas, risk taking, and creativity. It should be an exciting, reinforcing environment that encourages and supports faculty members to engage in professional activities and challenges.

### Tolerate Differences
A university, of all places, ought to be a venue for challenging ideas and conventional wisdom. Faculty members should be encouraged to engage in invigorating intellectual debate with their colleagues. Likewise, they should be reminded that while professional differences of opinion are to be expected, these differences should not be carried over into their personal lives.

In most ways, faculty members love their jobs, but they are worried. "The rewards for their jobs are eroding; their autonomy to define their work priorities is under attack; and they do not see the current leadership or system of governance capable of protecting their personal and professional interests" (Johnsrud, p. 118).

You can do your part to enhance faculty morale by implementing low-cost and no-cost responses to faculty morale issues.

### Factors that Produce High Morale
In their study of faculty morale, Rice and Austin (1988) found four key features that produced high morale at 10 liberal arts colleges. They discovered that colleges where high morale exists share certain factors (p. 3):

1) They have distinctive organizational cultures which are carefully nurtured.

2) They have strong, participatory leadership that provides direction and purpose while conveying to faculty the empowering conviction that the college is theirs.

3) They have a firm sense of organizational momentum. They were colleges "on the move."

4) Faculty have an unusually compelling identification with the institution that incorporates and extends the other three characteristics contributing to high morale.

Rice and Austin (p. 58) list the following characteristics of high-morale colleges:
- Involvement of faculty in decision making
- Environment supportive of faculty and their work
- Collaborative environment
- Encouragement of risk taking and new ideas

- Significant anticipatory long-range planning
- High proportion of faculty who attended liberal arts colleges
- Gap between perceived and desired involvement in decision-making is narrow
- Individual career orientations are likely to be accommodated by the organization
- Administrators and faculty have relatively similar views about the academic workplace

## THE CHAIRPERSON'S ROLE IN MAINTAINING MORALE

Studies of faculty morale show that faculty members, by and large, lack confidence in their institutions' leadership, and that is a major cause of low morale. However, while faculty members lack confidence in the upper levels of leadership, they have the most confidence in their chairpersons. "These findings suggest that faculty feel more trust for those they know better and presumably communicate with more frequently. This finding may serve to alert senior administrators to the need for increased communication and interaction with all members of the campus community" (Johnsrud, 118). Increasing the level and quality of communication is a forceful vehicle for improving faculty morale. Another finding on the study of faculty morale that is important for department chairpersons to know about is that "Relations existing between the chair and faculty members and within the department as a whole are crucial to the morale of faculty" (Johnsrud, 120).

> One of the primary roles of the department chair should be to build and nurture a positive collegial climate in the department for all faculty. To accomplish this objective, the selection of chairs should be monitored carefully and ongoing training instituted. Training should include attention to issues of professional work climate, professional development, academic support, evaluation, sexual harassment, and affirmative action. Department chairs should also be trained to recognize and confront inappropriate conduct. Chairs are in key positions to recognize and eliminate discrimination at the department level. (Johnsrud, 120)

Low faculty morale may in fact be difficult to define, but not impossible. As chairs and deans, we must be aware of factors that contribute to low or high morale, and we must do what we can to bolster the latter. There is much we can do, and the rewards are significant, but the work is constant and ongoing. Bolstering low morale and keeping high morale high requires vigilance, determination, and sensitivity.

## REFERENCES

Johnsrud, L. K. (1996). *Maintaining morale: A guide to assessing the morale of midlevel administrators and faculty.* Washington, DC: College and University Personnel Association.

Kerlin, S. P., & Dunlap, D. M. (1993, May/June). For richer, for poorer: Faculty morale in periods of austerity and retrenchment. *Journal of Higher Education, 64* (3).

Partin, B. L. (1991, Fall). The unilateral contract: A faculty morale nightmare. *The Department Chair, 2* (2), 1, 20.

Rice, R. E., & Austin, A. E. (1988, March/April). High faculty morale. *Change.*

Rosner, F. (1997, May). Post-tenure review: Accountability in Texas. *Academic Leader.*

# Putting All the Pieces Together to Be a Better People Manager and Leader

## 13

*Deryl R. Leaming*

> *Your ethics must be beyond reproach. Remember that no matter how much you may dislike the idea of being a role model, you are one. Moreover, if you expect to have the trust and respect of faculty and staff members, then you must possess honesty and all other qualities of strong ethical character.*

Today's chairs and deans spend more time dealing with the problems of faculty and staff members than they do on any other single matter. If you have a large department or are a dean, the array of personnel problems you face is staggering, and many of them have no easy answers. About the time you think you've dealt with every known problem, a new one crops up. And unless you possess considerable leadership skills, you will not likely survive as a chair or dean unless you can master the people-handling problems that you face day in and day out.

When I was a liberal arts dean of a college with numerous departments, never a day went by when there were not faculty members who were in the hospital, or so it seemed. I had faculty members who tried to commit suicide. In this college there were faculty members who had serious substance abuse problems. Divorce was common. Sexual harassment charges seemed to be weekly fare.

In this book, seasoned administrators have labored to put down their thoughts about leading and managing faculty and staff. These individuals have more than 200 combined years of administrative experience. Furthermore, they are exceptionally talented individuals and good problem solvers. In addition to the good advice you've been given by these writers regarding managing and providing leadership for faculty and staff, I will attempt in this chapter to summarize some of the pointers that will help you in your role as chair or dean.

Even though this is the final chapter, I believe it's an ideal time to pause for a moment to develop a brief definition of the word leadership. You should, when time permits, take a look at the variety of different definitions for the word in the many books written on the subject. Let me turn to James MacGregor Burns (1978), who, in my judgment, offers so many useful ideas about leadership. He discusses transactional, transformational, and moral leadership; it is the latter I have selected:

> The last concept, *moral leadership*, concerns me the most. By this term I mean, first, that the leaders and the led have a relationship not only of power but of mutual needs, aspirations, and values; second, that in responding to leaders, followers have adequate knowledge of alternative leaders and programs and the capacity to choose among those alternatives; and, third, that leaders take responsibility for their commitments—if they promise certain kinds of economic, social, and political change, they assume leadership in the bringing about of that change. (p. 4)

Burns's definition of moral leadership mirrors my ideas about what academic leadership should be. It's from this perspective that I approach ideas about leaders and leadership.

Malcomb Gladwell (2000) in his book, *The Tipping Point*, introduces interesting ideas that are important for leaders. As Gladwell explains, ". . . [T]he world of the Tipping Point is a place where the unexpected becomes expected, where radical change is more than a possibility. It is—contrary to all expectations—a certainty" (p. 14). Gladwell's ideas center on the notion that "little changes can somehow have big effects" (p. 10).

One encouraging belief that Gladwell advances is "a bedrock belief that change is possible, that people can radically transform their behavior or beliefs in the face of the right kind of impetus" (p. 258). This, of course, should encourage all academic leaders. He also adds that "we are actually powerfully influenced by our surroundings, our immediate context, and the personalities around us," which is an idea most of us accept without question.

## BE A CHANGE AGENT

Every good leader must be able to create a vision and communicate it to those who work with him or her. "The effective leader must assemble for the organization a vision of a desired future state. While this task may be shared and developed with other key members of the organization, it remains the core responsibility and cannot be delegated," write Bennis and Nanus (1997, p. 131).

I believe leaders want to improve whatever situation they find themselves in—regardless of the condition. If leaders discovered themselves in Utopia, they would undoubtedly find a way to inspire others to build on the existing social order in an effort to improve on it. In his clever book, *Who Moved My Cheese*, Spencer Johnson (1998) tells a story about change. One character discovers little tidbits that help him deal with change. After he is finally able to overcome lethargy and arrogance, he reluctantly sets out on a quest for cheese. Cheese is a "metaphor for what we want to have in life, whether it is a job, a relationship, money, a big house, freedom, health, recognition, spiritual peace, or even activity like jogging or golf" (p. 12). During his journey to find the cheese, the character (Haw) leaves messages for his friend (Hem) who refuses to change, hoping that the things he discovers might help Hem should he change his mind and begin his own search for the cheese. In the end Haw summarizes what he's learned. This summary becomes "The Handwriting on the Wall." Here's what Haw had learned (p. 72):
   1. Change happens.
   2. Anticipate change.
   3. Monitor change.
   4. Adapt to change quickly.
   5. Change.
   6. Enjoy Change!
   7. Be ready to change quickly and enjoy it again and again.

Leaders create a climate for change, and they invite others to go where they would not likely go without a leader. They see opportunities where others don't, and they take risks. They are builders. There is a litany of ideas that defines leaders and leadership, but continuing this attempt would, in the final analysis, lead me to listing trademarks and traits that define most leaders. The following are but a few that may help you to successfully lead and manage people:

## USE COMMON SENSE

There are times when you'll need to call upon the decision-making that is controlled by simple common sense. What should I do in this situation? What makes good sense given what I know about the situation? What values do I hold that will guide me with this decision? What is the practical way of my dealing with this problem? These are all good questions that most of us ask from time to time, and using good common sense will help us answer them and make the right decisions.

I like the simplicity that James Evans (2001) brings to the notion of leadership. Evans, who is the president and CEO of Best Western International, addresses ideas about leadership from experience and study of the subject. He says that common-sense leadership is "the ability to do the right thing at the right moment, most of the time" (p. 1). Makes common sense to me.

## SERVE YOUR CONSTITUENTS

Use your personal and position power to serve faculty, staff, and students. If you use it to your own self-aggrandizement, then others will see this, and they will work against you. You will not have their respect, and they won't do their best work for you. Lyles (2000) writes that "People who rely on negative, coercive power try to get all they can usually by making others feel weaker. They fight for positional authority. They fight for status. They fight to keep others from getting power, because they think the more power others have, the less powerful they themselves will be. The problem with that in today's world is that people don't respond to this kind of power like they used to. Formal authority as a source of power has eroded" (p. 40).

Remember, always, that students are essential constituents—keep their interests at the forefront. I've settled more faculty disputes by asking these questions: "What's best for our students in this situation? Are we properly serving the student interests by our actions?"

## BE FLEXIBLE

Policies conceived and developed by university officials have good reason behind them. But sometimes it makes good sense to apply common sense to them, particularly when others are not harmed by the decision you make. Caroselli (2000, p. 53) says, "If we regard leadership on a continuum—with the autocratic leader at one end, the laissez-faire at the other, and the democratic or participative leader in the middle—where would you place yourself?" The point here is that good leaders must remain flexible.

## HAVE COMPASSION

"How would I like to be treated?" is always a good guiding question whenever you are dealing with complex situations that involve people. If I were in this situation, how would I want my dean or department chair to react, and what would I like him or her to do? In my judgment, few things enhance a leader more than the qualities of compassion and empathy. I know those whom I most enjoy working for, and the ones I will work hardest for and do my best for are compassionate leaders. As Evans (2001) points out, "Common sense leaders know that it's only common sense to treat their people with professional and personal respect, making them feel part of the plan, see the vision" (p. 2).

Any time you and your colleagues set out on a mission that is time-consuming and requires massive amounts of effort, your faculty and staff members will become exhausted. As Kouzes and Posner (1995) suggest, they'll also become frustrated and disenchanted. It's a leader's job to give colleagues encouragement. Kouzes and Posner (p. 14) go on to say, "If people observe a charlatan making noisy pretenses, they turn away. But genuine acts of caring can uplift the spirits and draw people forward." Encouraging the heart is a worthy goal and will pay dividends, and those who engage in the effort will gain considerable respect.

## TREAT EACH PERSON AS AN INDIVIDUAL

This means treating each person differently, of course, and being fair toward all other faculty members and staff. Each person who comes to you with problems sees those problems as real. They stand in the way of his or her being happy, productive, or satisfied. Listen carefully and know that this person isn't really concerned about the problems of others; he or she needs to have his or her own problems resolved.

Remember that every faculty and staff member has worth and deserves your undivided attention—even if the individual is difficult. There are times when we may feel like discounting the worth of others just because of personality conflicts. We must guard against that. It doesn't become leaders when they fail to see the worth of all who are working with or for them.

## BE HONEST

Honesty is essential to good leadership, in all areas. It is particularly critical in the area of faculty evaluation. Keep in mind that honest performance appraisals are worth the effort and critical to smart management and strong leadership. Recognize, however, that you're not likely to fundamentally change many of your faculty. That's the reason that early and honest performance appraisals are so critical. If the person who is hired turns out to be an incompetent teacher and an inadequate scholar, then that's probably what you'll be stuck with unless you decide to terminate him or her before the person earns tenure. One of the valid points Buckingham and Coffman (1999) make over and over is "People don't change that much. Don't waste time trying to put what was left out. Try to draw out what was left in. That is hard enough" (p. 79).

Do not give performance appraisals short shrift. In the end, you and others in your department or college—and perhaps more especially your students—are the losers. Even when a leader is doing a good job of providing an honest performance, appraisal is time-consuming. Believe me, you'll pay dearly if it's not done. Moreover, you lose credibility as a leader when this is not done well.

## HAVE ETHICS THAT ARE BEYOND REPROACH

Remember that no matter how much you may dislike the idea of being a role model, you are one. Moreover, if you expect to have the trust and respect of faculty and staff members, then you must possess honesty and all other qualities of strong ethical character. Bethel (1990) defines ethics as "High standards of honesty and honorable dealings based on our morals. Ethics are a set of basic working tenets for life and business. How we act and what we do, our methods of functioning, and how we apply our moral judgment is our ethical behavior. Ethics are applications" (p. 2). She goes on to say, rightly I think, that "The stronger our ethical behavior, the better leaders we become."

## EMPOWER OTHERS

As I attempted to point out in Chapter 4, accomplishing a goal or realizing a vision can't be done alone. It takes teamwork, and therefore it's important that you enable others to act. As Kouzes and Posner (1995) point out, "The individuals in our study recognized that grand dreams don't become significant realities through actions of a single leader. Leadership is a team effort" (p. 11).

Another point that Gladwell (2000) makes that seems important to the notion of team effort is that merely by manipulating the size of a group, we can dramatically improve its receptivity to new ideas. By tinkering with the presentation of information, we can significantly improve its stickiness. Simply by finding and reaching those few special people who hold so much social power, we can shape the course of social epidemics. In the end, Tipping Points are a reaffirmation of the potential for change and the power of intelligent action (p. 259).

Ken Blanchard (Lyles, 2000), author of *Unleash Your Power Today*, writes in the foreword of Dick Lyle's book, *Winning Ways: 4 Secrets for Getting Great Results by Working Well with People*, "Today, the key to success is one's ability to exercise peer leadership. The most successful individuals shine because of their ability to influence, empower, and energize others" (p. x).

## GET AROUND

Get around your department or college. It's important for you to know what's going on and to listen to what your faculty and staff are talking about. They need to have you inquire about their work. Sometimes it's important just to stop by to ask how their classes are going and to listen to anything they have to say. Cohen (1990, p. 50) says that by seeing and being seen you can:

- Know what's going on in your organization every day
- Help those who need help
- Get help from those who can supply it
- Discover the real problems
- Uncover opportunities you didn't know existed
- Praise and recognize those who deserve it
- Correct or discipline those who need it
- Get your word out fast
- Communicate your vision for the organization
- Ensure everyone understands your goals and objectives.

Deans and department chairs must have the support of their faculty and staff members if they are to accomplish their goals. Without the support of faculty and staff in your college or department, it is impossible to make progress, accomplish your goals, or see your vision become reality.

Good leaders also get around to other campus leaders. Most other deans and department chairs are willing to give you their best advice. Perhaps they've faced similar problems and worked out solutions that are agreeable. We must not think that seeking the wisdom of others is a sign of weakness. All good leaders turn to others if they believe others can help them realize their vision or accomplish an objective.

## BE SECURE IN WHO YOU ARE

We cannot be good leaders if we are insecure people. Such individuals tend to be thin-skinned and too often are timid about doing some things because they are fearful they will make mistakes. Buckingham and Coffman (1999) quote a person who is leaving a company because she has to deal with an insecure manager: "He's not a bad man. He's just not a manager. He's insecure, and I don't think you can be insecure and [be] a good manager. It makes him compete with his own people. It makes him boast about his high-style living, when he should be listening to us. And he plays these silly little power games to show us who's the boss" (p. 35).

## UNDERSTAND YOURSELF

This book started with the concept: We must know and understand ourselves if we are to know and understand others, which is important for any leader. Bennis (1989, p. 54) says, "Know thyself, then, means separating who you are and who you want to be from what the world thinks you are and wants you to be." It is vital for our own self-worth and security to know who we are. Knowing and understanding yourself takes a lot of work, and it never stops, but good leaders know themselves, which gives them the self-confidence they need to be decisive.

## THINK BIG

Remember that if we can dream it, it can happen. Of course if this is true, we must manage faculty and staff problems so that those in our department or college can help us reach our dreams. Leaders know where they want their department or college to be in the future, and they have the ability to communicate that vision to others. As Evans points out, "Without that ability [to communicate], they are not leaders—just dreamers" (p. 4).

In the academy, teamwork is essential and as a dean or chair you have the responsibility to see that every faculty and staff member is a part of the team. Even if one faculty member becomes a nonteam player, the department suffers to some extent. The strong dean or department chair recognizes the need for team work, and he or she also knows how and when to delegate.

Giving time to helping faculty and staff members is never a waste. It's part of your job. Solving their problems is both critical and fulfilling. It marks you as a leader. It's tempting at times to give up on certain faculty members, but you can't, in my judgment. There have been times when I wanted to, but I have found that persistent attention helped them realize that I had no intention of giving up on them. Moreover, I discovered that with some, I have achieved success. I've been able to improve the productivity of some, and they began taking pride in their work. Others noticed and commented to them on their change, which served to reinforce their changed behavior. Students and staff did the same. To me there are few more satisfying things as a leader than helping faculty members improve their behavior and self-worth. And as newly committed team players, they have a powerful influence on other faculty and staff members. I must confess that I've not always been successful. I'm still working on some. I'll keep trying; I'm not ready to give up.

Leadership has many rewards. Few are more satisfying than seeing your faculty and staff members working together for the good of the college or department and being focused to accomplish established goals. When this happens, the disappointments fade and hope revives us.

There is no one answer for most problems—even when the problems seem identical. You'll find that what works one time will fail another time. When that happens we must draw on our experience to look for other solutions. Unfortunately there are times when nothing seems to work, and then there are serendipitous moments that we can be thankful for. Somehow—almost by accident, it seems—we hit upon something that seems to satisfy the problem of the particular faculty or staff member. Fortune has smiled upon us. I suspect it happens because we care, because we want to make a difference, because we are leaders.

Leadership is one of the most studied fields. Yet, there is so much to learn. Leadership as a concept is sometimes hard to wrap your mind around. Good leaders come in different shapes and sizes and their approaches can be very different. Some leadership approaches that work well for some will not work at all for others. Despite this, there are some common principles that are agreed upon by most scholars. This book attempts to discuss these. We hope they help in your job of developing strategies for leadership and management of your faculty and staff.

## REFERENCES

Bennis, W. (1989). *On becoming a leader*. Cambridge, MA: Perseus Books.

Bennis, W., & Nanus, B. (1997). *Leadership: Strategies for taking charge*. New York, NY: Harper Business.

Bethel, S. (1990). *Making a difference: 12 qualities that make you a leader*. New York, NY: Berkley Books.

Buckingham, M., & Coffman, C. (1999). *First, break all the rules: What the world's greatest managers do differently.* New York, NY: Simon & Schuster.

Burns, J. M. (1978). *Leadership.* New York, NY: Harper & Row.

Caroselli, M. (2000). *Leadership skills for managers.* New York, NY: McGraw-Hill.

Cohen, W. (1990). *The art of the leader.* Paramus, NJ: Prentice Hall.

Deem, R. (2001). *New managerialism and the management of UK universities.* Unpublished report.

Evans, J. P. (Spring, 2001). Common sense leadership for uncommon times. *The Online Journal of Academic Leadership.* http://www.academicleadership.org.

Gladwell, M. (2000). *The tipping point.* Boston, MA: Little, Brown.

Johnson, S. (1998). *Who moved my cheese?* New York, NY: G. P. Putnam.

Kouzes, J., & Posner, B. (1995). *The leadership challenge.* San Francisco, CA: Jossey-Bass.

Lyles, D. (2000). *Winning ways: 4 secrets for getting great results by working well with people.* New York, NY: G. P. Putnam.

Adams, S. (1996) *The Dilbert principle.* New York, NY: Harper Collins.

Adams, S. (1997). *Casual day has gone too far.* Kansas City, MO: Andrews & McMeel.

Altman, H. B. (2000). The departmental voice in the faculty reward system. In A. F. Lucas and Associates, *Leading academic change: Essential roles for department chairs* (pp. 138–157). San Francisco, CA: Jossey-Bass.

American Council on Education, American Association of University Professors, & United Educators Insurance Risk Retention Group. (2000). *Good practice in tenure evaluation.* World Wide Web: http://acenet.edu/bookstore/.

*The American Faculty Poll* (2000). TIAA-CREF and Chicago. New York, NY: National Opinion Research Center.

Anderson, P. A., & Guerrero, L. K. (1989, February). *Avoiding communication: Verbal and nonverbal dimensions of defensiveness.* Paper presented at the meeting of the Western Speech Communication Association, Spokane, WA.

Angelo, T., & Cross, K. P. (1993). *Classroom assessment techniques.* (2nd ed.). San Francisco, CA: Jossey-Bass.

Arreola, R. A. (2000). *Developing a comprehensive faculty evaluation system: A handbook for college faculty and administrators on designing and operating a comprehensive faculty evaluation system* (2nd ed.). Bolton, MA: Anker.

Ashforth, B. E., & Lee, R. T. (1990). Defensive behavior in organizations: A preliminary model. *Human Relations, 43* (7), 621–648.

Astin, A., & Astin, H. (2000). *Leadership reconsidered: Engaging higher education in social change.* Battle Creek, MI: W. K. Kellogg Foundation.

Austin, A. E., Rice, R. E., & Splete, A. P. (1991). *A good place to work: Sourcebook for the academic workplace.* Washington, DC: Council of Independent Colleges.

Avolio, B. J. (1999). *Full leadership development: Building the vital forces in organizations.* Thousand Oaks, CA: Sage.

Baker, W. H. (1980). Defensiveness in communication: Its causes, effects, and cures. *Journal of Business Communication, 17* (3), 33–43.

Baldwin, R. J. (Ed.). (1985) *Incentives for faculty vitality.* San Francisco, CA: Jossey-Bass.

Baldwin, R. J. (1989). Super Highway or Scenic Route: What Is the Best Path to Faculty Vitality? In H. B. Altman (Ed.), *Faculty vitality in Kentucky: Proceedings of the fourth annual conference on faculty development in Kentucky higher education.* Louisville, KY: University of Louisville Center for Faculty and Staff Development.

Barbuto, J. E., & Scholl, R. W. (1999). Development of new scales to measure an integrative taxonomy of motivation sources. *Psychological Reports, 82,* 1011–1022.

Bass, B. M. (1985). *Leadership and performance beyond expectations.* New York, NY: Free Press.

Bennett, J. B., & Figuli, D. J. (1993). *Enhancing departmental leadership: The roles of the chairperson.* Phoenix, AZ: Oryx.

Bennis, W. (1989). *On becoming a leader.* Cambridge, MA: Perseus Books.

Bennis, W. (1997). *Managing people is like herding cats.* Provo, UT: Executive Excellence Publishing.

Bennis, W., & Nanus, B. (1997). *Leadership: Strategies for taking charge.* New York, NY: Harper Business.

Bensimon, E. M., Ward, K., & Sanders, K. (2000). *The department chair's role in developing new faculty into teachers and scholars.* Bolton, MA: Anker.

Bergquist, W., & Phillips, S. (1995). *Developing human and organizational resources: A comprehensive manual.* Point Arena, CA: Peter Magnussen Press.

Bess, J. (2000). *Teaching alone, teaching together.* San Francisco, CA: Jossey-Bass.

Bethel, S. (1990). *Making a difference: 12 qualities that make you a leader.* New York, NY: Berkley Books.

Bissell, B. (1989). *Dealing with difficult people* (video). Richmond, VA: W. R. Shirah.

Bland, C. J., & Bergquist, W. H. (1997). *The vitality of senior faculty members: Snow on the roof—fire in the furnace.* ASHE-ERIC Higher Education Report, 25-7. Washington, D.C.: Graduate School of Education and Human Development, George Washington University.

Bland, C. J., & Schmitz, C. C. (1988). Faculty vitality on review. *Journal of Higher Education, 59* (2), 190–224.

Boice, R. (1990). Mentoring new faculty: A program for implementation. *Journal of Staff, Program, and Organization Development, 8* (3), 143–260.

Boice, R. (1992). *The new faculty member.* San Francisco, CA: Jossey-Bass.

Bolton, R. (1986). *People skills.* New York, NY: Touchstone.

Brand, M. (2000, November/December). Changing faculty roles in research universities: Using the Pathways strategy. *Change, 32* (6), 42–45.

Braskamp, L. A., & Ory, J. C. (1994). *Assessing faculty work: Enhancing individual and institutional performance.* San Francisco, CA: Jossey-Bass.

Bringle, R. (1999). *Service at Indiana University:* Defining, documenting, and evaluating. Indianapolis, IN: Center for Public Service and Leadership.

Brinko, K. T. (1993). The practice of giving feedback to improve instruction: What is effective? *Journal of Higher Education, 64* (5), 54–68.

Brown, W. (1985). *13 fatal errors managers make and how you can avoid them.* New York, NY: Berkley Books.

Buckingham, M., & Coffman, C. (1999). *First, break all the rules: What the world's greatest managers do differently.* New York, NY: Simon & Schuster.

Burns, J. M. (1978). *Leadership.* New York, NY: Harper & Row.

Caroselli, M. (2000). *Leadership skills for managers.* New York, NY: McGraw-Hill.

Centra, J. A. (1993). *Reflective faculty evaluation: Enhancing teaching and determining faculty effectiveness.* San Francisco, CA: Jossey-Bass.

Chism, N. V. N. (1999). *Peer review of teaching: A sourcebook.* Bolton, MA: Anker.

Chodron, P. (2001). *The places that scare you.* Boston, MA: Shambala.

Clark, D. J., & Bekey, J. (1979). Use of small groups in instructional evaluation. *POD Quarterly, 1,* 87–95.

Clark, S. M., & Lewis, D. R. (Ed.). (1985). *Faculty vitality and institutional productivity: Critical perspectives for higher education.* New York, NY: Teachers College Press.

Cohen, W. (1990). *The art of the leader.* Paramus, NJ: Prentice Hall.

Conrad, C. (1985). *Strategic organizational communication: Culture, situations, and adaptations.* New York, NY: Holt, Rinehart, and Winston.

Conrad, C., & Poole, M. S. (1998). *Strategic organizational communication: Into the twenty-first century* (4th ed.). Fort Worth, TX: Harcourt Brace.

Council of Colleges of Arts and Sciences. (1992). *The ethics of recruitment and faculty appointment.* Columbus, OH: The Ohio State University.

Covey, S. R. (1989). *The seven habits of highly effective people.* New York, NY: Simon & Schuster.

Creswell, J. W., Wheeler, D. W., Seagren, A. T., Egly, N. J., & Beyer, K. D. (1990). *The academic chairperson's handbook.* Lincoln, NE: University of Nebraska Press.

Daft, R. L. (2001). *Organization theory and design* (7th ed.). Cincinnati, OH: Southwestern.

Deem, R. (2001). *New managerialism and the management of UK universities.* Unpublished report.

Delbecq, A. L., Van de Ven, A. H., & Gustafson, D. H. (1975). *Group techniques for program planning.* Glenville, IL: Scott Foresman.

Ellison, S. (1994). Powerful, non-defensive communication home page. [online] .Available: http://www.pndc.com/summary .htm.

*Employee assistance program: Supervisor's guidebook.* (n.d.). Hershey, PA: Hershey Foods Corp.

Evans, J. P. (Spring, 2001). Common sense leadership for uncommon times. *The Online Journal of Academic Leadership.* http://www.academicleadership.org.

Finnegan, D. E., Webster, D., & Gamson, Z. F. (Ed.). (1996). *Faculty and faculty issues in colleges and universities* (2nd ed.). Needham Heights, MA: Simon & Schuster.

Gibb, J. (1961). Defensive communication. *Journal of Communication, 11* (3), 141–148.

Gladwell, M. (2000). *The tipping point.* Boston, MA: Little, Brown.

Glassick, C. E., Huber, M. T., & Maeroff, G. I. (1997) *Scholarship assessed: Evaluation of the professoriate.* San Francisco, CA: Jossey-Bass.

Gmelch, W. H. (1995). The department chair's role in improving teaching. In P. Seldin & Associates, *Improving college teaching.* Bolton, MA: Anker.

Gmelch, W. H., & Miskin, V. D. (1995). *Chairing the academic department.* Thousand Oaks, CA: Sage.

Hammond, S. A. (1996). *The thin book of appreciative inquiry.* Plano, TX: Thin Book.

Hammons, J. O., & Murry, J. W. (1995). Applying group decision-making to meetings. *The Department Chair,* (5) 3, 10-11.

Hecht, I. W., Higgerson, M. L., Gmelch, W. H., & Tucker, A. (1999). *The department chair as academic leader.* Phoenix, AZ: Oryx.

Higgerson, M. L. (1996). *Communication skills for department chairs.* Bolton, MA: Anker.

Higgerson, M. L. (1999). Building a climate conducive to effective teaching evaluation. In P. Seldin & Associates, *Changing practices in evaluating teaching: A practical guide to improved faculty performance and promotion/tenure decisions* (pp. 194–212). Bolton, MA: Anker.

Hutchings, P. (November 1996). The pedagogical colloquium: Focusing on teaching in the hiring process. *AAHE Bulletin, 49* (3), 3–6.

Johnson, S. (1998). *Who moved my cheese?* New York, NY: G. P. Putnam.

Johnsrud, L. K. (1996). *Maintaining morale: A guide to assessing the morale of midlevel administrators and faculty.* Washington, DC: College and University Personnel Association.

Kerlin, S. P., & Dunlap, D. M. (1993, May/June). For richer, for poorer: Faculty morale in periods of austerity and retrenchment. *Journal of Higher Education, 64* (3).

Kotter, J. P. (1990). *A force for change: How leadership differs from management.* New York, NY: Free Press.

Kouzes, J. M., & Posner, B. Z. (1995). *The leadership challenge: How to keep getting extraordinary things done in organizations.* San Francisco, CA: Jossey-Bass.

Leaming, D. R. (1998). *Academic leadership: A practical guide to chairing the department.* Bolton, MA: Anker.

Lenze, L. F. (1997). Small group instructional diagnosis (SGID). In K. T. Brinko and R. J. Menges (Eds.), *Practically speaking: A sourcebook for instructional consultants in higher education* (pp. 143–146). Stillwater, OK: New Forums Press.

Leonard, R. (1980). *The defensiveness cycle.* Symposium conducted at the North Carolina Public Manager's Program, Raleigh, NC.

Licata, C. (2000). Post-tenure review. In A. F. Lucas and Associates, *Leading academic change: Essential roles for department chairs* (pp. 107–137). San Francisco, CA: Jossey-Bass.

Lucas, A. F. (1994). *Strengthening departmental leadership. A team-building guide for chairs in colleges and universities.* San Francisco, CA: Jossey-Bass.

Lyles, D. (2000). *Winning ways: 4 secrets for getting great results by working well with people.* New York, NY: G. P. Putnam.

Mallard, K. (2000, Winter). Lending an ear: The chair's role as listener. *The Department Chair: A Resource for Academic Administrators, 10,* 11–13.

Marchese, T. J., & Lawrence, J. F. (1989). *The search committee handbook: A guide to recruiting administrators.* Washington, DC: American Association of Higher Education.

Marincovich, M. (1999). Using student feedback to improve teaching. In P. Seldin & Associates, *Changing practices in evaluating teaching: A practical guide to improved faculty performance and promotion/tenure decisions* (pp. 45–69). Bolton, MA: Anker.

Martin, R. P. (1980, September). *Cognitive factors in consultee defensiveness.* Paper presented at the meeting of the American Psychological Association, Montreal, Quebec, Canada.

Massy, W. F., Wilger, A. K., & Colbeck, C. (1994, July/August). Overcoming "hollowed collegiality," *Change, 26* (4), 10–20.

McDaniel, T. R. (1999, November). Faculty morale: A dean's duty? *Academic Leader.*

McDaniel, T. R. (2000, January). President-faculty relations: A dean's dilemma? *Academic Leader.*

McDaniel, T. R. (2000, October). Dilbert on deaning. *Academic Leader.*

McDaniel, T. R. (2000, November). Dean–department chair relations. *Academic Leader.*

McDaniel, T. R. (2001, February). The dean's detractors. *Academic Leader.*

Menges, R. J. (1999). Dilemmas of newly hired faculty. In R. J. Menges & Associates, *Faculty in new jobs: A guide to settling in, becoming established, and building institutional support* (pp. 19–38). San Francisco, CA: Jossey-Bass.

Menges, R. J., & Associates. (1999). *Faculty in new jobs: A guide to settling in, becoming established, and building institutional support.* San Francisco, CA: Jossey-Bass.

Menges, R. J., & Rando, W. (1989). What are your assumptions? *College Teaching, 37* (2), 54–60.

Merry, U., & Allerhand, M. E. (1977). *Developing teams and organizations.* Reading, MA: Addison-Wesley.

Mosvick, R. K., & Nelson, R. B. (1987). *We've got to start meeting like this!* Glenview, IL: Scott, Foresman and Co.

Myers, M. T., & Myers. G. E. (1982). *Managing by communication: An organizational approach.* New York, NY: McGraw-Hill.

Nikola, M. P. (1999). Maximize departmental collaboration through effective facilitation and meeting management techniques. *The Department Chair,* (9) 3, 6–7.

North, J. (1980, Summer). Guidelines and Strategies for Conducting Meetings. *POD Quarterly, 2,* 79–91.

Oncken, Jr. W., Wass, D. L., & Covey, S. R. (1999, November-December). Time management: Who's got the monkey? *Harvard Business Review, 77* (6), 178–187.

Partin, B. L. (1991, Fall). The unilateral contract: A faculty morale nightmare. *The Department Chair,* 2 (2), 1, 20.

Perlman, B., & McCann, L. I. (1996). *Recruiting good college faculty: Practical advice for a successful search.* Bolton, MA: Anker.

Peters, T. J., & Waterman, R. H., Jr. (1982). *In search of excellence: Lessons from America's best-run companies.* New York, NY: Harper & Row.

Peters, T. (1988). *Thriving on chaos: Handbook for a management revolution.* New York, NY: Harper and Row.

Rice, R. E., & Austin, A. E. (1988, March/April). High faculty morale. *Change.*

Rice, R. E., Sorcinelli, M. D., & Austin, A. E. (2000). Heeding new voices: Academic careers for a new generation. *New Pathways Working Paper Series, 7.* Washington, DC: American Association for Higher Education.

Richlin, L., & Manning, B. (1995). *Improving a college/university teaching evaluation system: A comprehensive, developmental curriculum for faculty and administrators* (2nd ed.). Pittsburgh, PA: Alliance Publishers.

Rogers, C. (1989). *On being a person: A therapist's view of psychotherapy.* Boston, MA: Houghton Mifflin.

Rojstaczer, S. (1999). *Gone for good: Tales of university life after the golden age.* New York, NY: Oxford University Press.

Rosner, F. (1997, May). Post-tenure review: Accountability in Texas. *Academic Leader, 13* (5), 3.

Sargent, A. (1983). *The androgynous manager.* New York, NY: AMACOM.

Satir, V. (1972). *People making.* Palo Alto, CA: Science and Behavior Books.

Sax, L. J., Astin, A. W., Korn, W. S., & Gilmartin, S. K. (1999). *The American college teacher.* Los Angeles, CA: Higher Education Research Institute.

Schein, E. H. (1978). *Career dynamics: Matching individual and organizational needs.* Reading, MA: Addison-Wesley.

Schuster, J. H., & Wheeler, D. W. (Ed.). (1990). *Enhancing faculty careers: Strategies for development and renewal.* San Francisco, CA: Jossey-Bass.

Seldin, P., & Associates. (1999). *Changing practices in evaluating teaching: A practical guide to improved faculty performance and promotion/tenure decisions.* Bolton, MA: Anker.

Shulman, L. (November/December, 1993). Teaching as community property: Putting an end to pedagogical solitude. *Change, 25* (6), 6–7.

Sorcinelli, M. D. (1992). New and junior faculty stress: Research and responses (pp. 27–37). In M. D. Sorcinelli & A. E. Austin (Eds.), *Developing new and junior faculty.* New Directions in Teaching and Learning, No. 50. San Francisco, CA: Jossey-Bass.

Sorcinelli, M. D. (1995). How mentoring programs can improve teaching. In P. Seldin and Associates, *Improving college teaching* (pp. 125–136). Bolton, MA: Anker.

Stamp, G. H., & Vangelisti, A. L., & Daly, J. A. (1992). Social interaction: The creation of defensiveness. *Communication Quarterly, 40* (2), 177–190.

Tierney, W. G., & Rhoads, R. A. (1994). Faculty socialization as cultural process: A mirror of institutional commitment. *ASHE-ERIC Higher Education Report, 6.* Washington, DC: School of Education and Human Development, George Washington University.

Timm, P. R., & DeTienne, K. B. (1995). *Managerial communication: A finger on the pulse* (3rd ed.). Upper Saddle River, NJ: Prentice Hall.

Tucker, A. (1993). *Chairing the academic department: Leadership among peers* (3rd ed.). Phoenix, AZ: Oryx.

Tucker, A., & Bryan, R. A. (1988). *The academic dean: Dove, dragon, and diplomat.* New York, NY: Macmillan.

Wergin, J. F. (1994). *Analyzing faculty workload. New Directions for Institutional Research,* No. 83. San Francisco, CA: Jossey-Bass.

Wunsch, M. A. (Ed.). (1994). *Mentoring revisited: Making an impact on individuals and institutions.* San Francisco, CA: Jossey-Bass.

# INDEX